Beyond Brexit

Beyond Brexit

Towards a British Constitution

Vernon Bogdanor

Professor of Government, King's College, London.

I.B. TAURIS

LONDON • NEW YORK • OXFORD • NEW DELHI • SYDNEY

I.B. TAURIS
Bloomsbury Publishing Plc
50 Bedford Square, London, WC1B 3DP, UK
1385 Broadway, New York, NY 10018, USA

BLOOMSBURY, I.B. TAURIS and the I.B. Tauris logo are trademarks of
Bloomsbury Publishing Plc

First published in Great Britain 2019
Reprinted 2019

Cover design: Adriana Brioso

A catalogu. .... Congress

ISBN: HB: 978-1-7883-1679-8
ePDF: 978-1-7883-1681-1
eBook: 978-1-7883-1680-4

Typeset by RefineCatch Ltd, Bungay, Suffolk

Printed and bound in Great Britain

To find out more about our authors and books visit
www.bloomsbury.com and sign up for our newsletters.

Contents

Acknowledgments vi
Introduction viii

1   Britain and Europe: The Poisoned Chalice 1

2   Europe and the Sovereignty of Parliament 51

3   Europe and the Referendum 87

4   Europe and the Collective Responsibility of Ministers 113

5   Europe and the Rights of the Citizen 135

6   Brexit and Devolution: The Future of the United Kingdom 169

7   Brexit: A Constitutional Moment? 257

Index 279

Acknowledgments

An earlier version of this book was scrutinised to its great benefit by Dr Rudolf Adam, Professor Conor Gearty, Sandy Sullivan, Dame Veronica Sutherland and Professor Derrick Wyatt, QC.

Much of Chapter 5 is based on a pamphlet I published for the Constitution Society in 2018 entitled *Brexit and Our Unprotected Constitution*. I am grateful to the Society for allowing me to re-use this material. This pamphlet was read in draft form by Lord Anderson QC, Professor Catherine Barnard, Dr Andrew Blick, Agata Gostynska-Jakubowska, Stephen Hockman QC, Sir Stephen Laws QC, Professor T.G. Otte, Lord Pannick QC, Anthony Speaight QC and Anthony Teasdale, all of whom made helpful comments.

I am particularly grateful to Andrew Blick who first suggested to me that Brexit might prove a constitutional moment and gave me the impetus to write this book.

But these generous friends are not in any way to be implicated in my arguments or conclusions. Indeed, I know that some of them will disagree with what I have written.

I should also like to thank my long-suffering publisher, Iradj Bagherzade and the incomparable London Library for meeting my requests for books so speedily and efficiently.

But my greatest debt is to my wife, Sonia, who has not only read and criticized an earlier draft of this book, but encouraged me at every stage.

Vernon Bogdanor
King's College, London,
September 2018

Introduction

B rexit is a momentous event. But so far discussion of it has been almost wholly confined to its economic consequences. Yet, Brexit will also affect the way we are governed. It will have fundamental consequences for our politics and our constitution. Entry into Europe in 1973 had a seismic effect on politics and the constitution. Brexit could be equally seismic.

Before we entered the European Community, as the European Union then was, in 1973, Parliament was thought to be sovereign. It could, it was believed, do what it liked. Judges did not, so most people thought, have the power, which they enjoyed in many other democracies, to strike down legislation as unconstitutional or contravening basic rights. Joining the European Community meant subordinating United Kingdom law to European law. It meant subordination to a higher legal order. In 1991, the judges disapplied part of an Act of Parliament because it went against European law, something which it had previously been thought they could not do. The judges took for themselves the power to review primary legislation in terms of its compatibility with European law.

Before we entered the European Community, our rights were protected primarily by Parliament, not by the judges. Our rights seemed at the mercy of government and MPs. But Europe gave us the Charter of Fundamental Rights, a Charter protecting rights against

Parliament when Parliament legislated on European Union matters and, indeed, providing much more extensive protection of human rights than the Human Rights Act which was enacted in 1998.

Before we entered the European Community, the referendum was thought to be unconstitutional, 'a device' in the words of Clement Attlee 'alien to all our traditions'. Yet, just two years after joining, in 1975, we had our first national referendum on whether we should remain. Since then we have had two further national referendums, climaxing in the Brexit referendum of 2016 and many referendums at sub-national level. The referendum has now definitely become part of the furniture of the British constitution.

Before we entered the European Community, there was much less constitutional debate than there is today. Indeed, many, even on the Left, felt that there was really little point in debating it, since it was hardly capable of improvement. In 1953, a visiting American academic, attending a dinner party at a British university, was surprised to hear 'an eminent man of the left to say – in utter seriousness – that the British Constitution was "as nearly perfect as any human institution could be". He was even more surprised that "No one even thought it amusing".[1] Mr Podsnap, a character in Charles Dickens's novel *Our Mutual Friend*, declared that we were 'Very Proud of our Constitution – It was Bestowed Upon Us by providence. No other Country is so Favoured as this Country'. Any such encomium today would be regarded as highly embarrassing. Indeed, over the past decades, radical reforms such as devolution and the Human Rights Act have totally transformed our system of government and our understanding of the constitution. We are now much more uncertain about the

---

[1] Edward Shils, 'British Intellectuals in the Mid-Twentieth Century', *Encounter*, April 1955, reprinted in Shils, *The Intellectuals and the Powers*, University of Chicago Press, 1972, p. 135.

merits of our system of government than we were before 1973. 'If', so
Bagehot writes, 'you are always altering your house, it is a sign either
that you have a bad house, or that you have an excessively restless
disposition – there is something wrong somewhere'.[2]

But will Brexit turn the clock back to the era before 1973? It seems
unlikely. Membership of the European Union has swept away too
many of our traditional landmarks for it to be possible to resurrect
them. We will remain marked by our European commitment, short-
lived though it has proved to be. Too much has changed and the past
is indeed another country.

Brexit, however, will give rise to two constitutional problems. The
first is how our rights are in future to be protected. Membership
of the European Community shifted power from government and
Parliament to the courts. But, as Chapter 5 shows, Brexit means that
we will no longer enjoy the protection of the European Charter of
Fundamental Rights, a Charter which indeed gave us much more
extensive protection than the Human Rights Act. Will we be happy in
future for our rights to be protected by government and Parliament
rather than the courts – or do we need the judges to ensure that our
rights are preserved?

Furthermore, Brexit will transform the relationship between the
British Government and the government of the devolved bodies in
Scotland, Wales and Northern Ireland. We will have to re-think the
balance of power between Holyrood, Cardiff Bay, Stormont and
Westminster. Brexit also resurrects the English Question. England,
of course, remains the only part of the United Kingdom without a
devolved body to represent its interests. England's interests are
represented by the British Government, which has an awkward

---

[2] Bagehot, *Collected Works, The Economist* 1974, vol. VII, p. 226.

dual role as the government of the United Kingdom as well as the government of England. Brexit, therefore, calls into question the current territorial division of powers and raises once again the question of how the United Kingdom is to be preserved. So, Brexit involves not just a new relationship between Britain and the Continent, but perhaps also a new relationship between the various components of the United Kingdom.

The greatest barrier to resolving all these difficult problems lies in the tenacious hold upon us of the concept of the sovereignty of Parliament, a concept undermined and perhaps abrogated by our membership of the European Community. Sovereignty is an absolute concept. Like virginity, once it is lost, it cannot be regained. Perhaps then, the problems raised by Brexit can only be resolved by further limiting the sovereignty of Parliament. Indeed, the central theme of *Beyond Brexit* is that the constitutional problems likely to result can only be resolved by radically rethinking our constitutional arrangements and moving towards a written or codified constitution. Brexit, therefore, could prove a constitutional moment. It will mark an end to our membership of the European Union. But it could also mark a new beginning in our constitutional development.

Beyond Brexit, then, has a specific but important theme – the effects of Britain's forty-five year membership of the European Union on the British constitution and the likely constitutional consequences of Brexit. *Beyond Brexit* steers clear of the debate on the merits or demerits of Brexit; it is not concerned with the negotiations between the British Government and the European Union nor the parliamentary processes by which Brexit is being achieved

Beyond Brexit is intended, not for the specialist, but for all those interested in the future of the United Kingdom. I hope that it will be widely read, since it deals with fundamental problems confronting our country and how it is governed. "The British Constitution", the Queen once said, 'has always been puzzling and always will.'[3] My hope is that *Beyond Brexit* will make the constitution seem just a little less puzzling.

1

Britain and Europe: The Poisoned Chalice

I

Britain's entry into the European Community, as the European Union then was, in 1973, led to profound changes in the constitution and the political system. Brexit is likely to lead to equally profound changes. It will, of course, mean the unravelling of forty-five years of our membership of European institutions. But we will not be able simply to return to the status quo as it was before 1973. Indeed, in politics, it is rarely possible to put the clock back. Too much will have changed since 1973; in any case, the Britain of 2019 is a very different place from the Britain of 1973. Our ideas about politics and the constitution have altered, almost out of all recognition. The atmosphere of the times, the spirit of the age, are quite different. The past is, as L.P. Hartley famously said, a foreign country. It would seem, as we leave the European Union, that our future will now be under our control, ours to mould as we wish – 'take back control' was a key slogan of the Brexiteers. But perhaps that is an illusion. For some consequences of our membership of the European Union are likely to remain with us even after Brexit.

Beyond Brexit seeks to chart the effects of our short-lived European commitment upon our constitution and our political system and to analyse how they will be affected by Brexit. *Beyond Brexit*, therefore, is an exercise both in past history and in futurology. Historians, it has been said, imagine the past and remember the future; or perhaps rather they interpret the past in terms of what they think the future will bring. What is clear is that our future will be shaped by our past and we will find it difficult to escape the consequences of our European involvement, comparatively brief though it was.

But why was that involvement so brief and why did it prove so problematic?

There are many reasons, but perhaps the fundamental one is that Britain, for profound historical reasons, remained outside and on the whole unaffected by the movement for European unity, which in the immediate post-war years animated so many on the Continent.

During the early post-war years, the idea of European unity became, for the first time, albeit briefly, part of the popular consciousness of Europe. But it did not become part of the popular consciousness in Britain.

In the eighteenth century, Edmund Burke had declared that no European could be a complete exile in any part of Europe. The idea of European unity was championed by philosophers such as Kant in the eighteenth century and by Saint-Simon in the nineteenth. Indeed, Saint-Simon believed that there was, in the continent, a developing *patriotisme europeén*. Nevertheless, until the twentieth century, European unity remained an idea for philosophers and prophets, rather than for politicians. However, in the twentieth century, by contrast, it was to move onto the political agenda and, after the Second World War, it was taken up by leading politicians on the Continent with some degree of popular support. This was, in part and paradoxically, a consequence of a sense of European weakness, a sense that the Continent was coming to be overshadowed by the growing power of the United States and Russia. European unity arose out of a perception of the decline of Europe, not of its strength. Even so, until the 1940s, the idea of Europe was promoted only by a few far-sighted political leaders – by Briand and Stresemann, foreign ministers of France and Germany during the 1920s and also by Winston Churchill, who, in *The Saturday Evening Post* in February 1930, wrote:

> The conception of a United States of Europe is right. Every step taken to that end which appeases the obsolete hatreds and vanished oppressions, which makes easier the traffic and reciprocal services of Europe, which encourages nations to lay aside their precautionary panoply, is good in itself.

But then, in words that prefigured his post-war approach, he wrote 'But we have our own dream and our task; we are with Europe, but not of it. We are linked but not compromised'.[1]

It took the Second World War for the idea of the unity of Europe to become, for the first time, an element in the *popular* as well as the political consciousness of the Continent and it was this growth in the consciousness of being European which was to make possible the creation and development of the European Community, established by the Treaty of Rome in 1957. The six founding members of the European Community – France, Germany, Italy and the Benelux countries – Belgium, Luxembourg and the Netherlands – had all suffered from National Socialism, from enemy occupation or both. Britain alone amongst the European belligerents had suffered neither. For many on the Continent, the struggle against Hitler had taken on the aspect of a supranational struggle. Hitler, so it appeared, had exploited divisions amongst the European powers to establish Nazi

---

[1] Cited in Michael Charlton, *The Price of Victory*, BBC Publications 1983, pp. 19–20.

domination over Europe. The war against him was not, therefore, merely a conventional war between nation-states, but seemed to take on the character of a war of faiths in which the nations themselves had been divided. The resistance to Nazism, therefore, seemed to have a supranational character. It sought not merely to defeat Hitler but to create the conditions under which any future Hitler would be impossible. It sought not merely to re-establish the nation states as they had been before the war, but to link them together permanently through the creation of some form of European government. Two of the most powerful elements in the resistance movements – socialism and Christian Democracy – were themselves supranational in nature and the wartime resistance seemed to hold open the possibility of these two political forces revivified and coming together in the common cause of European unity. The war, therefore, seemed pregnant with possibilities for a new Europe in which future national conflicts would become impossible.

'I have known two Europes,' declared the French writer, Maurice Druon, in 1946, 'two Europes that existed. One, the Europe of the night, which began for us and for other peoples even earlier, was a Europe in which for a moment the same sun rising in the Caucasus set in the Atlantic – I have known another Europe, a weak Europe being born, having its seat in London, a Europe made up by a few exiles, of certain volunteers, all Europeans, because they did not merely belong to the nation of their birth, but because they truly belonged to a common struggle, and it is this Europe which, in the end, had won.'[2]

On the Continent, therefore, the European idea was seen by many and, in particular, by the Christian Democrat founding fathers of the

---

[2] Cited in John Lukacs, *The Last European War*, Routledge and Kegan Paul, 1977, p. 496.

European Community – the leaders of West Germany, Italy and France, Konrad Adenauer, Alcide de Gasperi and Robert Schuman – as a reaction against nationalism, of which Fascism and National Socialism were but perverted forms. From the shock of defeat and occupation, they and other European leaders drew the lesson that the nation-state had failed and that Europeans could avoid future wars and restore the influence of a ravaged continent only if they combined together to create new supranational institutions.

Maurice Druon had written that the seat of the new Europe had been in London. But, not having suffered the shock of occupation or defeat, Britain drew very different lessons from the Second World War. For Britain, the war seemed to have shown not the weakness of nationalism and the need for supranational organization; rather, it had shown the beneficent value of British patriotism. We would, Churchill insisted, defend our 'island', the fortress which kept us safe from invasion. The rhetoric of our 'finest hour' and victory in 1945 proved the strength and vitality of Britain and her Commonwealth – or, as Churchill always preferred to call it, her Empire. There was therefore no reason to crib or confine British patriotism nor to submerge it in European supranational institutions. While it was difficult for the Germans, the Italians or the French to feel pride in their national past – indeed many had cause for shame in what they or their parents might have done during the war – the British could rejoice in their past and, in particular, in their wartime solidarity. Protected by their geographical position, by the Channel and by their wartime experience, Britain's political leaders did not find it easy to understand the very different psychology of the Continental nations which the war had ruined. European identity, then, had been constructed in reaction to war, British identity was reinforced by it.[3]

---

[3] Ben Wellings, *English Nationalism and Euroscepticism: Losing the Peace*, Peter Lang, 2011.

As Jean Monnet, leading architect of the Coal and Steel Community and the European Community put it, 'Britain had not been conquered or invaded. She felt no need to exorcise history'.[4]

Britain, nevertheless, had seemed, for a short period during the early stages of the war, to share in the development of a European consciousness. Maurice Druon, after all, had spoken of the new Europe as having its 'seat' in London. When, in March 1940, Britain and France signed a treaty pledging not to make a separate peace with Hitler, they declared also that they would maintain, after the war:

> A community of action in all spheres for so long as may be necessary to effect the reconstruction with the assistance of other nations, of an international order which will ensure the liberty of peoples, respect for law and the maintenance of peace in Europe.

This declaration led *The Times* to comment, on 29 March 1940, that:

> Anglo-French unity has already reached a more advanced point than at any period during the last war, and what is more it is realized in both countries that this point is but the first step towards a closer and more lasting association.

In *Le Figaro*, on 30 March, Wladimir d'Ormesson insisted that 'England is now in Europe'.[5]

In June 1940, Winston Churchill, seeking to forestall French surrender, offered indissoluble union between Britain and France,

---

[4] Quoted in Jaqueline Tratt, *The Macmillan Government and Europe: A Study in the Process of Policy Development*, Macmillan 1996, p. 11.

[5] Max Beloff, 'The Anglo-French Union Project of June 1940', in *The Intellectual in Politics*, Weidenfeld and Nicolson, 1970, pp. 172–99 at p. 174. This was first published in the *Melanges Pierre Renouvin*, Press Universitaires de France, 1966. See also David Thomson, *The Project for Anglo-French Union in 1940*, Clarendon Press, 1940.

'in their common defence of justice and freedom against subjection to a system which reduces mankind to a life of robots and slaves'.[6] This proposal was to be revived by French Prime Minister, Guy Mollet, in 1956, at the height of the Suez crisis. In 1940, following the French surrender, the French Prime Minister, Paul Reynaud, had remarked that Churchill's offer 'might have marked the beginning of a United States of Europe'[7] and one authority has commented that:

> If it was right for Britain at the crisis of the war's fortunes to take the tremendous risk of the unknown inherent in the merging of the two sovereignties, then it must have been the case already for a long time that Britain's security was inextricably involved in preserving a balance on the continent and that this could only be done by a total commitment of her material and moral strength for European objectives.[8]

However, the fall of France and the further progress of the war were to sever the connection between Britain and the Continent. Instead of binding Britain closer, the war served to undermine Britain's incipient Europeanism and to confirm the British in the view that their fate was separate from that of the Continent and that they, unlike the shattered nations of the Continent, remained a great power, with a reach far beyond Europe. The experience of the Second World War, and of the immediate post-war years therefore served to reinforce contrasts between Britain and the Continent.

---

[6] The text of the Declaration can be found in *Their Finest Hour*, vol. II of *The Second World War* by Winston Churchill, Cassell 1949, pp. 183–4.

[7] Beloff, at 199. Reynaud was speaking to the Deputy Ambassador of the United States.

[8] Ibid, p. 198. It is only fair to add that, towards the end of his life, Max Beloff changed his view completely, and became a vehement Eurosceptic. See his final book, *Britain and European Unity*, significantly subtitled *A Dialogue of the Deaf*, Macmillan, 1996.

These differences in psychology were reflected in differences in post-war constitutional experience. For, after 1945, known in Germany as *jahr null* – year zero – the countries of the Continent were forced to begin again, to reinvent constitutions and political systems. The German constitution dates from 1949, the Italian from 1947; the French enacted a new constitution in 1946 and then another in 1958. The Continental countries had, perforce, to rethink the preconditions of constitutional and political order. The contrasts between the historical experience of Britain and her Continental neighbours, therefore, came to be reinforced in constitutional and institutional structures. The democracies of the Continent developed quite different political systems and constitutions from our own, because their basic assumptions and preconceptions were so very different. These were carried over into the institutions of the European Community. By the time Britain joined that Community in 1973, European institutions were firmly established and it was not easy for politicians raised in the very different political culture which prevailed on this side of the Channel to understand them.

Brexit, therefore, was not a chance development. It was the culmination of a long-term trend of disenchantment in Britain towards the European Union, a long-term trend towards Euroscepticism. There were, admittedly, periods between 1973 and 2019 when it appeared that such scepticism had been quelled and that public opinion was becoming more favourably disposed towards Europe. But these periods were relatively short and Europhilia never struck deep roots amongst the British public. More frequently, Britain's relationship with the Continent seemed fraught with difficulty. Charting the story of Britain's involvement shows that Europe posed powerful challenges for Britain's constitution and her political system, challenges which proved difficult, if not impossible, to resolve.

II

The story of Britain's involvement with the movement for European unity begins in 1950. In that year, Britain was invited to join the European Coal and Steel Community, a precursor to the European Union. But she declined the invitation and six Continental countries – France, Germany, Italy and the Benelux countries – the same countries which were later to sign the Treaty of Rome establishing the European Community in 1957 – went ahead without her. The Treaty had been preceded by a conference at Messina in 1955. The six founder members sent senior ministers to the discussions. Britain sent an Under-Secretary at the Board of Trade, Russell Bretherton. He had instructions to make no prior commitments. When it became apparent that the Six were intent on creating a customs union and that Britain was not sympathetic, Bretherton was asked to withdraw.

It used to be thought that, on withdrawing, Bretherton had said 'Gentleman, you are trying to negotiate something you will never be able to negotiate. But, if negotiated, it will not be ratified. And, if ratified, it will not work'. Apparently, however, he never said anything of the sort and the version that he did was mischievously put about, it appears, by a French official. The comment certainly bears no relation to what he actually thought. His son wrote to *The Economist* 30 November 2013 denying that Bretherton had ever made such a comment. Bretherton was, apparently, sympathetic to the Six and wrote to his political masters in August 1955: 'We have, in fact, the power to guide the conclusions of this conference in almost any direction we like, but beyond a certain point we cannot exercise that power without ourselves becoming, in some measure, responsible for the results.' Bretherton later apparently believed that: 'If we had been able to say that we agreed in principle, we could have got whatever kind of common market we wanted.' But his brief was not to commit

Britain, so he was asked to withdraw from the Messina conference, which he did with some regret. The Permanent Secretary at the Board of Trade, Sir Frank Lee, later a strong advocate of British entry, believed at the time that 'there will be nothing for it but to let this elaborate and embarrassing comedy of manners be played through to the end'.[9] This was one of the first but certainly not the last occasion on which British politicians and officials underestimated the determination of Continental leaders.

In forming the Coal and Steel Community and then the European Community, the Six had been anxious to secure British leadership. Britain's prestige stood enormously high after the Second World War, but their success in forming the Community on their own convinced European leaders that the movement towards European unity could go ahead without British leadership, indeed without British involvement. This meant, in consequence, that if Britain later wished to participate in the European movement, she would have to accept rules which had been laid down by others. Dean Acheson, the US Secretary of State at the time, called his memoirs of this period, *Present at the Creation*. This was a good title, since this period was a formative one in world politics – especially on the Continent where new relationships were being formed and a new mould was being created. During the immediate post-war period, Britain had a great deal of freedom of manoeuvre and her allegiance was much sought after. But, from the late 1950s, alignments came to be frozen and it was to prove difficult to alter them. What happened in 1950, therefore, was to prefigure Britain's post-war relationship with the movement for European unity. For, since that year, Britain has, on the whole, remained outside the mainstream of that movement. Britain was a

---

[9] Alan Milward, *The United Kingdom and the European Community, Volume 1: The Rise and Fall of a National Strategy 1945–1963*, Frank Cass, 2002, pp. 203, 207.

critic until around 1960, then, from 1961, a supplicant seeking membership of the European Community, then, after finally joining in 1973, a querulous member, seeking exemption from some of the rules – in the form of opt-outs, exceptions and rebates – and now, once again, an outsider and a supplicant. Hardly ever was Britain an enthusiast.

In 1961, Britain's Conservative government under Harold Macmillan reversed his government's previous policy and decided to seek membership of the European Community. It did so, not because it had been converted to the European ideal, but primarily for economic reasons. The Continent seemed to be thriving economically while the British rate of growth remained sluggish. Exposure to the wider market on the Continent would, it was hoped, provide new opportunities for British manufacturers. There seemed much less danger at that time of the European Community leading to political federation. Certainly, Charles de Gaulle, France's president since 1958, was strongly opposed to such a step. He favoured a Europe of states – Europe des États – and could therefore be relied upon to oppose measures of political integration.

Macmillan, however, failed to achieve British entry into the Community. The British application was vetoed by de Gaulle in January 1963, primarily because he believed that British membership would prevent the introduction into the Community of the Common Agricultural Policy, which he believed to be vital for France's economy, but also because he feared that Britain would prove an American Trojan horse and that her transatlantic ties would prevent the development of the Community as a real European power in world politics.

Since the time of Macmillan's application, Europe has been a toxic issue in British politics. It has destroyed prime ministers and split political parties. It has not only emphasized divisions between the parties. It has also caused divisions and splits *within* the parties. Indeed, the European issue was to become the major cause of a split in the Labour Party in 1981. At that time, most Labour MPs and Labour Party members were hostile to Britain's membership of the European Community. So was its leader, Michael Foot. Indeed, Labour's election manifesto in 1983 proposed that Britain leave the European Community without a referendum. But many leading figures on the Right of the party, led by former Cabinet ministers – Roy Jenkins, David Owen and Shirley Williams – were pro-European. They decided to break from Labour in 1981 and to form a new party – the Social Democratic Party – SDP – which, in 1988 would merge with the Liberals to form the Liberal Democrats. More recently, Europe has divided the Conservatives as well. The Conservatives, unlike Labour, have not split, but divisions within the party over Europe have caused serious problems for every Conservative leader since the time of Margaret Thatcher's administration in the 1980s. Indeed, the split over Europe was probably a major cause of the heavy defeat of the Conservatives in the general election of 1997 which brought New Labour to power under Tony Blair. But, as well as splitting parties and ruining governments, Europe has also destroyed the careers of many politicians. Had it not been for the European issue, Roy Jenkins in the 1970s and Kenneth Clarke in the 1990s might well have become leaders of their respective parties. There is, indeed, a plausible case to be made that the fundamental conflict in post-war British politics has been not so much between Left and Right, but between those who favoured a closer commitment to Europe and those who did not. That profound political divide has cut across the parties and united some odd bedfellows. Amongst the pro-Europeans have been Harold Macmillan, Edward Heath, Roy Jenkins, Kenneth Clarke and Tony Blair. The anti-Europeans, by contrast, have included Hugh Gaitskell, Enoch Powell, Michael Foot, Tony Benn, Margaret Thatcher and Boris Johnson.

III

More recently, the European issue has transformed electoral behaviour and has revealed a profound cultural divide in British politics which has both polarized the two major political parties and divided them internally. It led also to the rise of UKIP, the United Kingdom Independence Party, which became the most successful non-nationalist minor party in modern British history. UKIP originated as the Anti-Federalist League, founded in 1991, but was renamed as UKIP in 1993, following the Maastricht Treaty. The party was, for a long time, greatly underestimated. David Cameron notoriously declared in 2006 that its supporters were 'fruitcakes, loonies and closet racists'.[10] Around the same time, a Labour cabinet minister told me that UKIP was 'the British National Party in blazers', while an *Observer* journalist, Nick Cohen, in a blurb for the book by Robert Ford and Matthew Goodwin, *Revolt on the Right*, claimed that UKIP offered 'a garish picture of what the British right looks like when it has had one beer too many'. But the party was to come first in the European Parliament elections in 2014, the only occasion in modern British history in which a major party did not come first in a nationwide election. In the 2015 general election, UKIP won 12.5 per cent – one-eighth – of the vote, but only one seat in Parliament. Its success, however, lay not in winning seats in the Commons, but in its appeal in the country and the ability of its leader, Nigel Farage, to communicate to those otherwise disillusioned with politics. The party played an important educative role in altering opinion and has achieved far more than other minor parties have done. It can claim much of the credit – or debit, depending on one's political viewpoint – for the fact that Brexit is coming about.

---

[10] Quoted in Robert Ford and Matthew Goodwin, *Revolt on the Right: Explaining Support for the Radical Right in Britain*, Routledge, 2014, p. 3.

By the time of the 2017 general election, admittedly, UKIP was in sharp decline since its main aim appeared to have been achieved. Nevertheless, the 2017 general election was to prove, even more than that of 2015, to be a Brexit election, polarizing voters according to their view on Brexit. The British Election Study asked: 'As far as you are concerned, what is the SINGLE MOST important issue facing the country at the present time?' The dominant issue was Brexit. More than one in three mentioned Brexit, as compared to fewer than one in ten who mentioned the National Health Service and one in twenty who suggested that it was the economy. In the general election of 2015, the favoured parties for those who were to vote Leave in the 2016 referendum had been either the Conservatives or UKIP. However, the resignation of Nigel Farage from the UKIP leadership and a belief that, for the Conservatives, in Theresa May's famous words, 'Brexit means Brexit' – in other words a so-called hard Brexit – meant that the bulk of Leave voters came to support the Conservatives in 2017. Survey evidence seems to show that over half of 2015's UKIP voters swung to the Conservatives in 2017 while just 18 per cent swung to Labour and 18 per cent remained with UKIP. Amongst Leave voters as a whole, over 60 per cent supported the Conservatives in 2017. Labour, by contrast, won over Remain voters from the Greens and, remarkably perhaps, from the Liberal Democrats, even though the Liberal Democrats were more obviously a Remain party, since they, unlike Labour, were proposing a further referendum on Europe to undo the consequences of that held in 2016. Nearly a quarter of those who had voted for the Liberal Democrats in 2015 supported Labour in 2017, as did nearly two-thirds of those who had voted Green in 2015. In total, around half of those who had voted Remain in 2016 voted Labour in 2017, one-quarter voted Conservative and just 15 per cent voted for the Liberal Democrats, a sign perhaps that they were once again coming to be seen as a minor party with no chance of being involved in government. The general election of 2017 showed that the Conservatives were coming increasingly to be seen as a Leave Party, while Labour was coming to be seen as a Remain party. That was paradoxical, since Theresa May and the majority of her Cabinet had been Remainers while Jeremy Corbyn and his allies had always been, to say the least, equivocal, on the virtues of the European Union. Indeed, Corbyn had advocated a 'No' vote in the 1975 referendum on Europe; he had been opposed to ratification of the Lisbon treaty in 2008 and has remained sceptical of the virtues of European integration which he and his closest colleagues regard as a constraint on the implementation of a socialist programme in Britain.

The party system has been deeply affected by the European issue and, in particular, by the two referendums on Europe. The first, in 1975, Britain's first national referendum, was on whether we should remain in the European Community which we had joined in 1973. The result was a two to one victory for Remain. The second referendum on Europe was in 2016 which resulted in a 52/48 per cent victory for Leave. Before 1975, referendums had been seen as unconstitutional, as a threat to the British constitution. In reality, as Chapter 2 shows, they in no way undermine the constitution. But they do threaten the party system.

The 1975 referendum on Europe prefigured the split in the Labour Party in the 1980s and the formation of the SDP. In 2014, there was a referendum on Scottish independence, which rejected independence by 55 to 45 per cent, a narrower majority for the United Kingdom than some had anticipated. The unexpected surge of support for independence in the referendum prefigured the SNP's electoral landslide in 2015, in which the party won fifty-six of the fifty-nine Scottish seats, totally eclipsing Labour, hitherto the dominant party in Scotland. The 2016 referendum on Europe has proved disruptive for both the major parties, realigning voters along the Remain/Leave axis.

The issue of Europe seems to have polarized the voters around the two main parties. That is profoundly ironic for both the 2016 referendum and the snap general election, as well as the 1975 referendum, had been intended to exorcise Europe from British politics. David Cameron had hoped that the 2016 referendum would legitimize Britain's membership of the European Union and stop the Conservatives from, in his own words, 'banging on about Europe'. Instead, the 2016 referendum did the opposite, ejecting Britain from the European Union and re-opening divisions within the Conservative Party. Theresa May had called the snap election in 2017 to resolve Brexit once and for all. Her failure to retain her overall majority served only to reopen the issue and to make the parliamentary passage of the Brexit legislation more difficult than it would otherwise have been. The election helped the Labour Party because it could finesse the issue of Europe. The Labour manifesto declared that the party accepted the outcome of the referendum, that a Labour government would leave the EU and institute a policy of 'managed immigration' in place of free movement and that it would seek to retain the benefits of the single market and the customs union. Yet, membership of the single market requires acceptance of free movement. Labour never made precisely clear how it would square this circle. But perhaps that did not matter. Labour was able to win the support of areas that had voted Remain in the referendum, even in seemingly safe Conservative constituencies such as Kensington and Chelsea, and Canterbury, while retaining the support of Leave voters in the party's working-class strongholds. The Conservatives, however, had secured a higher share of the vote in 2017 than they had won in 2015 in areas of the country that had voted to leave the European Union – and indeed the six seats that the Conservatives gained from Labour – Copeland, Derbyshire North East, Mansfield, Middlesbrough South, Stoke South and Walsall North – were all areas with heavy Leave majorities in the 2016 referendum.

This new constituency alignment shows how class has come to be less important in voting behaviour. Kensington and Chelsea, and Canterbury are, after all, primarily middle-class constituencies. Yet they were won by Labour – and remarkably – by a Labour Party markedly more left wing than it had been in the past. Constituencies such as Mansfield, Middlesbrough, Stoke and Walsall, by contrast, are located in post-industrial Britain, areas hollowed out by the processes of industrial change and deserted by many of the ambitious who have moved away to the larger, more cosmopolitan, conurbations. Yet these constituencies were gained by the Conservatives. Brexit was an important factor in this realignment. So was education. Those with educational qualifications were much more likely to be Remain supporters and Labour voters, while those without were more likely to be Leave supporters and Conservative voters. Of those with no educational qualifications, 52 per cent voted Conservative and 35 per cent Labour. Of those with a degree or higher educational qualification, 33 per cent voted Conservative and 48 per cent Labour.

Brexit, then, seems to have overcome the traditional class alignment in British politics. The Conservatives secured a net gain over Labour of 4 per cent amongst the skilled working class and 6 per cent amongst the semi-skilled and unskilled working class, but a net loss of 9 per cent amongst the upper and middle classes – a striking outcome. Labour, whose policy was perhaps the most Left wing the party has ever seen, gained votes amongst the more affluent classes and lost them amongst the poorer classes. In total, amongst manual workers, 44 per cent voted Conservative and 41 per cent Labour, while amongst non-manual workers 42 per cent voted Conservative and 39 per cent Labour. Paradoxically, those who might be presumed to be the victims of austerity swung to the Conservatives, while those who had suffered least or perhaps even benefited swung to Labour. Brexit has transformed the impact of class on politics; perhaps it has even turned class politics upside down. The general election of 2017 was a Brexit election. There is some evidence that the 2018 local elections were also Brexit elections, even though, of course, local authorities have no responsibility for European Union matters. The Conservatives gained seats in local authorities where there had been a majority for Leave, but lost seats where there had been a majority for Remain.[11]

Brexit has served to replace issues of economic ideology with issues of identity in British politics. During most of the twentieth century the political debate, with the significant exception of Northern Ireland, was essentially concerned with the role of the state and of the distribution of income – did voters want a greater or lesser degree of state control – did they want a redistribution of income or a retention of incentives for the better off. But the general elections of 2015 and 2017 were elections in which the prime issue had become identity: How British are you? How English are you? Is being British or being English compatible with also being European? In Scotland, the questions were: How Scottish are you? Is being Scottish compatible with being British? The parties of identity – UKIP and the SNP – attacked their political opponents not for being too left-wing or too right-wing, but for being insufficiently British or being insufficiently Scottish. That marked a sea change in British politics. These elections also showed that 'strength-of-identity' politics was greatest in areas that were not strongly connected to global growth, areas of relative economic decline, seaside towns and those parts of provincial England hollowed out by the decline of manufacturing industry – in contrast to the large conurbations which, on the whole, benefit from

---

[11] John Curtice and Ian Montague, 'Scotland: How Brexit has Created a new Divide in the Nationalist Movement', in *British Social Attitudes Survey*, Sage 2018, pp. 1–2. This chapter ranges far more widely than its title would suggest, and offers an excellent broad overview of how Brexit has altered voting behaviour in the whole of the United Kingdom.

globalization and which are the centre of the new knowledge and creative economy. The former areas tend to have stronger community ties than the large conurbations, ties which globalization has undermined and they have found immigration more unsettling than those living in London or Manchester. They are likely to be more pessimistic and fearful of the future than those who have benefited from globalization precisely because their communities are being undermined by change. The former areas tended to vote for Leave, the latter for Remain. Labour's strength is increasing in the conurbations and in the university towns, while the strength of the Conservatives, paradoxically, is increasing in provincial England and amongst those struggling to manage – many of whom voted for UKIP in 2015 but returned to the Conservative fold in 2017. It is the contrast between Hampstead and Hartlepool. It has led, in England, to a tilting of the political axis, a bifurcation, resulting from the uneven impact of globalization on different parts of the country.[12] It is, of course, not at all clear whether the 2017 general election signifies a new pattern in British politics or whether it was an untypical election based on a single issue. Will Brexit still prove to be an issue in 2022 – indeed, could there be another Brexit election before 2022? Brexit has already contributed to the fall of one government – that led by David Cameron – and contributed to the failure of her successor – Theresa May – to retain the Conservatives' overall majority in the House of Commons. Will Brexit continue to disrupt governments and political parties? Might there be a resurrection of UKIP if the Conservatives appear to be failing to secure a hard Brexit? These are, of course, at present unanswerable questions.

---

[12] Will Jennings and Gerry Stoker, 'The Bifurcation of Politics: Two Englands', (2016) 87(3) *Political Quarterly* pp. 372–82.

IV

Why is it that Europe has produced such profound divisions? The answer surely is that it has given rise to that most basic of political concerns – national identity. It raised the fundamental question – what does it mean to be British? Is being British compatible with being European? These are questions that we have found difficult to answer. For our history seems to point us in two different directions.

At the end of the nineteenth century, Britain was detached from the Continent. At that time, Britain was primarily an Imperial power. Since the end of the Napoleonic wars, her energies had been concentrated upon her Empire; in particular, upon her Empire in the East based on the possession and government of India. Her main strategic commitment was the defence of India – of the Indian Empire – not so much against Indian nationalism which was only just beginning at that time – but against Russia which was thought to be casting envious eyes over India. 'As long as we rule India', Lord Curzon, the Viceroy, had declared in 1901, 'we are the greatest power in the world. If we lose it we shall drop straight away to a third-rate power'.[13] Earlier, in 1866, Benjamin Disraeli, leader of the Conservative Party, had gone so far as to say that Britain was 'more an Asiatic power than a European'.[14] In 1900, we had no Continental commitment. We had no troops on the Continent. Indeed, we did not agree to maintain troops on the Continent in times of peace until 1954. We had no alliances with any European power except Portugal. We lived in what seemed splendid isolation, protected by the navy and the empire.

---

[13] Quoted in Evgeny Sergeev: *The Great Game 1856–1907: Russo-British Relations in Central and East Asia*, Johns Hopkins University Press, 2013, p. 230.
[14] Cited in Sneh Mahajan, *British Foreign Policy 1874–1914: The Role of India*, Routledge, 2002, p. 7.

Perhaps that period of Imperial isolation, though it has long gone, still leaves some of its impact upon the British psyche. Its consequence would be to confirm for many the perception that Britain was not fundamentally a European power. That was certainly what de Gaulle thought. In the 1963 press conference in which he announced that he would veto Britain's application to join the European Community, he contrasted the economies and the historical experience of the Six with that of Britain. The Community, he declared, had been created by six countries 'which are, economically speaking, one may say, of the same nature – joined in solidarity, especially and primarily, from the aspect of the consciousness they have of defining together an important part of the sources of our civilisation; and also as concerns their security, because they are continental states – Thus it was psychologically and materially possible to make an economic community of the Six, though not without difficulties'. But 'the nature, the structure, the very situation (*conjuncture*) that are England's differ profoundly from those of the continental states'. Britain, de Gaulle said, was 'insular, she is maritime, she is linked through her exchanges, her markets, her supply lines, to the most diverse and often the most distant countries; she pursues essentially industrial and commercial activities, and only slight agricultural ones'. That was why she was so opposed to the Common Agricultural Policy, which the French regarded as an essential element of the European Community. She was, therefore, not fundamentally European, though de Gaulle did concede that Britain might evolve 'little by little towards the Continent'. He proposed that, instead of Britain joining the European Community, there be 'an accord of association', an association agreement. That may have been a prescient prediction. Perhaps, indeed, Britain will negotiate such an agreement with the European Union after Brexit. Sometimes one's opponents see one's situation more clearly than one's friends. Certainly, many on the Continent would argue that de Gaulle had predicted the effect of British membership on Europe while, in Britain, Brexiteers would argue that de Gaulle's perception of Britain's geopolitical position was more acute than that of the British Government.

Indeed, in the 1950s, many in Britain would have agreed with de Gaulle's critique. Anthony Eden, speaking as Foreign Secretary at Columbia University in January 1952, told the Americans who were eager that Britain should be part of a European political unit:

> If you drive a nation to adopt procedures which run counter to its instincts, you weaken and may destroy the motive force of its action. – You will realize that I am speaking of the frequent suggestions that the United Kingdom should join a federation on the continent of Europe. This is something which we know, in our bones, we cannot do.

Few, even of the most most enthusiastic supporters of the European Union would have favoured Britain joining 'a federation on the Continent of Europe'. That, indeed, was something which they knew 'in our bones we cannot do'. Pro-Europeans, however, argued that the mindset which had produced detachment from Europe was formed during the era of empire, an era which had pulled Britain away from the Continent by the coat tails. Britain's separation from the Continent, therefore, far from being a fundamental axiom of her existence, was a deviation, so that, even though empire may have so strongly coloured Britain's sense of national identity, it was but an aberrant period, albeit a long one. For during so much of Britain's long history, her fate had been intertwined with that of the Continent. Indeed, we had fought two world wars because of conflicts that had arisen in Europe. Perhaps, therefore, Britain was, in reality, European or at least might become so?

Britain's splendid isolation had ended as long ago as the Boer War which lasted from 1899 to 1902. During that war, the hostility of the

Continent to British imperialism convinced most of her leading statesmen that she needed friends. In 1902, an alliance with Japan was signed and, in 1904, the *entente cordiale* with France which, although not an alliance, did gradually bring Britain back into the affairs of the Continent. Even so, Britain remained aloof from formal alliances until the outbreak of war in 1914. Her obligations to France were obligations of honour. There was no formal commitment; it is by no means clear that the Liberal government would have remained united in going to the aid of France had not Germany invaded neutral Belgium. Following the experience of four years of war, Britain again sought to remain aloof from the Continent for much of the inter-war period when, remembering the blood-letting of the Somme and Passchendaele, the common sentiment was 'Never Again'. Never Again would British troops be sent to the Continent. Never again would Britain be involved in a European war. In 1938, Prime Minister, Neville Chamberlain, horrified that Britain might have to go to war on account of what seemed an obscure frontier dispute in Czechoslovakia, spoke of 'a faraway country of which we know nothing', a sentiment which shocked Winston Churchill and his supporters, but may well have reflected the feelings of many people in Britain at the time.

The experience of the Second World War did seem, however, to lead to a fundamental change in British thinking and both Labour and Conservative governments drew the lesson that it was no longer possible for Britain to remain detached from the Continent. Post-1945 Britain was by no means hostile to engagement with the Continent. Quite the contrary. During the immediate post-war years, Britain participated in a number of international organizations, committing herself to defence and economic cooperation with her Continental neighbours. In 1947, she signed the Treaty of Dunkirk with France, a treaty of alliance and mutual assistance; this was broadened into the Treaty of Brussels in 1948, which brought in Italy and the Benelux countries. This Treaty in turn led to the 1949 NATO alliance with other European powers and with the United States and Canada, an explicit commitment to collective security so that an attack on any of the members of that alliance, which included most of the western European powers, was to be understood as an attack on all; the other members were under an obligation to go to the aid of any country that was attacked. This was of, course, a great contrast to British policy in the period before 1939 when her leaders were adamant about not accepting a Continental commitment.

There were, in addition, important economic agreements. In 1948, Britain had been a leading participant in founding the Organization for European Economic Cooperation whose main purpose was to administer Marshall Aid to the shattered economies of post-war Europe; in 1950, she helped found the European Payments Union which provided for the elimination of discriminatory financial measures and a liberalized and multilateral payments regime. Britain had also been instrumental in creating the Council of Europe in 1949 and was one of the first countries to ratify the Council's European Convention on Human Rights in 1951; in 1954, Britain took the lead in establishing the Western European Union and committed herself, for the first time in her peacetime history, to station her troops and a tactical air force on the Continent. Britain, therefore, far from isolating herself from the Continent as had been the case in earlier periods, had taken the lead in creating and involving herself in post-war European organizations.

Although Britain was instrumental in creating the Council of Europe, her basic attitude towards European integration had not changed. Indeed, Ernest Bevin, Foreign Secretary in the post-war Labour government, had at first been sceptical of the Council of Europe. 'I don't like it', he told his officials and he explained why. 'If you open that Pandora's box, you never know what Trojan 'orses will fly out.'[15] That, perhaps, was the most prescient remark ever made about Britain's involvement with the European movement.

What did Bevin mean? What was he frightened of?

What he was frightened of was the idea of European unity. For, in the view of Bevin and almost all of Britain's leading politicians at the time, there should be very strict limits on the extent of British participation in European organizations. Britain would participate – indeed she would be an enthusiastic proponent – of intergovernmental organizations. But she could play no part in any organization which went beyond the intergovernmental, any organization which sought European integration.

The Council of Europe proved in fact, in large part due to British insistence, an intergovernmental rather than a supranational organization and it had no law-making powers. So, Britain had no reason to be frightened of it. What Bevin had feared was that it might become an instrument for European integration. He and his government had feared integration: the sharing of power. That would impinge upon the central principle of the British constitution, the sovereignty of Parliament.

The treaties that Britain had signed had all been intergovernmental in nature. Until 1961, no British government, whether Labour or Conservative, was prepared to go beyond that. They were not prepared to participate in any project of European integration. The Coal and Steel Community, which in 1950 Britain had declined to join, was, however, quite different in kind from other European organizations. What it sought to do was to create a common market for coal and steel products with a common policy on imports and common measures to enforce competition and harmonize state aids. The Coal

---

[15] Quoted in Roderick Barclay, *Ernest Bevin and the Foreign Office, 1932–1969*, Latimer, 1975, p. 67.

and Steel Community contained the germ of the European Community and of the European Union. It was to be governed by an institution, the High Authority of the Coal and Steel Community, which was the prototype of the Commission of the European Union. This High Authority was to be composed of international civil servants, nominated by the member states of the Community, and it would make decisions which would be binding on the member states, overriding their parliaments and governments. The great objection of the British government was that these decisions would be made by a body which was not elected. This hardly seemed compatible with parliamentary democracy. The High Authority, moreover, would not be responsible to the member states. Instead, it would represent the common European interest. It was to be an explicitly supranational organization. The European Commission, its successor organization, was also intended to represent a common European interest. In the Coal and Steel Community, in addition to the High Authority, there would be a Court of Justice, prototype of the European Court of Justice, to arbitrate disputes.

The purpose of the Coal and Steel Community, which put two industries essential to the waging of war under supranational control, was to make war between the two ancient enemies, France and Germany, impossible; for the French at least, it had a further purpose: to 'build the first concrete foundations of the European Federation which is indispensable to the preservation of peace'. Indeed, in his Declaration of 9 May 1950, French foreign minister, Robert Schuman, had insisted that 'the pooling of coal and steel production should immediately provide for the setting up of common foundations for economic development as a first step in the federation of Europe'. This aspiration was to be repeated in the preamble to the Treaty of Rome in 1957 committing the members of the European Community to 'ever closer union'. In 1950, the future Conservative Prime Minister,

Harold Macmillan, summarized for the Council of Europe the nature of British objections to the Coal and Steel Community. He explained why the British took a different view from the Continental countries:

> So great have been the political convulsions, so many the changes of regime, so frequent the revolutions, so unstable the political system within the nations, that they naturally look for safety and permanence to some supra-national authority – In the reaction against democratic weakness men have sought safety in the technocrats. There is nothing new in this. It is as old as Plato. Frankly, it is not attractive to our British point of view. We have not overthrown the divine right of kings in order to fall down before the divine right of experts. This is not a purely British point of view. It is shared by all those who are truly attached to democracy and parliamentary institutions.[16]

On 2 June 1950, the British government decided not to join the Coal and Steel Community. The Cabinet minutes explain why. 'M. Schuman's original memorandum said in terms that his plan would be a step towards the federation of Europe. It has been our settled policy hitherto that in view of our world position and interests, we should not commit ourselves irrevocably to Europe either in the political or in the economic sphere unless we could measure the extent and effect of the commitment. This is in effect what we are now being asked to do.' In the House of Commons, Prime Minister Attlee was more terse. 'It was made clear', he declared, 'that we could not accept in advance of discussions the principle that the most vital economic forces of this country should be handed over to an authority which is not responsible to Governments'.[17] One backbench MP,

---

[16] Quoted in 'Anglo-French Split Widens over the Schuman Plan', *Guardian*, 16 August 1950, p. 8.

[17] House of Commons, vol. 477, col. 472, 5 July 1950.

however, making his maiden speech, said that this decision was a mistake and that Britain should at least have played a more constructive part in the discussions. His name was Edward Heath. Britain's failure to follow Heath's advice was a pivotal moment in her relationship with the Continent. Since 1985, the date of the Schuman Plan, the ninth of May, has been known on the Continent as Europe Day. In Britain, it is ignored.

V

The proposal in the Coal and Steel Community to surrender national powers to a body that would not be responsible to national legislatures was, then, a striking contrast to the other treaty organizations to which Britain had acceded. These had required a sacrifice, or sharing, of *national* sovereignty. Indeed, any international commitment requires such a sacrifice. But the Coal and Steel Community required, in addition, a sacrifice of *parliamentary* sovereignty, which, unlike national sovereignty, cannot be shared.

National sovereignty and parliamentary sovereignty are two quite different concepts which are often confused. Every treaty or international commitment requires a sacrifice of national sovereignty and it is a matter of political debate how much national sovereignty it is reasonable to share in the national interest. National sovereignty is a matter of degree. It is a pragmatic concept. Unlike parliamentary sovereignty, national sovereignty is a tradeable asset. The general view when Britain signed up to various treaty obligations in the years immediately following the end of the Second World War, including obligations on the Continent, was that these treaties would increase British security and therefore her capability and room for manoeuvre in an increasingly threatening world dominated by two superpowers – the United States and the Soviet Union. Britain's freedom to manoeuvre would otherwise be restricted by her small size in comparison with the superpowers; it was becoming clear that the Commonwealth would not become a political bloc enabling Britain herself to become a superpower.

Parliamentary sovereignty, however, is a quite different concept from national sovereignty. It proclaims that Parliament can enact any law that it wishes and that no authority can declare an Act of Parliament void. The concept of parliamentary sovereignty is not like that of national sovereignty a tradeable asset. It is not like baldness a mere matter of degree. It is, rather, an absolute, like virginity; just as one cannot be a qualified virgin, so also one cannot be a qualified sovereign. A parliament is either sovereign or it is not. What the Coal and Steel Community and later attempts at European integration entailed was a sacrifice not only of national sovereignty, which would have caused few problems to Britain, but also of her fundamental constitutional concept, parliamentary sovereignty. Proposals for European integration beginning with the Coal and Steel Community required the sharing of legislative power with a European body. It was this which almost all British politicians in the 1950s and a sizeable proportion of British politicians since, have found unacceptable; it was resistance to the sharing of power which lay behind the Brexit slogan of 2016 'Take back control'.

The concept of parliamentary sovereignty is peculiar to Britain. It is one of the main reasons why Britain does not have a codified constitution. For there is clearly no point in having such a constitution if any part of it can at any time be overridden by a sovereign Parliament. Indeed, the whole purpose of having a constitution is to entrench certain provisions, including those protecting human rights and placing them beyond the reach of parliamentary majorities so that they cannot be overruled by a simple majority of the legislature. The

British constitution, by contrast, had no such entrenched provisions; or at least it did not have until Britain joined the European Community in 1973. Until then, the British constitution could have been characterized in just eight words: 'Whatever the Queen in parliament enacts is law.'

The great nineteenth-century constitutional lawyer, A.V. Dicey, who first provided an analysis of the concept of parliamentary sovereignty, argued that it was not a purely abstract doctrine derived from deductive principles or any theory of jurisprudence. It was, rather, so he believed, a generalization drawn from English legal history. For Dicey, the roots of the idea of parliamentary sovereignty, 'lie deep in the history of the English people and in the peculiar development of the English Constitution'.[18] The idea of parliamentary sovereignty is a product of an evolutionary history, but also an expression of it; the history of a country which has seen no fundamental break in its constitutional development for over 300 years. There is a sense, indeed, in which England, the core of the United Kingdom, never began. For it is hardly possible to fix a date at which England began as a modern state. There has been no formal breach in the historical continuity of England since 1689, when James II was deposed. Even then, the breach of continuity was masked by the use of traditional forms since it was held that James, rather than being deposed, had voluntarily 'abdicated'. The brief republican interlude earlier in the seventeenth century, between 1649 and 1660, was followed by what was significantly called a Restoration, not a new beginning, but the return of a traditional institution, the monarchy. It is precisely because there has been no sharp break in Britain's constitutional history since the seventeenth century that, unlike

---

[18] A.V. Dicey, *Introduction to the Study of the Law of the Constitution*, 10th edn, Macmillan, 1959, p. 69fn.

almost every other democracy, there seems in Britain to have been neither the desire nor the need to enact a constitution.

The emphasis on evolutionary adaptability and on the supremacy of Parliament in Britain's constitutional arrangements was strengthened in the nineteenth century by the Great Reform Act of 1832. The Acts of Union with Scotland in 1707, with Ireland in 1800 and the Anglo-Irish treaty of 1921 all defined the boundaries of the British state. But it was the Great Reform Act which went far to define its character. It was passed because the governing elite was prepared to respond in conciliatory fashion to a widespread popular demand for extending the franchise. Perhaps 1832 is the nearest that Britain has ever come to a constitutional moment. The Great Reform Act seemed to show that the British constitution was flexible enough to develop through a process of evolution. The Act also served to reinforce the centrality of Parliament in Britain's political arrangements. It showed that pressure on Parliament could be used to achieve improvement and reform and that there was no need for a constitution to constrain Parliament.

In Dicey's lectures on comparative constitutions, unpublished in his lifetime, he argued that the British constitution was unique amongst modern constitutions in being a 'historical' constitution. By this, he meant not only that it was very old, but also that it was original and spontaneous, a product of historical development and evolution rather than specific enactment or deliberate design.[19] This view was to be echoed by other writers on British government. In a book published in 1904 entitled *The Governance of England*, (sic), the author, Sidney

---

[19] Dicey's characterization of the British Constitution as an 'historical' constitution can be found in his unpublished lectures on the Comparative Study of Constitutions, now collected and edited by J.W.F. Allison in A.V. Dicey, *Comparative Constitutionalism*, Oxford University Press, 2013, pp. 172–86.

Low, wrote that: 'Other constitutions have been built; that of England has been allowed to grow ...' 'Our constitution', Low declared, 'was based not on codified rules but on tacit understandings' although, as he ruefully remarked, 'the understandings are not always understood'.[20] It is easy to understand how Dicey and his successors saw the supremacy of Parliament as lying at the heart of the British constitution. British constitutional history, with the striking and significant exception of the Irish Question, has overall been peaceful and evolutionary. That explains why the doctrine of parliamentary sovereignty has proved so long-lasting and why it has been so widely accepted. Entry into the European Community, however, was to prove not an evolutionary adaptability but a quantum leap. It was incompatible with the idea of an 'historical' constitution.

The concern that participation in the process of European integration would be incompatible with our parliamentary system was to be powerfully articulated in 1962 in a speech by the then Leader of the Opposition, Labour's Hugh Gaitskell, delivered at a time when the Conservative government under Prime Minister Harold Macmillan had applied to join the European Community and when it was not yet apparent that the application would be vetoed by de Gaulle. Gaitskell claimed that he was not opposed in principle to membership of the European Community, but only to the likely terms which the Conservative government was negotiating. Yet his criticisms were in fact fundamental and went to the heart of the whole European project. Gaitskell was the first major politician to emphasize the crucial issue of parliamentary sovereignty in relation to the European Community. The intergovernmental organizations which Britain had joined operated, so Gaitskell argued, by consensus and did not seek to bind member states against their will. The European Community was

---

[20] Sidney Low, *The Governance of England*, T. Fisher Unwin, 1904, p. 12.

quite different. It involved Britain handing over powers currently exercised by Parliament to a European body. It involved a transfer of legislative power away from Westminster. Those powers would in future be exercised by the European Community. The initiation of legislation in relation to the powers transferred would in future be the responsibility of the European Commission, which was both unaccountable and unelected. Britain, therefore, would be bound by legislation made by a body which it had played no part in electing and which it could not remove.

The Commission, like the High Authority of the Coal and Steel Community, was a hybrid institution, part civil service, part executive, a combination more familiar on the Continent than it was in Britain. Its powers were, admittedly, restricted to the initiation of legislation. The power of decision lay with the Council of Ministers, composed of the ministers of the member states. At the time that Britain was making its first application to join the European Community, in 1961, it seemed that the Council took and would in future take its decisions by unanimity rather than by majority vote. That was certainly the view of President de Gaulle and it was also the position of Harold Macmillan and the Conservative government in Britain. But, so Gaitskell pointed out with some prescience, there was a real possibility that, eventually, decisions on political and economic issues would be made based on a majority vote. This would mean that Britain could be over-ruled and required to accept policies which Parliament would not have supported. 'Do we want that?' Gaitskell asked. It is perhaps ironic that the Council in fact did begin to take decisions by majority vote following the Single European Act in 1986, an amendment to the Treaty of Rome, which Margaret Thatcher, later a Eurosceptic, was to champion. She did so because she believed that it was in Britain's interests to secure an internal market in the European Community by the removal of non-tariff barriers to trade. It would, however, be almost impossible to achieve this were every member state to enjoy a veto over the removal of each of around 300 of these non-tariff barriers. For this reason, Margaret Thatcher pressed for majority voting, a decision which she later came to regret. But it was clear, as Gaitskell was to point out in 1962, that once the Council came to make decisions by majority vote, British ministers could no longer be wholly responsible for their decisions to Parliament. A minister defending an unpopular decision in Parliament would be able to escape responsibility by saying that he had argued strongly against it in the Council of Ministers but had been overruled by ministers in the other member states. This raised questions of what substitute mechanism could be found for the responsibility of ministers to Parliament, an issue, as Gaitskell saw it, which was fundamental to the British constitution.

Gaitskell stressed that the issue of supranationality was bound up with that of parliamentary democracy. Under the Treaty of Rome, the European Community had the power to make laws, called 'regulations', 'decisions' and 'directives' which had binding force on the member states. Some of these laws required Parliament to decide how they should best be formulated in accordance with national traditions, but many did not. So, for the first time in Britain's modern constitutional history, laws binding on British citizens could be made by an external authority not elected by the British people and not accountable to the House of Commons. There would, therefore, be a democratic deficit. How could it be remedied? The suggestion by proponents of European integration was that the Commission should be made accountable to the European Parliament and the European Parliament should be directly elected. At that time, representatives of the European Parliament were not elected but nominated by national parliaments, although from 1979 they would be directly elected. After direct elections to the European Parliament, the Commission would then be in a position to become, according to some pro-Europeans, the executive of the European Community, responsible to the European Parliament, while the Council of Ministers, composed of the governments of member states, would be, in effect, an upper house, a Senate, rather as, in Germany, the upper house, the Bundesrat, composed of the members of the various Land or provincial governments is a Senate. But this proposed solution, while it might remove the democratic deficit, posed a further and even more fundamental problem, at least as far as Britain was concerned. For it would mean that the European Parliament would become a federal assembly with powers of its own. This was something that Gaitskell presciently drew attention to in 1962: 'When it is pointed out that the Commission is a body which has powers but is not responsible or under anybody's control, what is the answer? The answer they give us is "That is why we should set up a Federal Assembly with powers over them". This is what they are arguing.'

Gaitskell then went on to ask: 'What does federation mean? It means that powers are taken from national governments and handed over to federal governments and federal parliaments. It means – I repeat it – that if we go into this we are no more than a state (as it were) in the United States of Europe such as Texas or California.' Gaitskell insisted that the aim of the founding fathers of the Community was, in fact, federation, saying 'we would be foolish to deny, not to recognise and indeed sympathise with, the desire of those who created the European Community for political federation'. But would this be the right path for Britain? 'This is what it means', Gaitskell went on, 'it does mean the end of Britain as an independent nation state. It may be a good thing or a bad thing, but we must recognise that this is so ... We must be clear about this: it does mean, if this is the idea, the end of Britain as an independent European State. I make no apology for repeating it. It means the end of a thousand years of history. You may say, "Let it end" but, my goodness, it is a decision that needs a little care and thought.'

The dilemma then was that, either legislation would be initiated by an unaccountable and unelected European Commission – or – if there were to be parliamentary control, it would be control by the European Parliament rather than national parliaments. The European Parliament would then have taken powers away from Westminster and be superior in authority to it. So, either one sacrificed the principle of parliamentary government, the principle that legislation should be enacted by a democratically elected body and that ministers should be responsible to it; or one sacrificed the principle of parliamentary sovereignty by making Westminster subordinate to a European parliament.

Gaitskell had summed up the essence of the constitutional objections to Britain participating in the project of European integration. These objections were succinctly reiterated by Tony Benn in a letter to his constituents, sent in 1975, just before the first referendum on Europe, in which he advocated withdrawal from the European Community. They form the nub of the constitutional case of the Eurosceptics against involvement and were to be the basis of the case for Brexit in the 2016 referendum.

Europe, Benn said, undermined five basic constitutional rights.

First, it undermined the requirement that consent of the House of Commons is needed for all new laws or taxes. For membership of the Community subjected Britain to laws and taxes not enacted by Parliament but enacted by authorities not directly elected and authorities who could not be dismissed through the ballot box.

Second, it undermined the right of MPs to alter any law and any tax by majority vote. For Community laws could not be altered or repealed by Parliament, but only by authorities not directly elected nor accountable to Parliament.

Third, it undermined the right of Parliament to alter or amend any law since the courts would be required to uphold and enforce Community laws not passed by Parliament and which overrode British law.

Fourth, it undermined the principle of parliamentary responsibility according to which ministers and civil servants under their control could act only within the laws of Britain and were accountable to Parliament for what they did and, through Parliament, to the people. But, in discharging the duties flowing from British membership of the Communities, ministers would not be wholly accountable to Parliament; for these duties might entail accepting laws which ministers did not support.

Fifthly, it undermined the accountability of Parliament to the people, since British membership of the Communities permanently transferred legislative and financial powers to Community authorities not directly elected by the British people, authorities which the people could not dismiss and which, therefore, would be under no pressure to remedy popular grievances.

But, over and above these constitutional problems, there was a further and even more fundamental issue raised by Gaitskell made in his 1962 speech. In that speech he argued that Europe was an issue of such transcendental importance that it could not be left to government alone to decide. He said that it must be decided by the British people, not by the government alone. 'We are now being told', Gaitskell declared, 'that the British people are not capable of judging this issue – the top people are the only people who understand it. This is the classic argument of every tyranny in history. It begins as a refined intellectual argument and it moves into a one-man dictatorship. We did not win the political battles of the nineteenth and twentieth centuries to have this reactionary nonsense thrust upon us again'. The argument that the government knew best was, he said, 'an odious piece of hypocritical supercilious arrogant rubbish'. Gaitskell did not mention the idea of a referendum on the European issue. Indeed, it was generally believed in 1962 that the referendum had no place in the British political system, that it was unconstitutional. He argued instead that a general election was needed to decide the European issue, an election at which the Labour Party would presumably oppose the European policy of the Conservatives. But, although Gaitskell did not mention it in his speech, his arguments made a strong case which could be used in the future by those who did favour a referendum. Gaitskell's argument, in fact, pointed the way towards the introduction of the referendum.

VI

Britain's first attempt to enter the European Community, under Harold Macmillan's government, failed when it was vetoed by President de Gaulle in 1963. In despair, Macmillan wrote in his diary: 'The great question remains: "What is the alternative?" – to the European Community. If we are honest we must say there is none – had there been the chance of a Commonwealth Free Trade Area we should have grasped it long ago.'[21] A second attempt, under Harold Wilson's Labour government in 1967, also met with a veto from de Gaulle. However, with de Gaulle's resignation from the presidency in 1969, the path lay open for British entry; this was achieved, at the third try, by Edward Heath's Conservative government in 1973.

Entry into the European Community did not, of course, end Britain's problems with the concept of European integration. Indeed, it intensified them. As Britain had not, in 1957, signed the Treaty of Rome,

---

[21] Ibid, p. 302.

the founding document of the European Community, the early stages of the development of the Community had been undertaken without British participation; therefore they naturally did not take account of British interests. So, when Britain finally joined, in 1973, difficulties immediately became apparent. One of Britain's official negotiators of British entry, Sir Con O'Neill, later wrote that there had been 'a number of European enthusiasts in public life who had always imagined that entering the Community would be an easy, pleasant and comfortable process. They had never bothered to discover how intensely technical and difficult the process was bound to be, and had relied too much on mere idealism and good fellowship to do the trick.'[22] For Britain found upon joining that she was required to make far greater adjustments than any of the other member states. The question was whether she could make them and, perhaps, whether it was in her interest to do so.

Pro-Europeans argued that the need for adjustment might well have been much less had Britain been a founding member of the European Community. Britain would then have had an opportunity to help shape the rules to suit her own interests rather than those of the Continental powers. But perhaps this argument should not be exaggerated, since the 'technical' difficulties to which O'Neill refers, largely reflect the fact that the constitutional attitudes and political practices of the founding members were so very different from those to which the United Kingdom was accustomed. These differences, therefore, were not merely 'technical'. They arose out of deep-seated factors, rooted ultimately in history. They flowed in the last resort from differences between Britain and her Continental neighbours, the result of profoundly different historical experiences.

Britain's economic and social arrangements were certainly different from those of the other member states. Her system of indirect taxation,

---

[22] Con O'Neill, *Britain's Entry into the European Community*, Frank Cass, 2000, p. 47.

for example, was different; so also was her system for subsidizing agriculture. But, above all, her constitutional arrangements, her party system and her electoral system, were different from those of her Continental partners.

The Continent offered a striking contrast to the evolutionary political stability of Britain. Indeed, of the original six countries which formed the European Communities – France, Germany, Italy and the Benelux countries – only France had existed as a unified country 200 years before. It was no doubt for this reason that France was, even after de Gaulle, the strongest defender in the European Union after Britain of the idea of national sovereignty. Germany and Italy had not been unified until the second half of the nineteenth century and the most recent German borders date from 1990, following the collapse of Communism in East Germany and the disappearance of the East German state. Belgium and the Netherlands assumed their present boundaries in 1830. Of the more recent member states, such as Poland, which entered the European Union in 2004 after the fall of Communism, most were not created until after the First World War; some – Slovakia and Croatia, for example – were not created until the 1990s. Their experience of nationhood is comparatively recent.

Moreover, political upheavals on the Continent had hardly any resonance in Britain. On the Continent, the fundamental dates of modern political history are 1789, the year of the French Revolution, 1848, the year of the failed liberal revolutions and 1917, the year of the Bolshevik Revolution. These moulded the party systems of most Continental countries, so that the characteristic Continental structure of party cleavages is quite different from that in Britain.[23] But Britain escaped the revolutions and attempted revolutions of 1789, 1848 and

---

[23] See S.M. Lipset and Stein Rokkan's 'Introduction' in *Party Systems and Voter Alignments*, Free Press, Glencoe, 1967.

1917, which left little more than echoes on this side of the English Channel. She had no experience of the turbulence that had marked the Continent.

This fundamental divergence was, as we have seen, widened by the experience of the Second World War and immediate post-war years, which seemed to reinforce the differences between Britain and the Continent. Most of the Continental countries were forced to rethink the preconditions of constitutional and political order. For Germany and later for Spain, Portugal and Greece, emerging from dictatorship, later still for the ex-Communist countries, the EU was a symbol of democratic respectability, a sign that they had come once more to be accepted into the world of civilized nations. Britain, of course, was fortunate in that she did not need such a sign of acceptance. In addition, most of the Continental countries had found themselves having to reconstruct the very foundations of the state following defeat and occupation. All had their constitutional moments. Britain did not. She alone amongst the European powers, apart from Russia – a part-European power – was a victor in the war. She and Russia were the only major European powers whose institutions had remained intact during the war. The other countries had to start again. France had been compelled to come to terms with the traumas both of 1940 when obedience to the state was treason and defiance of its dictates the only true loyalty and then the Algerian crisis of 1958, which led to the overthrow of the Fourth Republic and the installation of the Fifth, and had almost led to the overthrow of democracy itself. The Netherlands had, since the *pacificatie* of 1917, a pact between the various groups in Dutch society, taken immense pains to conciliate Protestants, Catholics, Liberals and Socialists within the framework of a single state; Belgium has spent much of the post-war period in a painful restructuring of its constitution so as to accommodate the two linguistic communities, the Flemish and the Walloon. It is hardly surprising if there was, on the Continent, a strong sense of the importance of constitutional arrangements, a constitutional sense which was, until recently at least, absent in Britain.

The evolution of the European Community and then the European Union has been strongly marked by this emphasis on the importance of constitutional arrangements. Indeed, during the last thirty-three years, there have been no less than five major amendments to the Treaty of Rome, in addition to the enlargement treaties – the Single European Act of 1986, the Maastricht Treaty of 1992, the Amsterdam Treaty of 1997, the Nice Treaty of 1999 and the Lisbon Treaty of 2008. Many in Britain have seen this process of constitutional change as quite unnecessary. Adaptation, many in Britain believe, could have been secured more pragmatically without such constitutional amendments. For the British approach to political change is quite different from that on the Continent. It relies more on the development of informal procedures of cooperation and consultation than on the reform of constitutional structures. In the imperial era, Britain had neither sought to formalize arrangements with the colonies nor to create a federal empire. Indeed, the British tradition of a sovereign parliament had made her instinctively resistant to federalism for herself, although she had been perfectly prepared to export it to the colonies. Above all, Britain has been sceptical of the extent to which integration could be secured by institutions. 'Institutions', declared Malcolm Rifkind, a future Foreign Secretary, in 1983, 'must be subservient to policies. Closer cooperation should not be forced but must grow out of practical ways in which as a Community we can work together for our common good. Substance and reality must come before form. That is the real cement of a closer Community cooperation.'[24] Such a view would not attract very

---

[24] Speech at Dundee, 23 September 1983, reprinted in Conservative Research Department, *Handbook for Europe*, 1984, p. 45.

much support on the Continent; it has often been difficult for British leaders to understand the law-governed structure of the European Union.

For England, the Glorious Revolution and the Great Reform Act emphasized the undivided sovereignty of Parliament. But, of course, the very notion of a European Community implied that Parliament could not remain sovereign, since the legal order of the Community would be superior to it. The doctrine of the primacy of European law meant that the European Community was bound to challenge the fundamental principle of the British constitution, the sovereignty of Parliament.

The European Union, unlike Britain, had no single sovereign institution. It was based, instead, on the principles of the separation of powers and the judicial review of legislation, principles hitherto alien to the British system of government.

The principle of the separation of powers is exemplified in Europe in both its central institutions and in the division of power between the Community and the member states. In the Community, constitutional authority was divided between the Council of Ministers, the Commission, the Court of Justice and the European Parliament. The Commission, as we have seen, was a curious hybrid; it was difficult for those brought up within the British constitutional tradition to understand it. In Britain, there is a strong separation of powers between elected ministers and unelected officials. Members of the government, who enjoy the right to make political decisions are, with the exception of a very small number of ministers in the House of Lords, empowered to do so by virtue of the mandate which they have received from the voters. They are elected and accountable to Parliament. Civil servants in Britain, by contrast, are unelected, but appointed on a career basis and required to observe strict political neutrality. But the Commission was composed of officials with the right to make the important political decision of initiating or not initiating, legislation. The Commission was composed of members chosen in a broadly similar way to that of civil servants in Britain, but with the power to make decisions which in Britain would be taken by ministers. British constitutional experience, however, has little role for the non-elected political leader, such as Jacques Delors or Jean-Claude Juncker.[25] So, from the British perspective, the European Union gave authority to institutions and people who are not accountable. Who, after all, elected Jean-Claude Juncker? Yet he claimed to speak for Europe.

The European Union, like Britain, has a Parliament. But the European Parliament is a quite different animal from that of Westminster, which is an executive-sustaining parliament. The role of the European Parliament, by contrast, is to sustain a dialogue with other Community institutions – the Commission and the Council of Ministers. The House of Commons, however, is fundamentally a debating chamber, dominated by the binary dialogue between government and opposition. It debates a series of measures to which the government is committed and which it must defend. The procedure adopted by standing committees, now called public bill committees, to scrutinize legislation is, in essence, an extension of the process of debate; indeed, it has been suggested that such committees would be more accurately described as 'debating committees'.[26] The procedures of Westminster are geared to informing the electorate of issues in dispute between government and opposition and they imply the existence of two disciplined armies in the House of Commons

---

[25] I once heard a Conservative MP at a meeting refer to a Commissioner, Finn Gundelach, as an 'official'. Mr Gundelach bristled. M. Delors would, one suspects, have bristled even more.

[26] J.A. Griffith, Michael Ryle and M.A.J. Wheeler-Booth, *Parliament: Functions, Practice and Procedures*, Sweet and Maxwell, 1989, p. 270.

articulating two quite different philosophies. Indeed, a student of parliament once suggested that the activities of the British Parliament were in the nature of a continuous election campaign.[27]

The European Union is quite different. For European Union legislation is neither being proposed by a government nor attacked by an opposition. European Union legislation does not conform to the binary pattern of politics which is dominant at Westminster; there is no party-supported government in the European Parliament seeking to promote its legislation or secure support for its policies. The Parliament is horseshoe-shaped rather than rectangular like Westminster. It is a working legislature rather than a debating one, geared primarily to legislative scrutiny. It is a legislature of a quite different kind from Westminster which, until the reforms of Robin Cook as Leader of the House of Commons following the 2001 general election, was geared to consider legislation only when it reached its final form, with the prestige of the government behind it. By contrast, a legislative proposal put forward by the Commission and a subsequent decision taken, in principle, by the Council of Ministers is expected to be subjected to considerable amendment as it goes through the legislative process. European legislation is scrutinized by strong specialized committees of the European Parliament whose functions, like those of the committees of the Bundestag, are both legislative and investigatory. In the House of Commons, by contrast, legislative committees do not normally begin to scrutinize legislation in detail until after Second Reading (i.e. after the principle of the legislation has been agreed) and there is a sharp distinction between legislative committees and the more investigatory and forensic Select Committees. The Commons, unlike the European Parliament, lacks

---

[27] Bernard Crick, *The Reform of Parliament*, 2nd edn, Weidenfeld and Nicolson, 1970.

specialized committees. British parliamentary processes, therefore, are of a quite different kind to those of the European Parliament, so it is not surprising that, even after Britain entered the European Community, she found it difficult to accommodate herself to the institutional practices which she found. In Britain, the executive – the government and the civil service – has, on the whole, been able to adjust itself to Europe. But Parliament has found it more difficult, although the most effective scrutiny of European legislation and perhaps the most effective in the whole European Union, is to be found in the non-elected House of Lords, rather than in the House of Commons.

The two parliaments are also elected in quite different ways. Indeed, Britain is alone in Europe in electing its popular chamber by the first-past-the-post system. Everywhere else, except in France, which uses the two-ballot system, legislatures, including the European Parliament, are elected by systems of proportional representation. Such systems generally lead either to coalition or minority governments, rather than single-party majority governments as in Britain. The European Parliament, unlike Westminster, is a multi-party parliament, which operates through carefully constructed coalitions, most frequently a coalition between the two dominant political groups, the European Peoples Party (the Christian Democrat group) and the Socialists – a party group of the moderate right and a party group of the moderate left. Coalitional politics of this kind is largely unfamiliar to British politicians. It is true that there had been experience of twentieth-century peacetime coalitions in Britain. There were coalitions between 1918 and 1922 and also after 1931. In the twenty-first century, there was to be a peacetime coalition between 2010 and 2015. But, otherwise coalitions have occurred either in wartime – from 1915–1918 and 1940–1945; or, if in peacetime, during a time of economic emergency – as in 1931 and after the hung parliament elected in 2010. These coalitions, moreover, were all seen as essentially temporary, as involving a suspension of normal adversarial party politics. On the Continent, by contrast, coalitions, in political systems characterized by multi-party politics and proportional representation electoral systems, are generally seen as involving a continuation rather than a suspension of party politics. The parties involved in a coalition (e.g. the Christian Democrats and the Social Democrats in the Federal Republic of Germany) continue to argue out their differences, but within government rather than outside it. This conception of politics has, for better or worse, been transferred to the European Union, but it is almost wholly alien to the British conception, which is based firmly on majority rule. By contrast, as Romano Prodi, President of the European Commission once put it in the European Union, 'each and every one of us is a minority because there is no majority'.[28]

The European Union, moreover, is based on the conception of a territorial division of powers between a European level of government and the level of government of the member states. This, too, was something difficult for Britain to understand; until the devolution legislation of 1998, Britain remained a profoundly unitary and centralized state, lacking any regional or provincial layer of government, with the rather unhappy exception of the Unionist-dominated Northern Ireland Parliament which sat from 1921 to 1972. France was, of course, equally centralized, but it was to establish a more decentralized form of government under the presidency of François Mitterrand in 1982. Germany, with her federal system of government, probably found it much easier to cope with the notion of a territorial division of powers than Britain. British experience has made it difficult to understand how two very different parliaments could be involved in a dialogue. Instead, the British conception has generally been one of two entirely

---

[28] Wellings, *English Nationalism and Euroscepticism* at p. 75.

separate parliaments competing with each other. Westminster and the European Parliament were, in the view of Enoch Powell, a fervent opponent of British membership of the European Community, 'involved in a duel in which only one of them can survive'.[29]

The British tradition of thinking in terms of undivided parliamentary sovereignty tended to inhibit understanding of European institutions. The concept of parliamentary sovereignty implies that in every political system there must be a supreme and unlimited institution such as the Queen in Parliament in Britain. That is why the debate in Britain was sometimes concerned with the question of who was the supreme political authority in the European Union – either the member states, in which case the decisions of the Union could only be the product of intergovernmental agreement and the Union itself could never be anything more than a Europe of states; or, if the supreme authority were the European Union, the national identity of the member states comprising the Union would be obliterated and this would mean, as far as Britain was concerned, the end, as Gaitskell put it, of 1,000 years of history. It is difficult for those possessed of the notion of undivided sovereignty to grasp that there may be a third alternative, a division and sharing of power between the Union and the member states in which neither controls the other, but each undertakes the tasks that it is best equipped to undertake.

VII

At the end of the Second World War, Georges Bernanos, the French Catholic novelist, declared 'We can no longer pretend that European

---

[29] Select Committee on the European Communities: *Relations between the UK Parliament and the European Parliament after Direct Elections*, vol. II: HL 256: 1977/78, p. 186.

Man is Man. But we believe that European civilization is inseparable from a certain conception of man'.[30] The British, of course, shared that 'certain conception of man'. Indeed, during the Second World War, they became for a time the sole defenders of it. Few doubted that, after the war, Britain would remain, not only a world power, but also a leading European power. It was overlooked that the bases of British strength were crumbling and that the countries of the Continent would recover economically with startling speed. Most British observers failed to appreciate the development of a European consciousness on the Continent, a development from which Britain remained aloof; they underestimated the fundamental differences in institutional structure and practices between Britain and her Continental neighbours, which were to make life so difficult for Britain even after she finally joined the European Community in 1973.

This does not, of course, mean that British policy towards Europe, culminating in Brexit, was predetermined by her history. There were, no doubt, a number of turning points where alternatives were possible, so that, as T.S. Eliot put it in his *Four Quartets*:

Footfalls echo in the memory
Down the passage which we did not take
Towards the door we never opened.

What is, however, clear, is that a European commitment did not follow from Britain's traditional understanding of her international position. It would have involved a radical discontinuity of approach, an imaginative leap, a leap of faith perhaps. It would have required bold leadership and a willingness to break with the past, a willingness to help liberate Britain from her history rather than accepting its

---

[30] Cited in Lukacs, *The Last European War*, p. 512.

constraints. Perhaps only Churchill in his prime could have persuaded the British people to make the necessary leap of faith. Even so, bold leadership would need to have been accompanied by popular enthusiasm and in post-war Britain there was little sign of that. The British never became emotionally committed to the European idea. Such as it was, their allegiance was transactional, based on the hope that it might help create better economic conditions at home. Europe was seen as something other, as 'them' and not 'us'. In his Declaration of 1950, the French foreign minister, Robert Schuman had spoken of the European powers as sharing 'a common destiny'. The question that the British people faced was whether they shared in that destiny. The answer which they gave in the referendum of 23 June 2016 was that they did not. In that referendum, 52 per cent voted to leave the European Union, while 48 per cent voted to remain. Turnout, at 72 per cent, was higher than in any general election since 1992. On 29 March 2017, the Prime Minister, Theresa May notified the Council of the European Union of the United Kingdom's intention to withdraw under Article 50 of the Treaty of the European Union. Under the terms of Article 50, this would mean that Britain would cease to be a member of the European Union two years after the notification (i.e. on 29 March 2019) unless either an agreement between Britain and the European Union was to be achieved before that date – a highly unlikely contingency – or the European Council acting by unanimity agreed to extend the deadline. The European Union Withdrawal Act 2018, passed by Parliament, gave legislative sanction to Brexit occurring on 29 March 2019. Unless this legislation is either modified or repealed then, at midnight European time, 11 p.m. United Kingdom time, Britain will cease to be a member of the European Union.

2

Europe and the Sovereignty of Parliament

I

Europe then, posed a challenge to the sovereignty of Parliament. But that challenge was not clearly perceived either by ministers, by MPs, by lawyers or by legal academics until well after Britain had joined the European Community in 1973. There was, in particular, a tendency to confuse parliamentary sovereignty with national sovereignty and to assimilate the European Community with other international commitments that Britain had subscribed to such as the Council of Europe or NATO.

Yet two landmark legal cases decided by the European Court of Justice in the early 1960s had made it clear that the European Community was a quite different kind of organization. In *Van Gend en Loos* in 1963, the European Court ruled that the government of the Netherlands was not entitled unilaterally to impose its own customs duties and, furthermore, that individuals and companies as well as national governments had the right to bring action against the government which was imposing the duties for infringing European law. The European Court's judgment established the doctrine that Community legislation had direct effect upon the law of the member states. The Court declared that:

> The objective of the EEC Treaty, which is to establish a common market, the functioning of which is of direct concern to interested parties in the Community, implies that this Treaty is more than an agreement which merely creates mutual obligations between the contracting states. . . . the Community constitutes a new legal order of international law for the benefit of which the States have limited their sovereign rights, albeit within limited fields, and the subjects of which comprise not only member states but also their nationals independently of the legislation of member states, Community law therefore not only imposes obligations on individuals but is also intended to confer upon them rights which become part of their legal heritage.'[1]

In consequence of this judgment, the courts and tribunals of the member states as well as the European Court of Justice, had a duty to ensure that member states complied with European law. This meant that courts and tribunals in the member states, including Britain after she joined, would become also constitutional courts, to ensure that member states observed the 'new legal order' of the European Community.

The doctrine of direct effect was to be complemented by the doctrine of the primacy of Community law. This doctrine was asserted in the European Court of Justice's judgment in the case *Costa/ENEL* in 1964. That case concerned the lawfulness of the nationalization by

---

[1] Case 26/62 [1963] ECR 1, at 12.

the Italian government of the electricity industry. The European Court ruled that Mr Costa, an Italian citizen, had the right to bring a case against his government in an Italian court, arguing that the nationalization was unlawful as it was in conflict with European law, which was superior to Italian law. The European Court in its judgment declared that:

By contrast with ordinary international treaties, the EEC Treaty has created its own legal system. By creating a Community of unlimited duration, having its own institutions, its own personality, its own legal capacity and capacity of representation on the international plane and, more particularly, real powers stemming from a limitation of sovereignty or a transfer of powers from the States to the Community, the Member States have limited their sovereign rights, albeit within limited fields, and have thus created a body of law which binds both their nationals and themselves.

The integration into the laws of each member state of provisions which derive from the Community and, more generally, the terms and the spirit of the Treaty, make it impossible for the States, as a corollary, to accord precedence to a unilateral and subsequent measure over a legal system accepted by them on a basis of reciprocity. Such a measure cannot therefore be inconsistent with that legal system.

It follows ... that the law stemming from the Treaty, an independent source of law, could not, because of its special and original nature, be over-ridden by domestic legal provisions, however framed, without being deprived of its character as Community law and without the legal basis of the Community itself being called into question.

Therefore, 'the transfer by the States from their domestic legal systems to the Community legal system of rights and obligations arising under the Treaty carries with it a *permanent limitation of their sovereign rights, against which a subsequent unilateral act incompatible with the concept of the Community cannot prevail*' (emphasis added).[2] The judgment in *Costa* made it clear that European Community law could not be allowed to vary as between member states. That was implicit in the concept of a common or single European market in Europe with the consequence that trade barriers and distortions of free and equal competition in the member states would be removed. That would require uniform rules operating throughout the area, with an impartial court, the European Court of Justice, to ensure that the rules were observed.

These two doctrines – the doctrine of supremacy and the doctrine of direct effect – would clearly have massive constitutional implications for all the member states and, in particular, for Britain with her doctrine of parliamentary sovereignty. For how could Parliament remain sovereign in the face of the 'higher law' of the European Community? Indeed, the two doctrines of supremacy and direct effect logically entailed a limitation of parliamentary sovereignty, if not its abdication. Yet, neither *van Gend* nor *Costa* were reported in the British press, nor even in any of the domestic law journals, with the exception of the *Common Market Law Review*, which had been founded in 1963; nor were the judgments analysed by any but a very small number of legal academics. In 1971, however, a leading constitutional lawyer, S.A. de Smith, one of the very few to perceive the momentous consequences of Community membership, defined the European Community as 'an inchoate functional federation' and argued that 'full recognition of the hierarchical superiority of Community law would entail a revolution in legal thought'. He declared that there was 'no sure means of predicting the constitutional

---

[2] Case 6/64 [1964] ECR 585, at 593.

impact on the United Kingdom of admission to such an association.[3] That was a wise admission.

De Smith, however, was a voice crying in the wilderness. During the 1960s and early 1970s, much of the debate on Europe was concerned with matters other than sovereignty – in particular, the effects of entry into the Community upon the Commonwealth and on food prices in Britain. The question of sovereignty was, admittedly, raised by a few back-benchers opposed to British entry, but most of the opponents tended to concentrate on other issues. It was no doubt easier to persuade the British public of the concrete disadvantages of entry, such as a rise in food prices, than upon the dangers which might arise from what seemed an abstract matter, the issue of sovereignty.

At the time of Britain's first application to join the Community, in 1961, there was, however, some private discussion amongst officials in Whitehall. The Foreign Office whose ministers, the Foreign Secretary, Sir Alec Douglas-Home and the Lord Privy Seal, Edward Heath, the chief British negotiator, were deeply committed to entry, tended to minimize the consequences for sovereignty and to glide over the differences between national and parliamentary sovereignty. Edward Heath wrote to Lord Kilmuir, the Lord Chancellor, in November 1960, 'I am myself inclined to feel that we have allowed ourselves to be over-impressed by supranationality, and that in the modern world if, from other points of view, political and economic, it should prove desirable to accept such further limitations on sovereignty as would follow from the signature of the Treaty of Rome, we could do so without danger to the essential character of our independence and without prejudice to our vital interests'; one Foreign Office official minuted in the early 1960s that, 'to make some surrenders in the constitutional

---

[3] S.A. de Smith, 'The Constitution and the Common Market: A Tentative Appraisal' (1971) 34(6) *Modern Law Review* 613.

sphere is ... to my mind to surrender a shadow for substance'. What Heath and the official meant was that it was worth accepting limits on Britain's national sovereignty to increase her freedom of manoeuvre and influence in the world. That, of course, was a perfectly reasonable political judgment to make, but it was a political, not a constitutional, judgment and it did not meet the point that Parliament might be transferring or abdicating its sovereignty. Lord Kilmuir, the Lord Chancellor, replied to Heath. Like Heath, he favoured British entry, but he took the view that the sacrifice of sovereignty would be more serious than Heath had suggested and that it was important to confront it directly to avoid disillusion when the concrete consequences of the loss of sovereignty became apparent. In his reply to Heath, Lord Kilmuir pointed out that the decisions of the Council of Ministers, once qualified majority voting came about, would bind Britain even against the wishes of Parliament and that an Act of Parliament giving the force of law to all Council regulations 'would go far beyond the most extensive delegation of powers, even in wartime, that we have ever experienced'. It would also require questions of law relating to the European Community to be decided by the European Court of Justice. This, he predicted, would be disliked by 'the whole of the legal profession'.[4] That, perhaps, was one prediction which was not wholly fulfilled! But even Kilmuir, concerned as he was with the notion of sovereignty, did not quite penetrate to the core of the issue. He did not point out that questions of law relating to the European Community would also have to be decided by British courts and tribunals and that the consequences of membership would go far beyond any 'delegation of powers', even an extensive one. It was, in any case, somewhat odd to speak of a 'delegation of powers'. Delegation, after all, implies a transfer of power from a superior law-making

---

[4] Alan S. Milward, *The Rise and Fall of a National Strategy,* pp. 444–5, 448.

system to an inferior one, a transfer which can be revoked at any time. To delegate is generally to give power to an agent or deputy. It was hardly possible, however, to view the European Community in these terms. For entry to the Community would mean a transfer of law-making power to a legal system enjoying primacy over United Kingdom law; although, as Brexit shows, it would be possible to revoke that transfer, by repealing the European Communities Act of 1972, that process would not be easy since it would involve disentangling Britain from a whole complex of European laws made during the period of membership. In the *Miller* case in 2017, Britain's Supreme Court was to decline to accept in paragraph 68 'the suggestion that, as a source of law, EU law can properly be compared with delegated legislation'.[5] Instead, the European Communities Act had operated 'as a partial transfer of law-making powers or an assignment of legislative competences by parliament to the EU law-making institutions (so long as Parliament wills it) . . .' because the European Union made laws independently of Parliament.

In 1967, when Britain made her second attempt to enter the European Community under the Labour government of Harold Wilson, a White Paper was issued entitled *Legal and Constitutional Implications of the European Communities*. This too failed to mention the *van Gend* and *Costa* judgments. It recognized that Parliament would have to pass legislation giving the force of law to those provisions of Community law intended to have direct effect. It then declared that 'the constitutional innovation would lie in the acceptance in advance as part of the law of the United Kingdom of provisions to be made in the future by instruments issued by the Community institutions – a situation for which there is no precedent in this country' (paragraph 22). It also recognized that Community law 'is

---

[5] *R (Miller) v Secretary of State for Exiting the European Union* [2017] UKSC 5.

designed to take precedence over the domestic law of the Member States'. But it minimized the significance of entry by again treating Community law, even though a form of higher law, as a form of delegation of power. 'Like ordinary delegated legislation', Community law 'would derive that force under the law of the United Kingdom from the original enactment passed by Parliament'. It also minimized the effect on individuals by stating that direct effect was 'in relation to industrial and commercial activities and does not touch citizens in their private capacities'. Lord Gardiner, the Lord Chancellor, endorsed this view in the House of Lords. 'Community law', he declared, 'has little direct effect on the ordinary life of private citizens. In so far as it imposes obligations, it does so mostly in relation to industrial and commercial activities and does not touch citizens in their private capacities'. Lord Gardiner declared that he agreed with what his Conservative predecessor, Lord Dilhorne, had said in August 1962: 'I venture to suggest that the vast majority of men and women in this country will never directly feel the impact of the Community-made law at all. In the conduct of their daily affairs they will have no need to have regard to any of the provisions of that law – nor are they at all likely ever to be affected by an administrative action of one of the Community institutions.'[6] But, as we have seen, the European Community had created new enforceable rights and obligations for individuals as well as for industrial and commercial companies, including the right to seek a legal remedy both in national courts and tribunals and in the European Court of Justice. European law was to apply in the fields of industry, employment, prices and food. These matters affected the individual citizen far more than did the criminal law in which the European Community had no competence. More importantly, perhaps, the Lord Chancellor's view failed to take account

---

[6] House of Lords, vol. 282, cols 1203–4, 8 May 1967.

of the fact that the European Community was a dynamic and not a static institution which would seek to legislate in new areas, areas which would come increasingly to affect the individual citizen.

The White Paper, however, drew the following conclusion from British entry. 'It would also follow that within the fields occupied by the Community law Parliament would have to refrain from passing fresh legislation inconsistent with that law as for the time being in force.' But it suggested in paragraph 23 that:

> this would not however involve any constitutional innovation. Many of our treaty obligations already impose such restraints – for example, the Charter of the United Nations, the European Convention on Human Rights [this was of course written before the Human Rights Act of 1998] and GATT [the General Agreement on Tariffs and Trade].

The White Paper entirely failed to appreciate that the European Community imposed a quite different kind of obligation, which was not a 'restraint' of a voluntary kind as with other treaty obligations, an obligation in international law, but not binding in national law. Instead, entry into the Community would give rise to an obligation in national law which national courts and tribunals and the European Court of Justice would be under a duty to enforce. In the parliamentary debates in 1967, no minister or MP referred to *van Gend* or *Costa*, while Sir Lionel Heald, a former Attorney-General and Conservative backbencher of great authority assured the House of Commons that 'the essentials of the whole law of this country are not touched in any way by the Treaty'.[7]

Edward Heath's Conservative government, returned in the general election of 1970, made a third attempt to enter the European

---

[7] House of Commons, vol. xxx, col. 1546, 10 May 1967.

Community. This time it was successful. A further White Paper was issued in 1971 entitled *The United Kingdom and the European Communities*, Cmnd 4715. That too made no mention of *van Gend* or *Costa*; it was hardly mentioned in the very extensive parliamentary debates in 1971 and 1972, even though, according to the Solicitor-General, Sir Geoffrey Howe, over 2 million words were spoken in the Commons debates and another 400,000 in corresponding debates in the Lords.[8] The bulk of the 1971 White Paper was concerned with making the case for British entry into the Communities. It discussed in detail economic matters and the transitional arrangements. In a 48-page document, only three paragraphs dealt with constitutional matters and these minimized the constitutional consequences of entry. It emphasized that: 'The Community is no federation of provinces or counties. It constitutes a Community of great and established nations, each with its own personality and traditions. The practical workings of the Community accordingly reflect the reality that sovereign Governments are represented round the table.' The White Paper drew comfort from the so-called Luxembourg Compromise of 1966 by which 'when a Government considers that vital national interests are involved, it is established that the decision should be unanimous'. But the veto which member states enjoyed under the Luxembourg Compromise, which was a convention rather than being embodied in statute, was to disappear following the Single European Act in 1986. In any case, it was irrelevant to judgments of the European Court of Justice. For in that court, neither Britain nor any other member state enjoyed a veto. The White Paper, however, went on to say, 'like any other treaty, the Treaty of Rome commits its signatories to support agreed aims; but the commitment represents the *voluntary*

---

[8] Geoffrey Howe, 'The European Communities Act 1972' (1973) 49(1) *International Affairs*, 1.

undertaking of a sovereign state to observe policies which it has helped to form' (emphasis added). It concluded with a sentence that was to give rise to much controversy: 'There is no question of any erosion of essential national sovereignty; what is proposed is a sharing and an enlargement of individual national sovereignties in the general interest' (para 28). That, of course, was a matter of opinion and it contrasted markedly with the argument for joining the European Community put forward by the Heath government that it was a step of major importance which would greatly enhance Britain's standing in international affairs. Even if, however, there was to be no erosion of 'essential national sovereignty' it did not follow that there would be no erosion of parliamentary sovereignty. The White Paper did not discuss this issue of parliamentary sovereignty at all, nor the altered role of the courts flowing from membership. Paragraph 31 contented itself with the statement that 'the English and Scottish legal systems will remain intact'. It did concede that 'in certain cases' the courts 'would need to refer points of Community law to the European Court of Justice' but declared that 'our courts will continue to operate as they do at present' and that 'all the essential features of our law will remain'. This gave a quite misleading impression of the consequences of membership. The role of the courts, as we have seen, would be transformed. They would become constitutional courts and the English and Scottish legal systems, although they might remain, from one point of view, 'intact', would now become subordinate to the Community legal system. Further, British allegiance to Community law would in no sense be a 'voluntary undertaking', but a legal obligation which, if not observed, would lead to proceedings being brought in national courts and tribunals or the European Court of Justice, with the possibility of penalties for non-compliance.

In 1972, Parliament passed the European Communities Act which provided for British entry. This Act secured parliamentary approval for the Treaty of Accession making Britain part of the European Communities on the terms which Edward Heath had negotiated with the other members of the Community; it provided statutory authority to make the necessary consequential alterations to United Kingdom law. The problem which the Act had to solve was one of defining the relationship between two very different systems of law, United Kingdom law and Community law. In theory, this could have been done by specifically incorporating every single provision of Community legislation into United Kingdom law. Indeed, that had been the implication of the 1967 White Paper, which had declared, in paragraph 20, that 'a substantial body of legislation would be required to enable us to accept the law [of the Communities]'. But such a process, as well as being highly complex, would have given a misleading view of the nature of Community law. This was a single and independent system of law which could not be translated into different forms in each of the different member states. If Community law had to be enacted separately for each member state by each national legislature, the rules might well not have a uniform effect; and that would defeat the whole conception of a common market. The European Communities Act, therefore, proved to be a short one, which reflected the view of Community law as an independent and uniform system. Sections 2(1) and 2(2) of the Act enabled ministers to introduce legislation giving effect to all European Community law, both past and future, in the United Kingdom. Community law, therefore, was to be treated as a legal system which British courts would be required to apply. That would probably cause no difficulty in principle from the point of view of incorporating current Community law. But how could Parliament bind future Parliaments to accept future Community law? The principle of parliamentary sovereignty implied that Parliament could not bind itself in the future not to enact legislation contrary to Community law. The problem was resolved through section 2(4) of the Act which provided that future United Kingdom legislation was to 'be construed and have effect' subject to the Act; section 3(1) provided that, for purposes of legal proceedings, issues on the meaning or validity of Community law would either be referred to the European Court of Justice or would be determined by national courts 'in accordance with the principles laid down by and any relevant decisions of the European Court'. In consequence, United Kingdom courts would, in consequence of this part of the legislation, become transformed into constitutional courts.

The Act, which would fundamentally alter the constitution of the United Kingdom, was a skilful form of pragmatism. Perhaps wisely from a political point of view, it elided crucial constitutional issues rather than resolving them. It did not provide for what was to happen if subsequent United Kingdom legislation could *not* be construed to be in accordance with Community law; and it did not state explicitly that a future Parliament could not enact legislation contrary to Community law. It therefore took no position on the crucial question of the primacy of Community law, whether future United Kingdom legislation would be subordinate to Community law. From the point of view of the Community, of course, future United Kingdom legislation would be subordinate. In 1979, in *Commission of the European Communities v United Kingdom of Great Britain and Northern Ireland*, the European Court of Justice was to declare that:

> For a State unilaterally to break, according to its own conception of national interest, the equilibrium between advantages and obligations flowing from its adherence brings into question the equality of Member States before Community law and creates discrimination at the expense of their nationals. This failure in the duty of solidarity accepted by Member States by the fact of their

adherence to the Community strikes at the very roots of the Community legal order.[9]

From the Community point of view, therefore, a country seeking to join was required to ensure that its future legislation would be subordinate to the Community legal order. If, for any reason, it was unable or unwilling to do so, it would be seeking entry under false pretences.

The parliamentary proceedings on the European Communities bill show, however, that responsible ministers did not believe that future Parliaments would be legally bound by British entry into the Community. Indeed, both Lord Hailsham, the Lord Chancellor and Sir Geoffrey Howe, the Solicitor-General, went further, declaring that it was logically impossible for Parliament so to bind itself by limiting its powers. Lord Hailsham declared that it was 'abundantly obvious' 'not merely that this bill does nothing to qualify the sovereignty of Parliament but that it could not do so' and that parliamentary sovereignty prevailed over 'any treaty you choose to name, including this one'. Sir Geoffrey Howe declared that 'the ultimate supremacy of Parliament will not be affected, and it will not be affected because it cannot be affected'.[10] In 1977, in a paper submitted to the House of Lords Select Committee on a Bill of Rights, this doctrine was defended by the Specialist Adviser to the Committee and by academic and judicial authorities. They took the view that an Act of Parliament could not protect itself even from implied repeal and that a later Act would always enjoy primacy over an earlier one. David Rippengal, the Specialist Adviser to the House of Lords Select Committee on a Bill of Rights, declared that 'an Act can no more protect itself from implied

---

[9] European Court of Justice. Case 128/78 [1979] ECR 419 at 429.

[10] House of Lords, 7 August 1972, vol. 334, cols 813, 911; House of Commons, 5 July 1972, vol. 840, col. 556.

derogation by a future Act than it can protect itself from express derogation.' He also doubted whether section 2(4) of the European Communities Act would protect Community law from implied repeal. This view was endorsed by Professor Hood Phillips, a leading constitutional authority and Professor of Law at Birmingham University and by Lord Diplock, a law lord. The Select Committee concluded that it would be 'very remarkable ... for the courts to assume a power quite suddenly out of the blue to overrule the express words of Parliament, whether put in inadvertently or otherwise' and that 'there is no way in which a Bill of Rights could be made immune altogether from amendment or repeal by a subsequent Act. That follows from the principle of the sovereignty of parliament which is the central feature of our constitution.' In particular, there was 'no way in which a Bill of Rights could protect itself from encroachment, whether express or implied by later Acts'.[11]

But the sovereignty of Parliament is a far more complex and, indeed, confused notion than either Lord Hailsham, Sir Geoffrey or the Select Committee were willing to acknowledge.[12]

The classic formulation of the doctrine of the sovereignty of Parliament is that Parliament can enact any law that it chooses except one to limit its powers and that the validity of an Act of Parliament cannot be challenged in any court. There are a number of problems with this classic formulation.

The first problem is that of determining whether the clause 'except a law to limit its powers' delineates a genuine exception, the one possible exception, to the doctrine of sovereignty; or whether it is,

---

[11] Report of the Select Committee on a Bill of Rights, HL 176, 1977–8. Minutes of Evidence, 2, paras 7, 9, 28, pp. 277–91; report, para. 14.

[12] See, for a more detailed account of the complexities and confusions, Vernon Bogdanor, 'Imprisoned by a Doctrine: The Modern Defence of Parliamentary Sovereignty' (2012) 32(1) *Oxford Journal of Legal Studies*, 179–95. This section draws heavily on that article.

by contrast, an exemplification of the doctrine. On the former interpretation, it is not clear why it should be the case that the inability of a law to limit its power should be the *only* exception to parliamentary omnipotence. If there can be one exception, why not others also? Therefore, so some argue, the inability to limit its powers is an exemplification of the doctrine of parliamentary sovereignty, not an exception to it. But that is equally peculiar. For it seems odd to suggest that one of the qualities of omnipotence, an omnipotence that is often said to yield flexibility, is something that one cannot do, that is, bind oneself. It is perhaps similar to the conundrum, as yet unresolved by theologians, as to whether an omnipotent God can enact a binding rule which destroys divine omnipotence for the future. Can God bind herself?

But there is an even more fundamental point to be made concerning the question of whether Parliament can bind itself. For it is not contrary to logic to suggest that a sovereign body could pass an Act limiting its powers. The question is whether it has, in fact, done so. In his classic work, *The Concept of Law*, the legal philosopher, H.L.A. Hart, distinguishes between *continuing* sovereignty, a form of sovereignty in which the sovereign authority *cannot* bind itself; and *self-embracing* sovereignty, a form of sovereignty in which the sovereign authority *can*, in fact, bind itself. Of course, once a sovereign legislature has bound itself, it is no longer sovereign; so a sovereign authority can only bind itself on a single occasion. Hart concludes, therefore, that the idea of sovereignty is 'an ambiguous idea ... It in effect makes a choice between a continuing omnipotence in all matters not affecting the legislative competence of successive parliaments and an unrestricted self-embracing omnipotence, the exercise of which can only be enjoyed once – Which form of omnipotence – continuing or self-embracing – our Parliament enjoys is an empirical question concerning the form of rule which is accepted as the ultimate criterion in identifying the law'.[13] It follows, therefore, that it cannot be a defining element of the notion of the sovereignty of Parliament that it cannot pass an Act limiting its power. Whether Parliament can do so is an empirical matter, not a matter of logic. The issue cannot be settled by a mere conceptual analysis. Hart, like Dicey before him, believed that Parliament enjoyed a continuing sovereignty; but in 1961, when *The Concept of Law* was published, the challenge to parliamentary sovereignty posed by the European Community was, as we have seen, hardly appreciated. Indeed, there is no mention of it in the book.

Dicey, who first codified the theory of parliamentary sovereignty, did not notice the ambiguity in the concept. He seems simply to have assumed that sovereignty must, as a matter of logic, be continuous. Indeed, it seems as if, at first sight, he would have shared the view of Lord Hailsham and Sir Geoffrey Howe that Parliament could *never* limit its sovereignty. But Dicey thought that it was perfectly possible for Parliament, if it so chose, to *abdicate* its sovereignty. In *The Law of the Constitution* he writes, 'The impossibility of placing a limit on the exercise of sovereignty does not in any way prohibit either logically, or in matter of fact, the abdication of sovereignty. This is worth observation, because a strange dogma is sometimes put forward that a sovereign power, such as the Parliament of the United Kingdom can never by its own act divest itself of sovereignty. This position, is, however, clearly untenable. An autocrat, such as the Russian Czar, can undoubtedly abdicate; but sovereignty or the possession of supreme power in a state, whether it be in the hands of a Czar or of a Parliament, is always one and the same quality. If the Czar can abdicate, so can a Parliament. To argue or imply that because is not limitable (which is true) it cannot be surrendered (which is palpably untrue) involves the confusion of two distinct ideas. It is like arguing that because no man

---

[13] H.L.A. Hart, *The Concept of Law*, Clarendon Press, 1961, pp. 149–50.

can, while he lives, give up, do what he will, his freedom of volition, so no man can commit suicide'. And one way in which Parliament could abdicate its sovereignty would be to 'transfer sovereign authority to another person or body of persons'.[14] Indeed, it seems contrary to common sense to deny that Parliament could abdicate its sovereignty. Suppose, for example, that Britain decided to enact a constitution which limited the powers of Parliament. It would then have abdicated its sovereignty in favour of a constitution. Whether or not it would be desirable for Britain to enact a constitution is, of course, a separate question. But it seems quite absurd to suggest that it would be logically impossible for Britain so to act. If, however, it is possible for Parliament completely and permanently to abdicate its sovereignty, it is not clear why it is that Parliament cannot also limit its sovereignty in some lesser way, by, for example, transferring its powers to legislate on some matters to another body, so putting an end to its own powers to legislate on such matters.

Dicey, in fact, did not share the view of Lord Hailsham and Sir Geoffrey Howe that, as a matter of logic, Parliament could *never* limit its supremacy. He seems rather to have believed that it could have done but had never as a matter of fact done so. For he argued in *Law of the Constitution* that 'the historical reason why Parliament has never succeeded in passing immutable laws ... lies deep in the history of the English people and in the peculiar development of the English constitution'. The implication of this remark, surely, is that Parliament might, at some time in the future, actually succeed in doing what it had 'never succeeded' at in the past, namely passing an immutable law. For, if it is not a logical impossibility for Parliament to bind itself, then it must be contingent, an historical fact to the effect that Parliament has never in the past bound itself. But there might be perfectly good

---

[14] A.V. Dicey, *Introduction to the Study of the Law of the Constitution*, pp. 68–69fn.

reasons why Parliament might decide to bind itself, for example, to entrench certain human rights in legislation to prevent future generations from abridging them; perhaps Parliament in 1972, in effect if not in intention, did, in fact, bind itself to secure allegiance to a new legal order superior to that of Westminster.

Perhaps, therefore, it would be more charitable to interpret the comments of Lord Hailsham and Sir Geoffrey Howe during the parliamentary debates on the European Communities bill as meaning that, while, no doubt, Parliament could, under certain circumstances, limit or even abdicate its sovereignty, it was not, in their view, in fact doing so in the European Communities Act. But, if the Act did not bind future parliaments, it would follow that, were Parliament in future to enact a statute which could *not* be construed in terms of the European Communities Act, it would be the duty, nevertheless, of the courts to give effect to that particular statute. That was indeed the view of Lord Diplock, whom Sir Geoffrey Howe quoted in the parliamentary debates. Lord Diplock had told the Association of Teachers of Public Law in December 1971, that 'if the Queen in Parliament were to make laws which were in conflict with this country's obligations under the Treaty of Rome, those laws and not the conflicting provisions of the Treaty would be given effect as to the domestic law of the United Kingdom'.[15] Lord Diplock told the House of Lords that, although legislation contrary to the provisions of the Treaty of Rome would clearly be a breach of that Treaty, nevertheless, 'the courts would be bound to give effect to a subsequent Act of Parliament under the law as it is administered in the courts today, and as it will continue to be administered, because the Bill does not alter that'.[16]

---

[15] House of Commons, 5 July 1972, vol. 840, col. 629.
[16] House of Lords, 8 August 1972, vol. 334, col. 1029.

Yet, to the lay person, the implication of Britain's membership of the European Community in the light of the *Van Gend* and *Costa* judgments would be that, in the event of a conflict between Community law and the law of a member state, Community law would take precedence; indeed, by virtue of the judgment of the European Court of Justice in *Simmenthal* in 1978,[17] it was to become the duty of every national court and tribunal to enforce Community law and to disapply any conflicting national law. The logical implication, therefore, was that a litigant could go to a domestic court in Britain to have a statutory provision enacted by Westminster set aside. In terms of this logic, British judges would be under a duty to evaluate legislation in terms of its compatibility with Community law. They would be under a duty to apply Community legislation and also to interpret Westminster legislation, where that was possible, so that it was in conformity with Community legislation; since future United Kingdom law was to be construed by the courts subject to Community law, it followed that any future statute would have to be interpreted with reference to Community law. This meant that a later statute could not repeal by implication a Community law. If Parliament wanted to repeal a Community law, it would have to do so explicitly; this would, of course, be in defiance of the Community legal order.

Yet, until Britain entered the European Community, it had been held by the courts that, when two statutes conflicted, the later statute should prevail even if it did not explicitly repeal the former. This is known as the doctrine of *implied repeal* and had been standard legal doctrine since two cases in the 1930s, *Vauxhall Estates v Liverpool Corporation* [1932] 1 KB 723 and *Ellen Street Estates Ltd v Minister of*

---

[17] Case 106/77 *Amministrazione delle Finanze dello Stato v Simmenthal SpA* [1978] ECR 629; [1978] 3 CMLR 263.

Health [1934] 1 KB 590. Implied repeal seemed a logical consequence of the continuing version of the sovereignty of Parliament; since, if an earlier statute could override a later statute, it would be possible for one Parliament to limit what a later Parliament could do. But, if every measure passed after the European Communities Act of 1972 was to be subject to implied repeal, Britain would be in regular breach of the principle of the supremacy of Community law. This dilemma was resolved in *Macarthys v Smith* [1979] 3 All ER 325 when the European Communities Act was held to be immune from implied repeal. Whether it could be subject to explicit repeal without repealing the European Communities Act itself was never clear; since no case presented itself in which Parliament enacted a provision such as: 'Notwithstanding the European Communities Act, it is hereby enacted that e.g. a tariff is to be imposed on French goods.' It is impossible to tell, therefore, what the attitude of the courts would have been to such an enactment.

The new doctrine – that implied repeal of Community law was not possible and that Parliament would have to make its intentions explicit – was first applied by Lord Denning, the Master of the Rolls, in *Macarthys v Smith*. In that case, however, he did concede that Parliament could, if it wished, explicitly repeal Community law. He commented, obiter, that 'If the time should come when our Parliament deliberately passes an Act with the intention of repudiating the Treaty or any provision in it or intentionally of acting inconsistently with it and says so in express terms then I should have thought that it would be the duty of our courts to follow the statute of our Parliament'. Sir Geoffrey Howe had agreed, telling the Commons in 1972: 'Most people have agreed that a subsequent United Kingdom statute … which began with the phrase "notwithstanding the provisions of … the European Communities Bill, black shall be white, would mean that the courts of this country would give effect to that limited proposition, certainly as the matter now stands".'[18] To which the reply might be, in the words of a noted constitutional lawyer, that 'it is impossible to remain within a legal order and to deny its consequences'.[19] Indeed, despite Lord Denning's comment made, obiter, there must still remain a doubt as to whether the British courts would have treated an Act of Parliament repudiating, not the Treaty as a whole, but a particular provision of it, as valid in their role as British courts; or whether, acting as constitutional courts for the European Community, they would have disapplied it. Were the courts to have treated the Act concerned as valid, the European Commission might have brought proceedings against the British government at the European Court of Justice at Luxembourg and if the British government had been found guilty of a breach of Community law, a penalty would have been imposed. Fortunately, perhaps, the issue of what the British courts would have done in the case of an explicit incompatibility between a British statute and Community law was never put to the test. However, the issue of implied repeal had been put to the test and was decided in favour of Community law.

An even more momentous step than in *Macarthys v Smith* was taken in the second *Factortame* case in 1991 – *R v Secretary of State for Transport, ex p. Factortame (No. 2)*.[20] In that case, it was established that, not only was Community law protected from implied repeal, but that it was also the supreme law of the land.

In 1988, Parliament had passed a Merchant Shipping Act, in effect restricting the right of foreign-owned vessels to fish in British waters. A Spanish company adversely affected by this Act brought an action

---

[18] House of Commons, 13 June 1972, vol. 838, col. 1320.
[19] J.D.B. Mitchell 'What Happened to the Constitution on 1 January 1973' (1980) 11 *Cambrian Law Review* 69 at 76.
[20] [1991] 1 All ER 70; [1991] 1 AC [603].

in the British courts claiming that the Merchant Shipping Act was incompatible with the European Communities Act. In the High Court, Lord Justice Neill spoke of a new 'state of affairs which came into being when the United Kingdom became a Member State of the European Community in January 1973. Twenty years ago, the idea that the High Court could question the validity of an Act of Parliament or fail, having construed it, to give effect to it would have been unthinkable. But the High Court now has a duty ... where there is a conflict, to prefer the Community law to national law'. Lord Justice Neill also accepted that Parliament had bound itself in the 1972 Act. The effects of that Act were, he declared, 'as I understand it, that directly applicable Community provisions are to prevail not only over existing but also over future Acts of Parliament (i.e. Acts subsequent to 1972) in so far as these provisions may be inconsistent with such enactments'. Lord Justice Hodgson declared that it used to be 'unthinkable that there should be in an English court a higher authority than an Act of Parliament, but there is now in English law such a higher authority'.[21] When the *Factortame* case reached the House of Lords, the Law Lords accepted the arguments put by the Spanish company and declared that the courts would, for the first time in British history, 'disapply' part of a Westminster statute, the relevant provisions of the Merchant Shipping Act, as being in conflict with Community law. Sir Geoffrey Howe had declared in 1973 that if 'a conflict *should* occur between Community law and a United Kingdom statute enacted in the future, our courts have not been given the power (for which some people have argued) of declaring the later United Kingdom statute invalid'.[22] *Factortame* proved Sir Geoffrey's prediction false. The Law Lords took that power.

---

[21] [1988] CMLR 353 at 373, 374 and 381.
[22] Howe, 'The European Communities Act' at 9–10.

It followed that, as long as Britain remained within the EU, Westminster was, in effect, a legislature of limited competence and that British courts and tribunals were, in effect, constitutional courts able to pronounce on the validity of Acts of Parliament. In a later case, *R v Secretary of State for Employment ex parte Equal Opportunities Commission*,[23] the Law Lords ruled that aspects of the Employment Protection (Consolidation) Act of 1978 were incompatible with European Community law. The Law Lords again over-rode a statutory provision as incompatible with Community law. On this case, *The Times* commented, 'Britain may now have, for the first time in its history, a constitutional court' and concluded, 'in any other society, such constitutional "revision" would be a subject for heated debate. Its significance must not be lost on Britain's citizens and its Parliament'.[24]

There was now in Britain judicial review of primary legislation, a concept hitherto unknown to the British constitution. Europe had altered the balance of power in the British system of government in favour of the judiciary at the expense of Parliament and government; the power of Parliament had come to be limited through the supremacy of European Community law. There was a shift of power from Parliament not only to the European Court of Justice but also to national courts. That, of course, was the case in all the member states, but it was of particular importance for Britain which had no history of the judicial review of primary legislation. The effect of European Community membership, therefore, was to entrench provisions of Community law into our legal system. 'Most of us', Margaret Thatcher, a former barrister, was to conclude in 1995, 'including myself, paid insufficient regard to the issue of sovereignty in consideration of the case for joining the EEC

---

[23] [1995] 1 AC 1.
[24] *The Times*, 5 March 1994.

at the beginning of the 1970s ... There was a failure to grasp the true nature of the European Court and the relationship that would emerge between British law and Community law'.[25]

What the European Communities Act of 1972 had done, therefore, was fundamental. It had, in the words of the majority of judges in the *Miller* case in 2017, provided 'a new constitutional process for making law in the United Kingdom'.[26] It had, therefore, altered the rule of recognition in the United Kingdom. For the European Community was clearly not a mere association of sovereign states but a higher legal order in which the doctrine of primacy had already been established. The basis for the doctrine of primacy was that, if all member states were equally to honour their obligations under the treaty, the law deriving from the treaties must be applied uniformly throughout the Community so that member states would not be able unilaterally to derogate from European Community law. This meant that national courts would have to apply European Community law in preference to inconsistent national law. From the Community's point of view, it would be inconsistent with Britain's continued membership of the Community to suppose that Parliament intended a statute to be enforced if it could not be construed as being in accordance with Community law, even if Parliament seemed to have indicated to the contrary.

II

It seems then that our entry into the European Community had produced a structural change in the constitution in relation to Community law. That seems to be the only way to interpret the

---

[25] Margaret Thatcher, *The Path to Power*, Harper-Collins, 1995, p. 497.
[26] See para. 62.

judgment of Lord Bridge in *Factortame*. He spoke of 'the duty of a United Kingdom court, when delivering final judgment, to override any rule of national law found to be in conflict with any directly enforceable rule of Community law'. The reason for this was that 'if the supremacy ... of Community law over the national law of member states was not always inherent in the EEC Treaty, it was certainly well established in the jurisprudence of the Court of Justice long before the United Kingdom joined the Community'.[27] Directly applicable European Community law therefore prevailed over national law and Parliament had, in the European Communities Act, so it appears, parted with its sovereignty. In the words of Hoffmann J, admittedly obiter and without reference to *Factortame*:

> The Treaty of Rome is the supreme law in this country, taking precedence over Acts of Parliament. Our entry to the Community meant that (subject to our undoubted but probably theoretical right to withdraw from the Community altoget\her) Parliament surrendered its sovereign right to legislate contrary to the provisions of the Treaty on the matters of social and economic policy which it regulated.[28]

One commentator summed up the consequence of *Factortame* by suggesting that 'For the first time since 1688 a court suspended the operation of an Act of Parliament. Contrary to Dicey's oft-quoted assertion, it appeared that there was now a body with power to set

---

[27] [1991] 1 AC 659 643. But, in other parts of his judgment, Lord Bridge declared that the supremacy of European Community law flowed from the European Communities Act 1972, not from the inherent nature of the Community as a superior legal order. My own view, by contrast, is that the supremacy of Community law was always inherent in the nature of the Treaty of Rome.

[28] *Stoke on Trent City Council v B&Q* [1991] 4 All ER 223 at 224. After the 2016 referendum, of course, our right to withdraw was no longer 'theoretical'.

aside the legislation of Parliament and that body was the House of Lords'.[29] If that is so, the Treaty of Rome had, in effect, created a constitutional court in the United Kingdom to which Parliament was subordinate.

It may be argued that this limitation exists only because Parliament willed it in 1972. Parliament could at any time have repealed the European Communities Act. But it does seem somewhat odd to say that Parliament had willed a limitation of its sovereignty. What does such a statement mean? What is the evidence for it? By what mechanism did it do so? In *Factortame*, Lord Bridge declared that 'whatever limitation of its sovereignty Parliament accepted when it enacted the European Communities Act 1972 was entirely voluntary'.[30] He explicitly *accepted* that Parliament had, in fact, limited its sovereignty, something that the orthodox doctrine had declared was, by definition, impossible. Before *Factortame*, it was generally held that parliamentary sovereignty implied that every statute enacted by Parliament was legally binding. Where, however, is the evidence that Parliament 'voluntarily' accepted a limitation of its sovereignty? In his judgment, Lord Bridge declared that: 'Under the terms of the Act of 1972 it has always been clear that it was the duty of a United Kingdom court, when delivering final judgment, to override any rule of national law found to be in conflict with any directly enforceable rule of Community law.' This statement was quoted with approval in a dissenting judgment by Lord Reed in the *Miller* case.[31] As the preceding discussion makes clear, it had been anything but clear that

---

[29] E. Wicks, *The Evolution of a Constitution: Eight Key Moments in British Constitutional History*, Hart, 2006, p. 156. This interpretation of the constitutional consequences of our entry into the European Communities was also put forward by J.D.B. Mitchell in 'What Happened to the Constitution' and by H.W.R. Wade in 'Sovereignty – Revolution or Evolution?' (1996) 112 *Law Quarterly Review* 568–75.

[30] *Factortame* at 659.

[31] *R (Miller) v Secretary of State for Exiting the European Union* [2017] UKSC 5 at para. 226.

the duty of a United Kingdom court was as Lord Bridge described it. The evidence of the parliamentary debates shows clearly that Parliament *intended* nothing of the kind and in no way 'voluntarily' accepted a limitation of its sovereignty. In the debates, ministers declared precisely the opposite; that the Act should not, indeed could not, limit parliamentary sovereignty, not even to the extent of limiting the rule of implied repeal. Far from voluntarily willing a limitation of sovereignty, they argued that such a limitation was logically impossible to achieve. Can one voluntarily do something that one does not intend, that one indeed regards as logically impossible? Can one voluntarily do something when one is convinced that one is doing the opposite? Can one voluntarily do something when one is not aware of doing it? The interesting question perhaps arises as to whether, if parliamentarians had appreciated the full consequences of the European Communities Act, as Margaret Thatcher claimed they did not, they would still have passed the legislation.

It may, perhaps, be argued that the actual intentions of legislators are not of fundamental importance and that the concept of Parliament willing something is a construct of the courts, who are seeking the objective meaning of legislation. Therefore, the courts construed the European Communities Act as having the meaning and effect of precluding implied repeal. So, the judges, on this argument, were identifying the true position in cases such as *Macarthys, Factortame* and later decisions. It is, however, difficult to find any prominent jurist or constitutional lawyer who took that view before these judgments were made. The truth, surely, is that these were creative decisions made by judges who might, without any great damage to legal logic, have discovered very good reasons for concluding that the European Communities Act had *not* made any fundamental alteration to the British constitution. The doctrine of the sovereignty of Parliament, it is clear, entails that judges refuse to give effect to legislation which purports to limit that sovereignty. In *Macarthys* and *Factortame*, the judges did not refuse to give effect to such legislation. It was therefore the judges who determined the significance of the European Communities Act of 1972 by interpreting it as imposing a limitation upon the sovereignty of Parliament. H.W.R. Wade in a seminal article in the *Cambridge Law Review* in 1955, declared that: 'The seat of sovereign power is not to be discovered by looking at the Acts of any Parliament but by looking at the courts and discovering to whom they give their obedience.'[32]

Even if the argument that Parliament had willed a limitation of the sovereignty of Parliament was accepted, it would hardly serve to rescue the doctrine. If, in a federal constitution, the right of secession is constitutionally recognized, that does not make the provincial units sovereign. Although most federal constitutions do, in fact, prohibit secession, it is not inconsistent with the notion of federalism for secession to be permitted under agreed rules. If I volunteer to surrender my freedom with the proviso that I can at any time break free of my chains, it would seem odd to say that my freedom has not really been curtailed during the period in which it had been surrendered. Parliamentary sovereignty would be lost, therefore, for as long as Britain remained in the European Community.

In any case, the interpretation that the limitation on the sovereignty of Parliament exists only because Parliament willed it in fact gives that concept a meaning quite different from that put forward by Dicey to the effect that Parliament had the right to make or unmake any law whatever and that no person or body could set aside the legislation of Parliament.[33] At the very least, therefore, the sovereignty of Parliament meant something different after we joined the European Community

---

[32] H.W.R. Wade, 'The Basis of Legal Sovereignty' (1955) *Cambridge Law Review* 172 at 196.
[33] See Dicey, *Law of the Constitution*, 39–40.

from what it had meant before. The rule of recognition was now not, as it had been before 1972, that Parliament could enact any law whatever, but that Parliament could enact any law whatever, except for a law implicitly repealing a European Community law. Moreover if, as had been believed before *Macarthys*, the concept of parliamentary sovereignty entailed implied repeal, then Parliament in enacting a statute which excluded implied repeal had, in fact, limited its sovereignty. It had moved from what Hart called continuing sovereignty to self-embracing sovereignty. However, as Hart pointed out, once Parliament had adopted that second version of the concept, it was no longer sovereign. It had exercised its sovereignty to limit its sovereignty. Just as someone who has lost their virginity can never recover it, so a Parliament that has sacrificed its sovereignty, could never recover that sovereignty.

Of course, the view that Parliament had limited its sovereignty in the European Communities Act raises an awkward question. If Parliament could voluntarily limit its sovereignty in the European Communities Act, why might it not also do so with respect to other statutes – the Human Rights Act, for example, or the devolution legislation? What, if anything, was unique about the European Communities Act?

The doctrine in *Factortame* was carried further in *Thoburn v Sunderland City Council* [2003] QB 151, the so-called 'Metric Martyrs case' in which Lord Justice Laws argued that there was a whole category of 'constitutional' statutes and measures which were not subject to implied repeal. He included in this category, in addition to the European Communities Act, also Magna Carta, the 1689 Bill of Rights, the Act of Union, the parliamentary Reform Acts, the Human Rights Act and the devolution legislation. But what was the criterion for saying that a statute was 'constitutional' in the absence of a codified constitution? Lord Justice Laws defined in paragraph 62 of *Thoburn* a 'constitutional statute' as one which '(a) conditions the legal relationship between the citizen and State in some general, overarching manner, or (b) enlarges or diminishes the scope of what we would now regard as fundamental constitutional rights'. The second part of this definition seems in part circular, while the definition as a whole excludes legislation which many would certainly regard as constitutional (e.g. the Parliament Act regulating the relationship between the two houses of Parliament and the Act of Settlement of 1707 regulating succession to the throne). More importantly, perhaps, constitutional issues can easily arise out of what seems at first sight non-constitutional legislation. To take one example almost at random – in 1976 the Labour government enacted an Education Act requiring local authorities to avoid selection in secondary education. Critics of the Act, which was repealed by the Conservatives in 1979, argued that this was an unconstitutional alteration of the balance between central and local government. In 1985, the Conservative government enacted legislation abolishing the Greater London Council and six metropolitan county authorities. Critics argued that this, too, was unconstitutional since it was abolishing an elected layer of local government and transferring most of its powers either to central government or to its agencies. Many would argue that the right to strike was constitutional, indeed that relationships between the government and the trade unions were a constitutional matter. The German socialist, Lassalle, once declared that the Stock Exchange was part of the constitution. The truth is, that in a country without a codified constitution, it can never be precisely clear which matters are 'constitutional' and which are not. With an elastic constitution such as the British, the definition of what is constitutional will also be elastic.

However, the implication of *Factortame* for the doctrine of parliamentary sovereignty is clear. The distinguished constitutional lawyer, H.W.R. Wade, who had argued in the *Cambridge Law Review* in 1955, that Parliament could not abridge its sovereignty, had changed his mind by 1996 and now concluded that *Factortame* had shown that 'Parliament can bind its successors. If that is not revolutionary, constitutional lawyers are Dutchmen'.[34] There had been a revolution, a judicial revolution. The constitution had become what the judges said it was. Wade added that 'the new doctrine' adumbrated in *Factortame*, 'makes sovereignty a freely adjustable commodity whenever Parliament chooses to accept some limitation'. Yet, if one exception to the unlimited power of Parliament is permissible, others are permissible also if, as seems to be the case, sovereignty is like virginity, an absolute, rather than baldness, a matter of degree. For, if Parliament could 'will' a limitation of sovereignty with regard to the European Union, why could it not equally 'will' a limitation of its sovereignty in relation to other enactments (e.g. a Human Rights Act or devolution legislation)? It would be absurd to believe that, because Parliament could, at any time repeal such legislation and return to the status quo ante, the rule of recognition had not been radically altered in the meantime.

Oddly enough, even the British government seems to have come to accept this view. In 2011, Parliament passed the European Union Act. This Act was intended to guard against further transfers of sovereignty from Parliament to the European Union. It provided that no such transfers should take place unless and until validated by a referendum. It sought to bind future parliaments by prohibiting the enactment of legislation-transferring powers without a referendum first being held. It is certainly possible that a court, if presented with legislation purporting to transfer powers without a referendum, would have disapplied it. If so, Parliament could enact legislation, seeking to stipulate the manner and form of future legislation in relation to the

---

[34] H.W.R. Wade, 'The Basis of Legal Sovereignty', 172–197; and 'Sovereignty – Revolution or Evolution?' (1996) 112 *Law Quarterly Review* 568–75 at 573.

European Union, so limiting the sovereignty of a future Parliament. 'To seek to bind future parliaments by prohibiting the enactment of legislation without a referendum first being held', declared David Goldworthy, the most sophisticated of the defenders of parliamentary sovereignty, 'is not consistent with the doctrine of parliamentary sovereignty'.[35] Nevertheless, the Act also declared that Parliament was sovereign! However, if the above interpretation of the European Union Act is correct, then such a declaration is hardly compatible with the concept of parliamentary sovereignty. It is perhaps ironic that the Act had been proposed by a government concerned by the erosion of that principle and seeking to reassert it in legislation against those who believed that it had been abrogated by Britain's membership of the European Union. The Act declared that Parliament was sovereign, but proposed to bind a future Parliament, by requiring it, if it sought to transfer powers to the European Union, to hold a referendum, whether it wished to do so or not, which would, presumably, also be binding. The Queen in *Through the Looking Glass* declared that it was possible to believe in six impossible things before breakfast. The European Union Act seemed designed to test that proposition. It is doubtful if a more absurd piece of legislation has ever been enacted at Westminster.

III

Macarthys and *Factortame*, then, had served to establish a new rule of recognition in United Kingdom law.[36] A rule of recognition is the ultimate rule of the legal system. It provides authoritative criteria by

---

[35] House of Commons European Scrutiny Committee, *The EU and Parliamentary Sovereignty*, HC 633–ii, 2010–11, Ev. 31, para. 9.
[36] This concept derives from Hart, *The Concept of Law*, chapter 6.

which one can recognize and identify its legal rules. In countries with codified constitutions, the constitution is generally the rule of recognition. In Britain, until its entry into the European Communities, it had been the sovereignty of Parliament that had been the rule of recognition – the rule declaring that whatever the Queen in Parliament had enacted was valid law. After *Factortame*, the rule of recognition had clearly been altered – it now declared that whatever the Queen in Parliament had enacted was valid law, provided that it did not implicitly conflict with a provision of Community law.

But can the judges alone alter the British constitution? Did an alteration of the rule of recognition rest with them or did such an alteration not require wider acceptance? Dicey, as we have seen, believed that the doctrine of the sovereignty of Parliament, far from being a deduction from abstract theory, was a generalization drawn from the history of the English people. Clearly, the idea of the supremacy of European law has no such deep roots in Britain. But, if Dicey's view is correct, then the judges alone could not supersede the principle of parliamentary sovereignty and alter the rule of recognition, unless Parliament itself and perhaps the people, as well, through a referendum, an instrument which Dicey favoured – see Chapter 3 – agreed to it. In chapter 6 of *The Concept of Law*, Hart suggested that the rule of recognition of a legal system, the ultimate norm as it were, was not itself a norm but a complex matter of sociological and political fact and that it was constituted not by the judges alone, but by 'a complex, but normally concordant practice of the courts, officials and private persons in identifying the law by reference to certain criteria'.[37] Judges, then, could hardly alter the rule of recognition on their own and should not seek to do so. Indeed, one authority has argued that the rule of recognition

---

[37] *The Concept of Law*, p. 109.

'*ought* not to be modified without the support of a broader consensus within the electorate' (emphasis added).[38] Surely parliamentary and popular approval are also required. The judges, it has been said, 'remain lions under a somewhat complex throne; they are not its occupants'[39] It may be that some politicians came to accept that British membership of the Communities entailed the undermining of Parliamentary sovereignty, but it is doubtful if the people ever did, although it is, of course, perfectly possible that they might have done so over a longer period of time. But in the forty-five years that Britain remained a member of the European Community/European Union, it is doubtful if the idea of the primacy of European law ever gained widespread popular acceptance. That, no doubt, is a further reason why British membership of the European Union never developed deep roots amongst the British public and it was perhaps a pointer to the outcome of the Brexit referendum.

But, as we have seen, if the sovereignty of Parliament can be abridged in one direction, it can also be abridged in another. The European Communities Act and Britain's membership of the European Communities and the European Union created a precedent, fundamentally altering the British constitution.

The European Communities Act transformed the character of the British constitution, the constitution which Dicey had called 'historical'. For the Act had the quality of fundamental law and perhaps it began what may prove a long and tortuous process along the road towards a codified constitution. Later, towards the end of the twentieth century, the devolution legislation of 1998 and the Human Rights Act of 1998 further exemplified that process and may prove to be further

---

[38] Jeffrey Goldsworthy, *Parliamentary Sovereignty: Contemporary Debates*, Cambridge University Press, 2010, p. 110.

[39] J.D.B. Mitchell, 'What Happened to the Constitution on 1 January 1973?' (1980) Cambrian Law Review 69 at 71.

steps along that road. By the end of the twentieth century, it was apparent that the British constitution was being refashioned in a highly conscious and deliberate way. It would be difficult to conceive of a more profound change in our constitutional arrangements. And this process began with the European Communities Act. Without that Act, without British entry into the European Community, it is possible that the process might not even have begun and perhaps the sovereignty of Parliament would not have been abridged. There can be no doubt, therefore, that membership of the European Community fundamentally altered the British constitution. Indeed, by means of the European Communities Act, Britain took a quantum leap from Dicey's 'historical' constitution to a legal constitution. The question now to be asked is whether Brexit will also fundamentally alter the constitution, either by returning us to the status quo ante, or by leaving embedded in the constitution changes which were a result of our membership of the European Community and European Union. I will seek to answer that question in Chapter 5 in which I analyse whether membership of the European Community and the European Union have fundamentally altered our conception of human rights; and in the concluding chapter, Chapter 7 in which I discuss whether Brexit is likely to prove the catalyst for a codified constitution. Whatever the future holds, as a result of Britain's European involvement, the sovereignty of Parliament has been irretrievably damaged.

3

Europe and the Referendum

I

Entry into the European Community, then, involved a constitutional revolution. It undermined the doctrine of parliamentary sovereignty. It showed that parliamentary sovereignty could be abrogated, that Parliament could be made subordinate to a superior law-making authority, that an Act of Parliament could be disapplied by the courts and that Parliament could, if it so chose, bind itself. Shortly after entry, Europe was to be responsible for another constitutional revolution – the introduction of the referendum into British politics, an innovation hitherto thought unconstitutional and rejected by most leading politicians. In a standard work on British government, published in 1964, it was stated that 'it has occasionally been proposed that a referendum might be held on a particular issue, but the proposals do not ever appear to have been taken seriously'.[1]

---

[1] A.H. Birch, *Representative and Responsible Government: An Essay on the British Constitution*, Allen and Unwin, 1964, p. 227.

Until the 1970s, the referendum was thought to be unconstitutional precisely because Parliament was sovereign. The British constitution, it has often been said, knows nothing of the people. One nineteenth-century constitutional theorist remarked that an identical resolution passed by the electors of every constituency in Britain would have no legal force and no court would pay the slightest attention to it.[2] Some early constitutional theorists suggested that, since Parliament represented the people, the people were somehow a party to laws made by Parliament. Nevertheless, in Dicey's words, 'the judges know nothing about any will of the people except in so far as that will is expressed by an Act of Parliament, and would never suffer the validity of a statute to be questioned on the ground of its having been passed or being kept alive in opposition to the wishes of the electors.'[3] Dicey did insist, however, that the constitution was made up not just of laws, but also of conventions and that these conventions had as their ultimate object 'to secure that Parliament, or the Cabinet which is indirectly appointed by Parliament, shall in the long run give effect to the will of that power which in modern England is the true political sovereign of the State – the majority of the electors or – the nation'. These conventions were 'intended to secure the ultimate supremacy of the electorate as the true political sovereign of the State'. The task of the legislature, therefore, was to 'secure the conformity of Parliament to the will of the nation.'[4] Dicey had, in fact, been the first to propose the referendum in an article in the *Contemporary Review* in April 1890, entitled 'Ought the referendum to be introduced into England?' The referendum would, he believed, yield 'formal acknowledgment of the doctrine which lies at the basis of English democracy – that a law

---

[2] Sir Frederick Pollock, *A First Book of Jurisprudence*, 5th edn, Macmillan, 1923, p. 274.
[3] A.V. Dicey, *Law of the Constitution*, 8th edn, Macmillan, 1915, pp. 57, 72.
[4] Ibid, pp. 249, 253.

depends at bottom for its enactment on the consent of the nation as represented by the electors'.[5] But, in accordance with the doctrine of the sovereignty of Parliament, a referendum could only be advisory. It could not bind Parliament.

The referendum, however, had not only been dismissed by many as unconstitutional, it was also thought to be undesirable because it was a weapon of dictators. In 1945, Winston Churchill had suggested that his wartime coalition government be continued into peacetime and that authority for its extension be given by the people in a referendum. Clement Attlee, the leader of the Labour Party, rejected this proposal, saying, 'I could not consent to the introduction into our national life of a device so alien to all our traditions as the referendum, which has only too often been the instrument of Nazism and Fascism. Hitler's practices in the field of referenda and plebiscites can hardly have endeared these expedients to the British heart'.

Neither the argument from the fact that referendums had been used by dictators nor the argument against the use of referendums from the doctrine of Parliamentary sovereignty are very strong. The fact that Hitler and Stalin misused referendums to sustain dictatorships is no reason why democracies ought not to use them to enable voters to choose between alternative policies, any more than the fact that Stalin held fraudulent one-party elections is an argument for not having democratically regulated elections. The referendum has, in fact, been used by most democracies at some time or another and it is a standard instrument of democratic government.

Nor is the argument from Parliamentary sovereignty very powerful. For, if Parliament can enact any legislation that it likes, surely it can enact legislation providing for a referendum. What Parliament cannot do – or rather could not do if it were to remain sovereign – is to be

---

[5] A.V. Dicey, *A Leap in the Dark*, 2nd edn, John Murray, 1911, pp. 189–90.

legally bound by the result. The 1975 referendum on continued British membership of the European Community was advisory, but the government agreed that it would be bound by the result. In the words of Edward Short, Leader of the House of Commons at the time, 'the Government will be bound by its result, but Parliament, of course, cannot be bound by it'. He then added that, 'one would not expect honourable members to go against the wishes of the people'.[6] The 2016 referendum was also advisory, but, as in 1975, the government had agreed to be bound by the result.

The 1975 referendum, Britain's first national referendum, was held on 5 June. In it, voters were presented, first with a statement and then a question.

The statement was: 'The Government have announced the results of the renegotiation of the United Kingdom's terms of membership of the European Communities.' The question which followed was: 'Do you think the United Kingdom should stay in the European Community (the Common Market)?'

The outcome of the referendum was a 2 to 1 victory for staying in the Community.

On a turnout of 64.5 per cent, 17,378,581 (67.2%) voted 'Yes' and 8,470,073 (32.8%) voted 'No', The 'Yes' majority was nearly 9 million – 8,908,508.

The result was announced on 6 June 1975, the thirtieth anniversary of D-day.

From that referendum, two conclusions might have been drawn.

The first was that it had been held because Britain's political leaders had a sincere wish to discover the views of the British people on continued membership of the European Communities; for that reason, they introduced the novel device of the referendum.

---

[6] House of Commons, 11 March 1975, vol. 888, col. 293.

The second was that the outcome of the referendum showed that the British people had become enthusiastic Europeans.

Both these conclusions would, however, be entirely mistaken.

The referendum was held primarily for tactical reasons, to prevent a split in the Labour Party – just as the 2016 referendum was to be held primarily for tactical reasons, to prevent a split in the Conservative Party.

Entry to the European Communities had been negotiated by the Conservative government of Edward Heath in 1972. The preceding Labour government of 1964–1970, led by Harold Wilson, had also sought to negotiate entry and many assumed that Labour would, in consequence, support British accession. But in opposition after 1970, Labour's Left wing, which was opposed to entry, became more powerful and it appeared that many MPs and a large majority of party members were against entry and wanted to commit the party to leaving the European Community when it was next returned to power. This was something that Wilson and the pro-Europeans in the Labour Party could not accept. There was some danger of a party split and the issue came to be entangled with that of the leadership of the Labour Party. Wilson's opponents on the left and various competing leadership aspirants were, so Wilson believed, seeking to supplant him and to use the European issue for that purpose. The referendum offered him a way both of drawing the teeth of his opponents in the party and of avoiding a Labour commitment to withdrawing from the Community.

A referendum to resolve the European issue was first suggested by Tony Benn. He had first raised it as early as May 1968 when he was Minister of Technology in Harold Wilson's Labour government. He was, at that time, in favour of British membership, but argued for the referendum on the grounds of popular participation. This argument was later to be combatted by those who argued that the issues involved in membership were too complex for the people to decide. Jean Rey, the ex-President of the European Commission, was to declare in London on 17 July 1974, that: 'A referendum on this matter consists of consulting people who don't know the problems instead of consulting people who know them. I would deplore a situation in which the policy of this great country should be left to housewives. It should be decided instead by trained and informed people.' But this argument, echoed in various respects by many of those opposed to referendums, went too far. For, if the people were not qualified to pronounce on a single issue, admittedly complex, such as Britain's continued membership of the European Community, were they not equally unqualified to pronounce on the whole complex of difficult issues which formed the basis of every general election? In a referendum, the voters would be the jury on just one issue. In a general election they would be the jury on a whole host of different issues. The latter task was far more formidable than the former. The argument of those opposed to the referendum on the grounds of the incapacity of the British electorate seemed to bear a striking resemblance to those used by opponents of extending the franchise before the Great Reform Act of 1832.

Tony Benn continued to pursue the case for the referendum. During the 1970 general election campaign in a letter to his constituents in Bristol South East, he implicitly rejected the doctrine of his great eighteenth-century predecessor as MP for Bristol, Edmund Burke, who had insisted that it was for Members of Parliament to exercise their own judgment on behalf of their constituents. Benn, however, declared in his letter that: 'If people are not to participate in this decision, no one will ever take participation seriously again . . . It would be a very curious thing to try to take Britain into a new political unity with a huge potential for the future by a process that implied that the British public were unfit to see its historic importance for themselves.'

Labour was defeated in the 1970 election, but Benn again proposed the referendum at a meeting of Labour's National Executive Committee later in the year. He failed to find a seconder. James Callaghan, the Shadow Foreign Secretary, declared presciently that the referendum was 'a rubber life-raft into which the party may one day have to climb' to avoid a split.[7] So it proved to be. In opposition, Wilson found a formula to hold the warring factions in his party together. He would oppose entry on what he regarded as 'Tory terms'. In government, he would renegotiate those terms and then present the results to the British people in a referendum. So, the prime reason for holding the referendum was not a desire to discover the views of the British people on the European Community but to prevent a split in the Labour Party.

After the referendum result was declared in June 1975, Wilson declared that: 'The verdict has been given by a bigger vote, by a bigger majority than has been received by any government in any general election'. He went on, rather over-optimistically to declare: 'It means that fourteen years of national argument are over.'[8] He seems to have assumed that the referendum result had settled the European issue for all time. *The Daily Express,* which had been opposed to Community membership, declared on the day after the referendum that Britain was now 'decisively' and 'irrevocably' European. But Europe was not to be purged from the body politic as easily as that.

The large majority for remaining in the European Communities did not show that the British people had become enthusiastic Europhiles. Fear was a more important motive than hope or confidence

---

[7] Quoted in David Butler and Uwe Kitzinger, *The 1975 Referendum*, Macmillan, 1976, p. 12. This book, based on interviews with many of the leading participants, still remains the best account of the politics of the referendum.
[8] Quoted Anthony King, *Britain Says Yes: The 1975 Referendum on the Common Market*, American Enterprise Institute, 1975, p. 205.

in Britain's European future. Indeed, the referendum had been held in a climate of fear. While the Continent appeared to be thriving, Britain seemed to be the sick man of Europe. Inflation was nearing 25 per cent, the highest percentage ever recorded, unemployment was rising and there was apprehension at the growing power of the trade unions which had brought down the Heath government in February 1974. The post-war political order seemed to be disintegrating. In November 1974, the Cabinet held an all-day session at Chequers and, according to Barbara Castle, 'Jim Callaghan [the Foreign Secretary] pessimistically said that every morning when he shaved he thought that he should emigrate but by the time he had eaten breakfast, he realised there was nowhere else to go'.[9] One of Britain's European Commissioners, Sir Christopher Soames declared that: 'This is no time for Britain to be considering leaving a Christmas club, let alone the Common Market.' Survey evidence showed that 32 per cent of those intending to vote 'Yes' believed that Britain had been wrong to enter the Community; but 53 per cent of those polled believed that a 'No' verdict in the referendum would lead to an immediate political and economic crisis.[10] One opinion pollster who had worked for the 'Yes' camp, declared shortly before it, '. . . the main factors underpinning the present majority in favour of continued membership form a vague amalgam of caution and conservatism . . . We have not managed to generate much enthusiasm or to appeal successfully to more idealistic motives'.[11] Two students of the referendum concluded that its verdict was 'unequivocal but it was also unenthusiastic. Support for membership was wide but it did not run deep'.[12] The referendum was a vote for the status quo, not an enthusiastic embrace of Europe.

---

[9] Barbara Castle, *The Castle Diaries 1974–1976*, Weidenfeld and Nicolson, 1980, p. 221.

[10] Butler and Kitzinger, *The 1975 Referendum*, p. 259.

[11] Anthony King, *Britain Says Yes*, p. 154.

[12] Butler and Kitzinger, *The 1975 Referendum*, p. 280.

Although the referendum was held for tactical reasons, as was the referendum of 2016 and, although it did not settle the argument over Europe, which the 2016 referendum might well succeed in doing, there were, on both occasions, principled and constitutional reasons for their being held. The constitutional issues were not, however, much discussed before the Labour Party had committed itself to the referendum. The European debate was instead concerned primarily with the substantive issues involved in membership, especially the economic issues involved. Most of the debate on the constitutional significance of the referendum was held only after Labour had already made its commitment to it.

There were, in fact, two strong and principled constitutional arguments for the referendum. The first was that in the last general election before Britain had entered the European Communities – the election of 1970 – all three main political parties had been in favour of British entry. There was therefore no way in which a voter could indicate by her vote that she was opposed to entry. On this fundamental issue of Europe, therefore, the party system was not working effectively. There was no way in which, whatever government had been elected in 1970, it could claim a mandate from the British people for entry. In the 2015 general election, the last before the referendum of 2016, the position was slightly different. While all three major parties were in favour of Britain remaining in the European Union, as the European Community had become, there was now a party – UKIP – which was unequivocally committed to withdrawal. However, few thought that UKIP could win the election and form a government and many voters might well have felt that a vote for UKIP, under a first-past-the-post system would be a wasted vote – as indeed it was. UKIP, although it achieved one-eighth of the vote, won just one seat in the House of Commons. A voter who rejected Europe but was also strongly opposed to the Conservatives might well feel that it was better to vote for the non-Conservative party most likely to form a government – Labour – while a voter who was strongly opposed to Labour might well have felt that it was more sensible to vote for the non-Labour party most likely to form a government – the Conservatives – than to waste her vote. In 2015, therefore, it could not be argued that the party system was really operating effectively enough to resolve the European issue.

But, even if the party system had in fact been working effectively, there was a further and even stronger argument for the referendum. It was the argument first raised by Gaitskell, that a decision on such a fundamental issue by Parliament alone would lack legitimacy. It is a weakness in the traditional doctrine of Parliamentary sovereignty that some decisions are so fundamental and a decision by Parliament alone may not be accepted as final by the people. That had already been shown in Northern Ireland where a referendum, a border poll, had been held in 1973 on whether the people of Northern Ireland wished to remain in the United Kingdom or join with the Republic of Ireland. The border poll showed a large majority for remaining in the United Kingdom, though its value was greatly reduced since most nationalist voters followed the advice of the nationalist politicians and decided not to vote. The implication of the border poll, however, was that it was for the people of Northern Ireland to decide upon their future rather than Parliament. That position was formalized in the Northern Ireland Constitution Act of 1973 which provided that Northern Ireland would not cease to be part of the United Kingdom without the consent of its people as expressed in a border poll and this remains the constitutional position which was reiterated in the 1998 Belfast or 'Good Friday' Agreement. The 1973 Northern Ireland border poll may have served to encourage supporters of a referendum on the European issue since it showed that it was not necessarily alien to the British political system.

The European issue seemed as fundamental to many in the United Kingdom as the constitutional position of Northern Ireland was to those living in that province. It seemed that there was some popular disquiet that the decision on entry had been made by the government without consulting the people; indeed, some of the votes in the House of Commons on the European Communities Bill had been carried on fairly narrow majorities. The Leader of the House of Commons, Edward Short, certainly believed that a popular vote was required to legitimize Britain's membership of the European Communities. In March 1975, he told the Commons that 'the issue continues to divide the country. The decision to go in has not been accepted. That is the essence of the case for having a referendum'.[13]

There was a clear constitutional rationale for the view that popular consent was required on the European issue. Voters, it might be said, entrust MPs with legislative powers as their agents. But they do not give MPs authority to transfer those powers to another body such as the European Community. In his Second *Treatise of Government,* John Locke declares that: 'The Legislative cannot transfer the power of making laws to any other hands. For it being but a delegated power from the people, they who have it cannot pass it to others'. MPs need, it might be argued, specific authority if they are to transfer legislative powers; they need, in addition, a specific mandate from the people in the form of a referendum. In a letter to his constituents in 1975, Tony Benn declared that the people lent their powers to Members of Parliament 'to use on their behalf, for the duration of a single Parliament only – Powers that must be returned intact to the electorate to whom they belong, to lend again to the Members of Parliament they elect in each subsequent general election'.

---

[13] House of Commons, 11 March 1975, vol. 888, col. 292.

Therefore, so it seems, far from being alien to the British constitution, the referendum is in accordance with traditional British liberal doctrine as put forward by Locke. For it gives Britain a form of constitutional protection. It is a safeguard against any transfer of legislative powers which the people do not want. In 1979, it prevented devolution to Scotland and Wales when referendums there failed to secure the necessary majorities. In 2004, it prevented devolution to the North East, which was rejected by a four to one majority in a referendum; and even though no referendum was held, fear of it prevented Britain joining the eurozone in the early years of the twenty-first century. Tony Blair and perhaps a majority of his Cabinet were in favour of joining the eurozone. But Blair had given a commitment that his government would not join the eurozone without a referendum. The referendum, however, was never held since not a single opinion poll had ever indicated a majority for it. Had the referendum not existed as a constitutional weapon, devolution to Scotland and Wales would have occurred in 1979 rather than 1997, the North-East would have had regional institutions which its people did not want and Britain might well have joined the eurozone in the early years of the twenty-first century. And, of course, Brexit would not be happening. Perhaps the referendum gives Britain the only form of constitutional protection that is possible in a country without an entrenched constitution.

The effect of the 1975 referendum was to give, for a time at least, popular legitimacy to Britain's membership of the European Communities. The result seemed to be accepted even by the opponents of British membership. When the result was announced, Tony Benn declared: 'I have just been in receipt of a very big message from the British people. I read it loud and clear. By an overwhelming majority the British people have voted to stay in and I'm sure everybody would want to accept that. That had been the principle of all of us who advocated the referendum.' One of Harold Wilson's advisers suggested that, while Edward Heath had, in 1973, taken the British Establishment into Europe, it had needed Harold Wilson to take the British people into Europe. By 2013, however, when David Cameron committed the Conservative Party to a further referendum, it had become apparent that, while the Establishment was, perhaps, still committed to Europe, the British people were not. In his Bloomberg speech in January 2013, proposing a further referendum on Europe, Cameron described the British people's consent to Europe as 'wafer-thin'. That, in his view, made the case for a further referendum. Like Wilson, Cameron sought a referendum to legitimize the status quo, to legitimize Britain's membership in Europe. However, while Wilson succeeded in his aim of keeping Britain in Europe, Cameron did not. Wilson told his Private Secretary on the day after the referendum, 'People say I have no strategy, cannot think strategically'.[14] Wilson is, indeed, the only British Prime Minister to have triumphed in confronting the European issue. He had been much criticized for his tactical manoeuvring and for accepting the constitutional innovation of the referendum. But he did succeed in averting the threat that his party would come to office either hopelessly split or committed to withdrawal from the European Community. The policy of renegotiation and referendum succeeded, in the short run at least, in holding the Labour Party together and of keeping Britain in Europe. In the book on his 1974–1976 government, *Final Term*, Wilson argues that, 'to bridge a deep political chasm without splitting a party or provoking dramatic ministerial resignations is sometimes regarded as something approaching political chicanery'. Nevertheless, 'the highest aim of leadership is to secure policies adequate to deal with any situation ... without major confrontations,

---

[14] Stephen Wall, *The Official History of Britain and the European Community: Volume II: From Rejection to Referendum, 1963–1975*. Routledge 2013, p. 590.

splits and resignations. It may be bad for the headlines and news placards, but it has been sought and achieved by our greatest leaders, Conservative as well as Labour. . . .'[15]

The outcome was indeed fortunate for Wilson and for the pro-Europeans in the government. There had been a large majority on a high turnout. The outcome was clear and indisputable. Had it been different, it is unclear whether the Wilson government could have continued. The majority of the Cabinet were committed to remaining in the European Community and the most pro-European ministers, Roy Jenkins and Shirley Williams, had indicated that they could not continue to serve in a government which took Britain out. It is not clear whether Harold Wilson would have remained in office to negotiate a British exit or whether, like David Cameron in 2016, he would have resigned as Prime Minister. The government and MPs would have been faced with the same embarrassment they were to be faced with just over forty years later in 2016.

A further fortunate feature of the outcome was that, again by contrast with 2016, the vote to remain was spread fairly evenly across all parts of the United Kingdom; in particular, Scotland, Wales and Northern Ireland had all voted to remain. In 1975, by contrast with 2016, the Scottish and Welsh nationalist parties were opposed to Britain remaining in the Community. The fear then had been that, while the rest of the United Kingdom might vote 'Yes', Scotland would vote 'No' so encouraging the separatists and igniting a constitutional crisis. The pro-Europeans might win the referendum at the cost of breaking up the United Kingdom.

The referendum had been held to legitimize Britain's membership of the European Community and to hold the Labour Party together.

---

[15] Harold Wilson, *Final Term: The Labour Government, 1974–1976*, Michael Joseph, 1979, p. 121.

Tony Benn had told his constituents in 1975 that the decision in the referendum 'once taken will almost certainly be irreversible'. Perhaps, if Labour had succeeded in retaining office in the 1979 general election, it would have been. In fact, however, Labour lost the election and, in opposition, the anti-European Labour Left gained influence. So, the gains of the referendum held only in the short term. In opposition, Labour moved to an anti-European stance; under the leadership of Michael Foot, its 1983 election manifesto committed the party to withdrawing from the European Community without a further referendum. Although Labour lost the 1983 election, the argument about Europe was to be reignited in the 1990s under John Major's Conservative government, as a result, first, of Britain's ignominious exit from the European Monetary System in 1992 and then, following the furious disputes raging over the Maastricht Treaty of 1992: disputes which nearly destroyed the Major government that had signed it. Well before that, the Labour Party had split on the European issue with the formation of the Social Democratic Party, the SDP. The 1975 referendum had helped to make the breakaway and the alliance between the new party and the Liberals possible by showing the pro-Europeans in the Labour Party that they might have more in common with the Liberals than with their anti-European colleagues on the Left of the Labour Party. Perhaps the alliance between the SDP and the Liberals was a natural consequence of the new alignments formed by the referendum, which had loosened tribal loyalties in the Labour Party.

II

The 1975 referendum was not intended to set a precedent. It was held, so the government declared in the White Paper, *UK Referendum on*

Membership of the European Community, 'because of the *unique* nature of the issue'[16] (emphasis added). Immediately after the referendum, a Conservative backbencher asked Harold Wilson:

'Will he keep to his determination not to repeat the constitutional experiment of the referendum?'

The Prime Minister replied:

'I certainly give the Right Honourable Member ... the assurance he seeks.'[17]

The unique nature of the European issue had been explained by Gerry Fowler, a junior minister in the government:

I have made absolutely clear that in my view and that of the Government, the constitutional significance of our membership of the EEC is of a quite different order from any other issue. It is not just that it is more important; it is of a different order. There is, and there can be, no issue that is on all fours with it. That is why we say that this issue is the sole exception, and there can be no other exception to the principle that we normally operate through parliamentary democracy'.[18]

But, as Roy Jenkins, who had resigned from the Shadow Cabinet in 1972 because he was opposed to the referendum, presciently noted: 'once the principle of the referendum has been introduced into British politics it will not rest with any one party to put a convenient limit to its use'.[19] In the debate on the referendum in the House of Commons, Margaret Thatcher, in her first speech as Conservative Party leader,

---

[16] Cmnd 5925, February 1975, p. 2.
[17] House of Commons, vol. 893, col. 37, 9 June 1975.
[18] House of Commons, vol. 881, cols 1742–43, 22 November 1974.
[19] Quoted in *The Times*, 11 April 1972.

declared: 'The immediate point may be towards registering a popular view towards staying in the European Economic Community. The longer term result will be to create a new method of validating laws . . . This will lead to a major constitutional change . . .'[20] For, just as it proved impossible to argue that Europe is the only issue on which a limitation of parliamentary sovereignty is justified, so it proved impossible to sustain the argument that Europe was the sole issue on which the principle of representative government could be qualified. But this raised the problem that, if Europe was, as proved to be the case, *not* a unique issue, how was one to distinguish between those legislative matters which required a referendum to validate them and those that did not? Some would argue that only constitutional issues should be made subject to a referendum. But, as we have already seen, it is not easy to distinguish, in a country without a codified constitution, between what is a constitutional issue and what is not. However, in perhaps a typically British unplanned and ad hoc way, conventions as to which issues needed to be put to referendum were to develop in due course.

Within just eighteen months of the 1975 referendum, the Labour government, now led by James Callaghan, was forced to concede a referendum on the bill providing for devolution to Scotland and Wales. Had he not made this concession, he faced the risk that Labour backbenchers opposed to devolution would defeat the bill in the Commons. The referendum commitment on devolution was to prove another life raft, this time for the opponents of the legislation. It enabled them to support devolution in the Commons and then campaign to defeat it in the referendum. 'It is', said Malcolm Rifkind, one of the few Conservative supporters of devolution, 'a unique constitutional matter that this Parliament is likely to put on the statute book a Bill in

---

[20] House of Commons, 11 March 1975, vol. 888, col. 316.

which it does not believe'.[21] This was to be even more true in 2018 when a Parliament composed predominantly of Remainers put the Brexit legislation on to the statute book. Enoch Powell, an opponent of devolution, speaking at Bexhill on 25 November 1977, noticed the constitutional innovation involved in the devolution referendums. He called it:

> an event without precedent in the long history of Parliament ... that members openly and publicly declaring themselves opposed to the legislation and bringing forward in debate what seemed to them cogent reasons why it must prove disastrous, voted nevertheless for the legislation and for a guillotine, with the express intention that after the minimum of debate the Bill should be submitted to a referendum of the electorate in which they would hope and strive to secure its rejection'.

The referendum, it seemed, had become 'the Pontius Pilate' of British politics.[22]

Back-bench rebels, opposed to devolution, added a further hurdle which it would have to surmount. In January 1978, an amendment was passed requiring 40 per cent of the electorate, as well as a majority of voters, to support devolution for it to be implemented. The rationale for this amendment was to test the government's claim that there was a pressing demand for devolution in Scotland and Wales. The rebels, while being opposed to devolution, indicated that they would be prepared to accept it if that pressing demand could be shown to be present. The referendums, held in March 1979, showed that there was no such pressing demand. While 33 per cent of the electorate in Scotland voted for devolution and 31 per cent opposed it, so

---

[21] House of Commons, 15 February 1978, vol. 988, col. 595.

[22] S.E. Finer, ed. *Adversary Politics and Electoral Reform*, Anthony Wigram, 1975, p. 18.

giving supports of devolution a narrow majority, that majority fell far short of the 40 per cent that Parliament had required. It proved, therefore, impossible to implement devolution and the Conservative government, elected in May 1979 accordingly repealed the Scotland Act which had provided for it. But, because of the controversy caused by the 40 per cent requirement and the feeling by many in Scotland that it had imposed an illegitimate extra hurdle, Parliament did not impose any similar hurdle in the 1997 devolution referendums nor did it seek to impose any similar threshold requirement in any other referendum legislation.[23]

The Labour Party in Wales had been opposed to the referendum commitment. It declared:

The question of a referendum involves much wider issues than devolution. The introduction of Government by referendum would be a complete reversal of our whole system of Government. Once this principle was accepted, then any party could call at any time for a referendum on any controversial proposal. Those who advocate a referendum must accept the full implications of this change, and must be aware that any radical changes proposed by a Labour government – whether extensions of public ownership or abolition of the 11-plus – would have to overcome this new hurdle before being carried out. In effect, Clause 4 of the Party Constitution would have to be rewritten – "To secure for the workers by hand or brain the full fruits of their industry etc – SUBJECT TO REFERENDUM".[24]

The assumption was that, by winning the October 1974 general election, the Labour government had a mandate for all the items in its

---

[23] See Vernon Bogdanor, 'The 40% Rule' (1980) 33(3) *Parliamentary Affairs*, 249–263.
[24] Labour Party Wales, *Why Devolution*, September 1976, p. 4.

election programme, including devolution. But, in the referendum held in Wales in March 1979, devolution was defeated by a margin of four to one, even though all the parties in Wales, with the exception of the Conservatives, were in favour of it. A similar outcome to that in Wales would occur in 2004, in a referendum in the North East on a directly elected assembly in that region. For even though the Labour government favoured the proposal and Labour was the dominant party in the North East, this too was defeated by a four to one majority.

When devolution came back on to the agenda with the election of another Labour government in 1997, led by Tony Blair, the government took the precaution of holding referendums *before* introducing legislation into the Commons to avoid wasting parliamentary time on a measure which was not wanted in Scotland or Wales. But this time, in referendums held in 1997, both Scotland and Wales voted in favour of devolution – albeit in Wales by a wafer-thin margin – and devolution to Scotland and Wales was accordingly enacted. The Blair government also held, under the terms of the Belfast Agreement of 1998, a referendum on a power-sharing form of devolution in Northern Ireland; this, too, showed a majority for devolution.

The referendums on devolution, like that on the European Community, were advisory. However, during the Commons proceedings on the Scotland and Wales Bill in 1977, when the government had responded to back-bench pressures by introducing, during the committee stage of the bill, a new clause providing for referendums, it had proposed that the referendums be binding, not merely advisory. Such a proposal had previously been regarded as unconstitutional since it contravened the sovereignty of Parliament. In the words of the edition of Erskine May's *Parliamentary Practice*, the parliamentary bible and guide to procedure, published in 1971, a binding referendum would be out of order since it proposed 'changes in legislative procedure which will be contrary to constitutional practice'.[25] On this occasion, however, in 1977, the chairman of the committee of the whole House considering the Bill accepted the amendment as in order, arguing that the precedent of the 1975 referendum had altered the constitutional position, even though that referendum had been, as we have seen, advisory. The action by the chairman of the committee of the whole House offers a striking illustration of how major alternations in the British constitution can take place under the guise of parliamentary procedure. This new precedent, however, had been created for no purpose, since the government later decided that the referendums should be advisory after all. Nevertheless, a precedent *had* been set that a referendum could be binding and that an Act of Parliament could become operative automatically following a referendum. Britain's second national referendum, on the alternative vote electoral system, held in 2011, was, by contrast with that on the European Community, binding to the extent that, had the voters favoured it – it was, in fact, rejected by a two-to-one majority – the government was required to bring forward an order to implement it without any further primary legislation. Parliament could, of course, have voted down the order. Nevertheless, this was a further development in the constitutional significance of the referendum, a development made possible and perhaps implicit in the referendum commitment of 1975 on Europe.

---

[25] Erskine May *Parliamentary Practice* 18th edn, Butterworths, London 1971, Chapter 21, p. 523. Cited by Maurice Macmillan MP in the House of Commons, vol. 925, col. 1674, 10 February 1977. The government announced that the referendums would, after all, be advisory on 15 February.

III

Enoch Powell, a fervent opponent of membership of the European Community, had declared that the outcome of the 1975 referendum on Europe was provisional since it depended upon the continuing consent of Parliament. Parliament, so he declared, could at any time change its mind and repeal the European Communities Act, so taking Britain out of the European Community. Perhaps Powell ought to have said that Britain's membership depended upon the continuing consent of the people, since it may be that Parliament alone would not be able to take Britain out of the European Union. Perhaps only the people could do so in a further referendum. After 2010, popular pressure for this referendum became so strong that the Prime Minister, David Cameron, felt that he had no alternative but to concede one.

The coalition government which came to power in 2010 had agreed in its coalition agreement that any petition which received over 100,000 signatures would be eligible for a debate in the Commons. A petition with over 100,000 signatures was duly received calling for a referendum on Europe. This was debated in the Commons in October 2011. The three major parties issued three-line whips instructing MPs to vote against the motion for a referendum, but 81 Conservative MPs defied the whip and voted for it, while some others abstained. It proved impossible to ignore so large a rebellion and impossible to ignore the growing strength of UKIP, which seemed to threaten the Conservatives' chances in a general election. In January 2013, David Cameron, in his Bloomberg speech, duly committed the Conservatives to a referendum. This was duly held in June 2016 and resulted in a majority for Brexit. The government having been repudiated, the Prime Minister, David Cameron, who had argued against Brexit, resigned. In 1979, when the voters in Scotland and Wales had rejected the advice of Prime Minister, James Callaghan, by opposing devolution, the Prime Minister did not resign immediately. Nevertheless, the referendums were interpreted as a vote of no confidence in the government and, just six weeks after the referendum, Callaghan was to lose a vote of confidence in the House of Commons. Perhaps Wilson too would have resigned had the 1975 referendum gone against his advice. The referendum, therefore, has taken on the character of another instrument of direct democracy, the recall; in a vote, it is not always easy to distinguish between rejection of a particular policy and rejection of the administration recommending that policy. That, perhaps, is one of the weaknesses of the referendum.

During the parliamentary proceedings on devolution, as we have seen, MPs voted for legislation to which they were opposed, hoping to defeat it in the ensuing referendums. The 2016 referendum was to take the subordination of Parliament a stage further by, in effect, requiring MPs to vote for legislation to which they were opposed.

At a seminar at King's College, London, held shortly after the Brexit referendum, the Professor of European Law, Takis Tridimas, declared that this referendum in 2016 was the most significant constitutional event in Britain since the Restoration in 1660. It showed or, perhaps, confirmed that, on the issue of Europe, the sovereignty of the people trumped the sovereignty of Parliament. Admittedly, the 2015 European Union Referendum Act had provided that the referendum should be advisory, like that of 1975 and not binding, as was the referendum on the alternative vote held in 2011. Nevertheless, the government had agreed in advance to be bound by the result and the outcome, even though the majority for Brexit was narrow, was regarded by nearly all MPs as decisive. Admittedly, the outcome is, constitutionally, as provisional as that of 1975. Indeed, three weeks before the 2016 referendum, the UKIP leader, Nigel Farage, believing that the Remainers would win, told the *Daily Mirror* on 16 May that a 52/48 verdict would be 'unfinished business by a long way'. He then told the BBC that 'there could be an unstoppable demand for a re-run of the EU referendum if Remain wins by a narrow margin'. 'Win or lose this battle', he concluded, 'we will win this war'. In logic, the Brexiteers could not in logic deny to their opponents the very right that they themselves were prepared to claim. Brexit, then, depends upon the continuing consent of the British people who could, at any time, through a referendum decide to put an end to the process or, once it had been completed, decide that they wished to reverse the decision, as 2016 reversed the decision of 1975, and re-enter the European Union. Finality, Disraeli once declared, was not the language of politics.

Nevertheless, Brexit is now coming about, not because government or Parliament want it, but because the people want it. Government and Parliament felt themselves constrained to do something that they did not wish to do. That is a situation quite without precedent in Britain's long constitutional history. The majority of the Cabinet which legislated for Brexit were Remainers; so were the majority in the Commons and even the majority of Conservative MPs; while the majority in the Lords for Remain was, almost certainly, even larger than the majority in the Commons. In the conflict between a supposedly sovereign Parliament and a sovereign people, the sovereign people have triumphed. Europe, therefore, has been responsible for the introduction of a new principle into the British constitution – the principle of the sovereignty of the people. The referendum had become, on the European issue, in effect, a third chamber of Parliament, issuing legislative instructions to the other two. The sovereignty of Parliament was now to be constrained, not by Brussels but by the people.

The constitutional consequences of the referendum, then, have been highly significant. As we have seen, Roy Jenkins predicted that it would not, in the future 'rest with any one party' 'to put a convenient limit to its use'. He feared that it could lead to an unregulated populism where almost any legislative proposal could be put to the people. In fact, however, the referendum has so far been used in a very circumscribed way and only for issues which, in countries with codified constitutions, would be regarded as constitutional. Referendums have been used not only for European matters but also for devolution. Indeed, it may now be said to have become a convention of the constitution that decisions involving the transfer of the legislative powers of Parliament – whether upwards to a European body or downwards through devolution – require the endorsement of the people. So also does a decision to join or leave the European Union and a decision by one part of the United Kingdom – for example, Scotland or Northern Ireland – to secede. So also does the introduction of a radically new constitutional mechanism such as a new electoral system. These are the issues which have been put to the people and which are held to require validation by referendum.

The principle of the sovereignty of the people which the referendum exemplifies has been generally deplored by political thinkers of both Right and Left. Socialists have tended to believe, with the Labour Party in Wales, that a general election victory is all that is required to give political leaders a mandate to govern. Liberals have feared a threat to liberties, while Conservatives have been fearful of mob rule. The French reactionary, Joseph de Maistre, went so far as to declare: 'The principle of the sovereignty of the people is so dangerous that, even if it were true, it would be necessary to conceal it.'[26]

In fact, however, the referendum, far from bringing mob rule, has proved an instrument of constitutional protection, providing a

---

[26] Joseph de Maistre, *Oeuvres Completes*, Libraire Générale Catholique et Classique, vol. 9, p. 494.

safeguard against major constitutional changes which the people do not want. It has become the people's veto. It was, Dicey believed, 'the only check on the predominance of party which is at the same time democratic and conservative'.[27] Whether it is favoured or not will depend on one's view of the efficacy of the party system. 'It is certain', Dicey declared, 'that no man who is really satisfied with the working of our party system will ever look with favour in an institution which aims at correcting the vices of party government'.[28] Had it not been for Europe, however, it is possible that the referendum would not have become part of the constitution and the principle of the sovereignty of Parliament would not have been abrogated.

---

[27] A.V. Dicey, 'Ought the Referendum to be Introduced into England?'(1890) *Contemporary Review*, 57.

[28] Dicey, 'Introduction' to *Law of the Constitution*, 8th edn, Macmillan, 1915, p.c.

4

Europe and the Collective Responsibility of Ministers

I

The introduction of the referendum into the British system of government in 1975 was to provoke another constitutional innovation, the suspension of collective responsibility under a single-party government, something that, like the referendum, had been hitherto regarded as unconstitutional.

On 23 January 1975, Prime Minister Harold Wilson announced that the convention of collective responsibility would be suspended for the period of the referendum campaign. Speaking in the House of Commons, he announced that:

The circumstances of this referendum are unique, and the issue to be decided is one on which strong views have long been held which cross party lines. The Cabinet has, therefore, decided that, if when the time comes there are members of the Government, including members of the Cabinet, who do not feel able to accept and support the Government's recommendation, whatever it may be, they will, once the recommendation has been announced, be free to support and speak in favour of a different conclusion in the referendum campaign.[1]

In the event, seven ministers in a Cabinet of twenty-three and thirty-one other ministers, including Whips, took advantage of this provision. The Cabinet dissentients included leading members of the Party – Michael Foot, Secretary of State for Employment and a future leader of the Party, Tony Benn, Industry Secretary, Barbara Castle, Health Secretary, Peter Shore, Trade Secretary, Willie Ross, Scottish Secretary, Eric Varley, Energy Secretary, and John Silkin, Minister for Local Government and Planning,

The convention of collective responsibility provides that Cabinet decisions are binding on all members of the government. It requires that ministers present a united front to Parliament and the country. They are committed to voting for all Cabinet decisions and are required to avoid publicly dissociating themselves from any Cabinet decision, even if they may have argued in private against it. The convention was given classic expression by Lord Palmerston as Prime Minister in the mid-nineteenth century, when he told his Chancellor of the Exchequer, W.E. Gladstone:

A Member of the Government when he takes office necessarily divests himself of that perfect Freedom of individual action which belongs to a private and independent Member of Parliament, and the Reason is this, that what a Member of the Government does or

---

[1] House of Commons Debates, 23 January 1975, vol. 884 col. 1745.

says upon public Matters must to a certain degree commit his colleagues, and the Body to which they belong if they by their silence appear to acquiesce; and if any of them follow his Example and express as public, opposite opinions, which in particular cases they might feel obliged to do, differences of opinion between Members of the Same Government are unnecessarily brought out into Prominence and the Strength of the Government is thereby impaired.[2]

Lord Salisbury, as Foreign Secretary in 1878, reiterated the doctrine.

'Now ... am I not defending a great constitutional principle, when I say that, for all that passes in Cabinet, each member of it who does not resign is absolutely and irretrievably responsible, and that he has no right afterwards to say that he agreed in one case to a compromise, while in another he was persuaded by one of his colleagues? Consider the inconvenience which will arise if such a great constitutional law is not respected. It is only on the principle that absolute responsibility is undertaken by every member of the Cabinet, who, after a decision arrived at, remains a member of it, that the joint responsibility of Ministers to Parliament can be upheld and one of the most essential principles of Parliamentary responsibility established.[3]

The principle had been stated in a more jocular manner by Lord Melbourne, as Prime Minister, in 1841 when his Cabinet were debating the Corn Laws. He apparently said, 'Bye the bye, there is one thing that we haven't agreed upon, which is, what are we to say? Is it better to make corn dearer, or cheaper, or to make the price steady? I

---

[2] Philip Guedalla, ed., *The Palmerston Papers: Palmerston and Gladstone Being the Correspondence of Lord Palmerston with Mr Gladstone, 1851–1865*, Gollancz, 1928, p. 288.
[3] House of Lords, 8 April 1878, vol. 239, col. 833.

don't care which, but we had better tell the same story'.[4] The political purpose of the convention is to enable a government to continue as a unity. Almost all ministers will, at one time or another, be in a minority on particular issues. But, if they are prepared to accept the decision of the majority, they can be assured that, when they themselves are in the majority, those ministers in the minority will nevertheless accept the decision and not seek to undermine the majority by making unauthorized declarations of policy. The convention, therefore, is important in creating an atmosphere of comity between members of the Cabinet. By 1889, John Morley was able to say, in a book which had received the imprimatur of Gladstone, that 'the doctrine of collective responsibility' was one of four 'principal features of our system of Cabinet government today'.[5] By 1947, L.S. Amery was able to go further and declare that 'the essence of our Cabinet system is the collective responsibility of its members'.[6]

II

The year 1975 was not, admittedly, the first occasion on which collective responsibility had been suspended. It had been suspended once before by the National Government, a coalition, in 1932, on the issue of tariff reform. The National Government had been returned with an overwhelming majority in the general election of 1931. In that election, the Liberal members of the National Government had declared that they were opposed to a tariff, but, in 1932, the government proposed a general tariff of 10 per cent on many products. The three Liberal ministers in the National Government cabinet,

---

[4] Spencer Walpole, *Life of Lord John Russell*, Longman, 1889, vol. 1, p. 369.
[5] John Morley, *Life of Walpole*, Macmillan, 1889, p. 154.
[6] L.S. Amery, *Thoughts on the Constitution*, Oxford University Press 1947, p. 70.

together with the former Chancellor of the Exchequer in the previous Labour government, Philip Snowden, now a member of the National Government cabinet, were strong free traders and refused to accept a tariff. By an agreement to differ, they were allowed to oppose the decision of the government while remaining in the Cabinet. The government issued the following statement:

> The Cabinet has had before it the report of the Committee on the Balance of Trade and after prolonged discussion it has been found impossible to reach a unanimous conclusion on the Committee's recommendation. The Cabinet, however, is deeply impressed with the paramount importance of maintaining national unity in presence of the grave problems that now confront this country and the whole world. It has accordingly determined that some modification of usual Ministerial practice is required and has decided that Ministers who find themselves unable to support the conclusions arrived at by the majority of their colleagues on the subject of import duties and cognate matters are to be at liberty to express their views by speech and vote. The Cabinet, being essentially united on all other matters of policy, believes that by this special provision it is best interpreting the will of the nation and the needs of the time.[7]

There were, however, a number of differences between what happened in 1932 and 1975, which make it difficult to regard 1932 as a precedent. The main difference was precisely that the government in 1932 was a coalition that had been deliberately formed in 1931 to embrace those with conflicting points of view; it had fought the 1931 election on that basis. The various parties fighting under the National banner – Conservatives, Liberals, Liberal Nationals,

---

[7] *The Times*, 23 January 1932.

National Labour – each issued its own programme and the Prime Minister, Ramsay MacDonald, said that the government was seeking a 'doctor's mandate'. It was known when the government was formed, by politicians and electors alike, that there was a fundamental disagreement on tariffs and that the Liberals had reserved their position on that issue. So, the National Government was a combination unlike any that had been seen before in Britain. The 'agreement to differ' was defended by the leader of the Conservative Party and effectively the deputy Prime Minister, Stanley Baldwin, on precisely that basis. 'The fate of no party', he declared, 'is at stake in making a fresh precedent for a National Government'. Baldwin then said that, in a sense, collective responsibility had been preserved since the decision to allow the agreement to differ had, in fact, been made collectively by the Cabinet: 'we have collective responsibility for the departure from collective action'.[8] The formula had been devised by the War Secretary, Lord Hailsham, who declared: 'The Government, having by its formation, provided one new precedent, need not be afraid of creating a second'.[9]

Ministers were given full freedom to express their dissent in speech and vote in Parliament. The dissidents were allowed to express their own views on the tariff policy, not only in the country, but also in Parliament. For the first time in British history, members of the Cabinet spoke from the government front bench on government legislation, the Import Duties bill providing for the tariff, on opposite sides of the debate and they went into the division lobby on opposite sides. In the House of Lords, Lord Snowden, Lord President of the Council, excoriated his Cabinet colleagues by saying 'the generation which knew from experience the horror and starvation of Protection is gone. The new generation must learn what Protection is from its

---

[8] House of Commons, 8 February 1932, vol. 261, cols 534–5.
[9] Quoted in Philip Goodhart, *Full-Hearted Consent*, Davis-Poynter, 1976, p. 219.

own experience and sufferings' and he denounced 'the patent fallacies, the unfounded claims and the contradictory assumptions upon which this measure is based'.[10] In the Commons, Sir Herbert Samuel, the Home Secretary and leader of the Liberal Party, spoke from the Treasury bench in favour of free trade, denouncing his colleague, the Protectionist Chancellor of the Exchequer, Neville Chamberlain and predicting that the abandonment of free trade would lead to a return to the 'hungry forties', to the years before Britain had adopted free trade by repealing the corn laws. Samuel was followed by Winston Churchill, then a backbencher, who declared that he accepted, but with reluctance, the 'agreement to differ', though he feared it might involve 'a grave and permanent alteration and possibly injury in the system of Cabinet government throughout the Empire'. However, he strongly deprecated a minister speaking from the government benches to oppose government policy. The government had called for a Doctor's mandate, but doctors, Churchill said, do not dispute in public. If they did, it would be deemed unprofessional. He excoriated 'the indecent and even scandalous spectacle of Ministers wrangling upon the Treasury bench and of important officers of State doing their utmost to discredit, impede and undermine the main policy of the Government of the day'.[11]

The agreement to differ did not hold the government together for long. In July and August, the Imperial Economic Conference at Ottawa agreed a system of Imperial Preference for the Empire with higher tariffs for countries outside; in September 1932, the Liberal ministers and Lord Snowden resigned from the government, though they continued to sit on the government benches until November 1933 when they crossed the floor. In the words of one constitutional

---

[10] House of Lords, 29 February 1932, vol. 83, col. 697.
[11] House of Commons, 4 May 1932, vol. 265, cols 1173–4.

authority, Sir Ivor Jennings, 'the dissenting ministers, having swallowed the camel of a general tariff, strained at the gnat of imperial preference and resigned within eight months'.[12]

Of the agreement to differ, Sir Ivor Jennings declared somewhat oddly that 'no harm was done by the precedent of 1932 provided that it is not regarded as a precedent',[13] though it is difficult to see how a precedent can be regarded as anything else. The precedent appeared to be very limited. It appeared to be a precedent only for a government formed on the very unusual basis of the National Government. Indeed, until 1975, it was generally accepted that an agreement to differ was possible only under a coalition government which, by its very nature, would modify the normal system of Cabinet government, a system normally based, at least in the Westminster Model, on single-party majority government. Baldwin had made this point explicit in 1932 and had declared that: 'Had the precedent been made for a party Government, it would have been quite new, and it would have been absolutely dangerous for that party....'[14] But Europe led to precisely that extension of the agreement to differ in a single-party administration, the Labour government elected in 1974.

That government had been committed to re-negotiating the terms of Britain's membership of the European Community, terms negotiated by Edward Heath's Conservative government and putting the outcome to referendum. On 21 January 1975, as Barbara Castle, the Health Secretary, recorded in her diaries, there had been:

'as someone said afterwards, an historic Cabinet! ... Harold [Wilson] announced a fundamental change in our constitutional convention as casually as if he had been offering us a cup of tea ...

---

[12] Sir Ivor Jennings, *Cabinet Government*, 3rd edn, Cambridge University Press, 1965, p. 281.
[13] Ibid.
[14] House of Commons, 8 February 1932, vol. 261, col. 534.

Harold came in quietly, "As soon as we have made our decision on the terms I am going to recommend that the minority should be free to campaign in the country on their own point of view". And he added, "This is unprecedented".[15]

Two days later, Wilson told the Commons that the government would be reporting the results of the re-negotiation and that it would be making a recommendation to the country based on the outcome. In due course that recommendation was that Britain should remain in the European Community. But Wilson then added that there would be an agreement to differ because, 'the circumstances of this referendum are unique, and the issue to be decided is one on which strong views have long been held which cross party lines'. Barbara Castle herself took the view that the agreement to differ was inherent in the decision to have a referendum. For, after all, a main reason for holding it was that the division of opinion on Europe did not run on party lines. The purpose of the referendum was precisely to allow opinions to be expressed across party lines. It would have seemed irrational if that freedom had been extended to everyone except leading figures in the Labour Party who were just as divided as other members and supporters of the party. Indeed, the division in the Labour Party exposed the government to some embarrassment, since the party outside Parliament, as represented by its National Executive Committee, came out against the re-negotiated terms, so the majority in the Labour Cabinet found itself in opposition to their party.

The agreement to differ was, by contrast with that of 1932, to be strictly limited in time until the referendum on 5 June. After that, Wilson declared on 29 May, it would come to an end. 'It was unprecedented because of the unprecedented nature of the referendum campaign. That

---

[15] *The Castle Diaries, 1974–1976*, p. 287.

ends after June 5, and I will see to it that normal collective responsibility and courtesy and comradeship will be renewed.[16]

There were two further contrasts with 1932. The first followed from the fact that in 1975, unlike 1932, there was to be a campaign in the country which was to decide the issue. In 1932, the issue had been decided entirely within Parliament. The main debate in 1975 was not to be in Parliament but in the country. For that reason, the agreement to differ was to be confined to the debate in the country. Freedom to dissent would not extend to speaking and voting in Parliament. On 7 April, the Cabinet approved guidelines which declared that the freedom to differ:

> does not extend to parliamentary proceedings and official business. Government business in parliament will continue to be handled by all ministers in accordance with Government policy. Ministers responsible for European aspects of Government business who themselves differ from the Government's recommendations on membership of the European Community will state the Government's position and will not be drawn into making points against the Government's recommendation. Where necessary Questions will be transferred to other Ministers.

In addition, ministers were asked 'not to allow themselves to appear in direct confrontation on the same platform or programme with another Minister who takes a different view on the government recommendations'. A junior minister, Eric Heffer, who broke the guidelines by speaking in the Commons against the government's policy, was summarily dismissed and told that he was no longer a member of the government. He was not even allowed the luxury of resignation.

---

[16] Butler and Kitzinger, *The 1975 Referendum*, p. 168.

The second further difference was that, in 1932, the free trade ministers had no departmental responsibility for trade policy, so would not be required to answer Parliamentary Questions which would contrast the government's policy on tariffs with their own commitment to free trade. But, in 1975, some of the dissenting ministers, most notably Tony Benn, the Industry Secretary and Peter Shore, the Trade Secretary did have departmental responsibility for European Community matters. When answering Parliamentary Questions, therefore, in accordance with the guidelines, they had to defend the government's policy even though they disagreed with it. This meant, in the view of Tony Benn, a leading dissenter, that the dissenting ministers were being taken into 'protective custody' for the period of the referendum.[17] The Conservative opposition frequently baited the dissentient ministers, who were reduced to somewhat unseemly expedients. On 5 May 1975, Peter Shore was asked whether his comment that 99 per cent of Britain's trade deficit was due to the European Community was in accordance with government policy. He replied: 'When I am speaking from the Dispatch Box of course I reflect the Government's policy as a whole – except when I am clearly reflecting my own policy.' During the period of the campaign, according to Barbara Castle, 'Cabinet government barely exists any more and is certainly going to be broadly in abeyance until the referendum is over. We antis noted that the popular version of the Government White Paper is being cooked up somewhere behind the scenes. There is no pretence about getting it approved by Cabinet'.[18] For the period of the referendum, Cabinet government was suspended.

On 23 May, two weeks before the referendum, Harold Wilson relaxed the guidelines saying that in the final four days of the campaign

---

[17] *Castle Diaries* p. 253.
[18] Ibid, p. 357.

ministers could confront each other on television programmes. On 27 May, the Home Secretary, Roy Jenkins, declared that 'I find it increasingly difficult to take Mr Benn seriously as an economics minister'.[19] Three days before the referendum, Jenkins appeared with Benn on a BBC *Panorama* programme in which the differences between them were starkly exposed.

Two different precedents had therefore been created for the abandonment of collective responsibility, each of them a response to a 'unique' circumstance. The first, in 1932, had been a response to a coalition government, the second a response to a referendum campaign. In 1977 there was a further agreement to differ and this time there was no pretence that the circumstance was unique or that a precedent was not being created. Again, the agreement to differ was on an issue connected with Europe. In 1976, the Labour government, by that time led by James Callaghan, proposed a bill providing for direct elections to the European Assembly, as the European Parliament was then called, in accordance with commitments that the member states had made in the European Council. Between the commitment by the government to legislation, which was made in the November 1976 Queen's Speech and the introduction of the legislation, the Labour government, which was in a minority in the House of Commons and was facing a no-confidence vote in which it was in serious danger of defeat, had agreed, in March 1977, to a pact with the Liberals to sustain it in office. One of the commitments of the Lib–Lab pact was to proceed with the legislation and to allow a free vote on the issue of proportional representation in the elections. The government proposed not only to allow a free vote on the issue, but also to allow dissenting ministers to vote against it, though Callaghan

---

[19] Butler and Kitzinger, *The 1975 Referendum*, p. 168.

hoped that the dissenters would content themselves with an abstention. At the Cabinet meeting of 26 May 1977, Callaghan, according to Tony Benn, said 'Yes, I would accept a vote against the principle. I hope people won't do it and I hope abstention will be sufficient – I hope they will consider what they are going to – but they can vote against'.[20] In this case, by contrast, with 1975 and even more by contrast with 1932, it seemed to have been the Prime Minister alone who made the decision on what the limits of dissent would be. Callaghan seems not to have sought collective agreement for the guidelines that he suggested, though no doubt the Cabinet tacitly consented to them. The Second Reading of the bill was passed by 394 votes to 147, but six Cabinet ministers – Michael Foot, Leader of the House of Commons, Tony Benn, Energy Secretary, Peter Shore, Environment Secretary, Albert Booth, Employment Secretary, Stan Orme, Northern Ireland Secretary and John Silkin, Agriculture Secretary, all voted against, together with twenty-five other members of the government. The bill, however, did not reach the statute book during that session, but a similar bill was introduced in the next session. On this occasion, there was a whipped vote and dissident ministers were given freedom to abstain but not to vote against. On the Second Reading, seven Cabinet ministers – the six mentioned above and Bruce Millan, the Scottish Secretary, abstained, as did twenty other members of the government. There was further provision for dissenting ministers in the vote in December 1977 on the regional list proportional representation voting system which the government was proposing based on a commitment in the Lib-Lab pact; then, on a guillotine motion in January 1978, four Cabinet ministers – Benn, Shore, Orme and Silkin – defied a two-line whip by abstaining.

---

[20] Ruth Winston, ed., Tony Benn: *Conflicts of Interest: Diaries, 1977–1980*, Hutchinson, 1990, p. 86.

The protracted debate on direct elections to the European Parliament with the provisions made for dissenting ministers were quite dissimilar to the agreements to differ of 1932 and 1975 precisely because of the long period which it covered – two sessions and two bills. It was beginning to appear that the convention of collective responsibility could be suspended whenever the Cabinet agreed to do so; or perhaps whenever the Prime Minister was prepared to announce that it was being suspended. At the beginning of the process, Callaghan, having been challenged by the Opposition leader, Margaret Thatcher as to whether collective responsibility applied at all to his government, replied, 'I certainly think that the doctrine should apply, except in cases where I announce that it does not'.[21]

Following the fall of the Callaghan government in 1979, there were to be no more explicit suspensions of collective responsibility for over thirty years. However, the doctrine was to come under further pressure with the formation of the Conservative/Liberal Democrat coalition government in 2010, the first peacetime coalition since the 1930s. For the first time in British history, an agreement to differ was agreed *before* the formation of a government, not, as was the case in 1932 and 1975, *after* it. The coalition government's *Programme for Stability and Reform* asserted, perhaps optimistically, that 'there is no constitutional difference between a coalition government and a single-party Government', though it then went on to admit that 'working practices need to adapt to reflect the fact that the United Kingdom has not had a coalition in modern times'. However, it declared that the government 'will work together ... on the basis of ... agreed procedures which further collective decision making and responsibility while respecting each party's identity'. But, at the same

---

[21] House of Commons, 16 June 1977, vol. 933, col. 552.

time, it declared that the principle of collective responsibility would apply *save where it is explicitly set aside*. A revised version of the Ministerial Code, issued after the formation of the government, declared that 'the principle of collective responsibility, save where it is explicitly set aside, applies to all government Ministers'. The coalition's *Programme for Government*, published in 2010, declared that there would be agreements to differ on five specific issues. They were.

1   Electoral reform. The coalition parties agreed to support a referendum on the alternative vote electoral system, but noted that, while the Liberal Democrats favoured reform, the Conservatives did not and accepted that there would be an agreement to differ on that issue. Collective responsibility, therefore, would be suspended in the referendum campaign, as it had been in 1975 and as it was to be again in the 2016 referendum campaign.

2   University tuition fees. The Liberal Democrat manifesto proposed the abolition of tuition fees and Liberal Democrat MPs had given a personal pledge that they would support abolition. The *Programme for Government* made provision for the abstention of Liberal Democrat ministers on this issue. In the event, the Cabinet minister with responsibility for tuition fees was a Liberal Democrat, the Business and Universities Secretary, Vince Cable. He and the other Liberal Democrat Cabinet ministers, including the party's leader, Nick Clegg, felt that they could not take advantage of the provision for abstention and so voted for legislation tripling university tuition fees from £3,000 per year to £9,000 per year. Only one Liberal Democrat Cabinet minister, Chris Huhne, Secretary of State for Energy and Climate Change, abstained.

3   The renewal of the Trident nuclear deterrent. Liberal Democrat ministers were to be allowed on this issue 'to make the case for alternatives'.

4   Nuclear power. The Liberal Democrats were to be allowed to maintain their opposition to new nuclear constriction and to nuclear power more generally.

5   Tax allowances for married couples. Liberal Democrat ministers were to be permitted to abstain on budget resolutions to introduce transferable tax allowances for married couples.

This, of course, was a far wider application of the agreement to differ than had ever before been seen in British politics. Moreover, previous agreements to differ had been of an ad hoc and improvisatory nature. The coalition government's suspension of collective responsibility, however, was planned well in advance of the legislation to which it was to apply. In addition, *The Programme for Stability and Reform* provided for even further unspecified agreements to differ: 'If on any future occasion any other exceptions are required they must be specifically agreed by the Coalition Committee and Cabinet'. However, 'in all circumstances, all members of both parties will be expected to support the Government on all matters of confidence'. It was difficult to see how all this could be made compatible with the thesis that 'there is no constitutional difference between a Coalition government and a single party Government'.

The Programme for Stability and Reform had allowed the Cabinet to allow for further exceptions to collective responsibility. The implication was that such further exceptions would have to be agreed by the Cabinet. However, on one occasion, the vote on the constituency boundary review in the Electoral Registration and Administration bill in 2012, Liberal Democrat ministers voted against their Conservative colleagues without such previous agreement by the Cabinet. Instead, they were given sanction after the event by the Prime Minister, David Cameron. The Electoral Registration and Administration bill in 2012 sought to implement part of the Parliamentary Voting System and Constituencies Act 2011. That Act was, in turn, implementing a promise in the coalition's proposals for government for a referendum on the alternative vote which was to be combined with the equalization of constituency boundaries and a reduction in the number of MPs in the House of Commons from 650 to 600. It was widely believed that the equalization of constituency boundaries would benefit the Conservatives, who had suffered from the movement of population from the inner cities to the suburbs and the countryside. This had led to Conservative constituencies becoming larger than Labour constituencies in the inner cities. Some believed that the Conservatives would gain up to twenty seats from equalization. It was also thought that the Liberal Democrats would suffer particularly severely, both from equalization and from the reduction in the number of constituencies, since many Liberal Democrat MPs held their seats as a result of local factors and a close identification with their constituencies. That would of course be lost when constituency boundaries were redrawn.

The referendum on the alternative vote led to heavy defeat for the reform. But between the referendum and the time of the Electoral Registration and Administration bill, the coalition government had sought to fulfil another of its commitments which was 'to bring forward proposals for a wholly or mainly elected upper chamber on the basis of proportional representation'. The Liberal Democrats were strongly in favour of an elected second chamber while most Conservatives were more sceptical. The government was not, however, committed to *supporting* such proposals only to bringing them forward. In the event, although the bill for Lords reform was supported by the Labour opposition and passed in the Commons with a majority of 338, no fewer than ninety-one Conservatives voted against the bill, defying a three-line whip and nineteen Conservatives abstained. Two ministers resigned from the government to vote against it. The government found itself unable to continue with the bill, since Labour declared that it would not support a timetabling motion, limiting discussion on it and there was insufficient Conservative support for the government to be confident of carrying a timetabling motion. The bill was dropped a few weeks after the second reading. Liberal Democrats argued that the Conservatives had broken the contract on which the coalition had been based and, in retaliation, refused to vote for the recommendations of the boundary commission. All fifty-seven Liberal Democrat MPs, including Liberal Democrat Cabinet ministers, voted against the recommendations; since the Labour opposition also voted against them they, too, had to be dropped. Nevertheless, the Conservatives had fulfilled the commitment in the coalition agreement 'to bring forward proposals' on Lords reform. In addition, they had applied collective responsibility to the legislation so that any minister who wished to vote against it was required to resign from the government as two, in fact, did; the issue of the equalization of constituencies was quite unrelated to Lords reform.

The Liberal Democrat revolt against the boundary review was a further stage in the undermining of collective responsibility. Previously agreements to differ could be defended by saying that they had been agreed upon by the Cabinet. There was, therefore, collective and, apparently, unanimous agreement to abandon, on specific issues, collective responsibility. At least, so it might be argued, the principle of collective unanimity remained. But, on this occasion, there was no agreement to differ. The breach of collective responsibility was unilateral and not endorsed until after the event by the Prime Minister.

In 2013, the Prime Minister, David Cameron, sanctioned a yet further breach of collective responsibility. In the Queen's Speech of May 2013, he declared that he was sufficiently 'relaxed' to allow Conservative ministers to vote for an amendment to the Speech regretting 'that a European Union Referendum Bill was not concluded'.[22] This, too, was a breach of the coalition agreement which had declared that 'in all circumstances, all members of both parties will be expected to support the government on all matters of confidence'. Later, there were conflicting responses by Conservative and Liberal Democrat ministers to the report of the Leveson Committee on media regulation, even though the government had itself appointed it.

The coalition agreement had explicitly defined certain issues on which collective Cabinet responsibility could be suspended. It seemed that, under the coalition, collective responsibility had become a freely adjustable commodity which could be ignored whenever it was expedient to do so. In a report on the working of the coalition, the House of Lords Select Committee on the Constitution, declared 'collective ministerial responsibility has been the convention most affected by coalition government'.[23] It may be indeed that there is a fundamental conflict between the principle of collective responsibility and the working of coalition government. For, in a coalition, the key decisions will often not be made by the Cabinet as a whole, but by the leaders of the parties comprising the coalition. It is they who will decide whether there is a collective view that the coalition Cabinet can support. The leaders will then seek to bind their followers. If it is not possible to achieve such collective agreement, then the parties to the coalition must decide whether they wish to continue the

---

[22] House of Commons, 15 May 2013, vol. 563, col. 749.
[23] *Constitutional Implications of Coalition Government*, HL 130, 2014, p. 4.

arrangement. If they do, they must then decide to suspend collective responsibility for the issue in question.

In the 2015 general election, the Conservatives under David Cameron won an overall majority. But collective responsibility was again to be suspended in the referendum on the European Union in 2016, just as it had been in the 1975 referendum. On 5 January 2016, David Cameron, now Prime Minister of a single-party Conservative government, told the Commons that, in the referendum on the European Union, to be held in June, while there would be a 'clear Government position' it would 'be open to individual ministers to take a different personal position while remaining part of the Government.'[24] In a Cabinet of twenty-two, four ministers – Chris Grayling, the Leader of the House of Commons, John Whittingdale, the Culture Secretary, Theresa Villiers, the Northern Ireland Secretary and Michael Gove, the Justice Secretary, took advantage of this provision, as did two ministers who, although not in the Cabinet, attended Cabinet meetings, Priti Patel, the Minister for Employment and Boris Johnson, the former Mayor of London.

On this occasion, there was some controversy concerning the role of the civil service. Sir Jeremy Heywood, the Head of the Civil Service, had issued guidelines declaring that it would 'not be appropriate or permissible for the civil service to support ministers who oppose the Government's official position by providing briefing or speech material on this matter.'[25] When the referendum resulted in a decision to leave the European Union, the civil service came under criticism since, so it was alleged, insufficient preparations had been made for that outcome. However, the role of the civil service in 2016, following

---

[24] House of Commons, 5 January 2016, vol. 604, cols 26–8.
[25] Letter from Head of the Civil Service, 'EU Referendum: Guidance for the Civil Service and Special Advisers', 23 February 2016, p. 2.

the guidance issued by Sir Jeremy, replicated the role of the civil service in 1975 and it would have been unconstitutional for officials to advise ministers who were in opposition to the policy of the government as to how best to conduct that opposition. The government had a clear policy, even though it was opposed by the dissenting ministers. The government was by no means neutral as to the outcome which it preferred. The task of the civil service, therefore, was to advise the government on its policy, not to advise ministers who might be opposed to that policy or on what the outcome would be if the government's policy failed as, in fact, it did.

By 2016, Callaghan's flippant comment that collective responsibility applied except when he determined that it should not, seems to have become a permanent truth of British government. It now meant something different from what it had meant forty years earlier. That had already been apparent in the revised Ministerial Code, published in May 2010, which had stated in paragraph 1.2: 'The principle of collective responsibility, *save where it is explicitly set aside*, applies to all Government Ministers' (emphasis added). That would not have been said before 1975. In the court proceedings on the publication of the Crossman diaries in 1975, Sir John Hunt, the Cabinet Secretary, while insisting that collective responsibility was 'a reality and an important part of the constitution', redefined it by saying that the agreement to differ in 1975 had not breached it because 'this was a decision by the Cabinet as a whole to waive collective responsibility on one particular issue for a limited time. It was not a decision which any Minister took unilaterally'. In other words, the convention was collective unanimity, not collective responsibility.[26] During the

---

[26] Cross-examination of *Sir John Hunt in A-G v Sunday Times*, cited in Hugo Young, *The Crossman Affair*, Hamish Hamilton and Jonathan Cape, 1976, p. 84. Ironically, one of the members of the Wilson Cabinet, Michael Foot, one of Crossman's literary executors, was opposed to his government's attempt to prevent publication of the diaries.

coalition government, it seemed to have become acceptable – as with the Liberal Democrats on the issue of the boundary review – for a party unilaterally to proclaim an agreement to differ as long as that agreement to differ was given ex post facto support by the Prime Minister. Collective responsibility for policy had become a maxim of political prudence and seemed no longer a fundamental convention of the constitution.

The convention of collective responsibility had developed with the rise of party government, first to ensure that the Cabinet presented a collective front to the king so that individual ministers could not be picked off one by one; then so that the Cabinet could present a united front to Parliament so that individual ministers could not be picked off one by one. Perhaps the convention was more relevant when the parties were more united on matters of policy than they are today and when such differences of view as existed could be kept within the knowledge of a small circle and withheld from the media. These conditions hardly exist today. Still, any prudent government will seek to limit the use of the agreement to differ. For it is in danger of subjecting the Cabinet to ridicule, as indeed any other executive, whether a Board of Directors or even the committee of a students' union, would be subject to ridicule if it diverged in public on fundamental issues. As Lord Palmerston had noted in the mid-nineteenth century: 'Differences of opinion between Members of the Same Government are unnecessarily brought out into Prominence and the Strength of the Government is thereby impaired.'

Nevertheless, the doctrine of collective responsibility has been irretrievably weakened; Europe was the occasion of its being weakened. Without the European issue, it might have remained as a fundamental convention of the constitution.

5

Europe and the Rights of the Citizen

I

Entry into the European Community, then, abrogated the sovereignty of Parliament by rendering British law subordinate to the law of the European Union. It also led to the introduction of the referendum into British politics. This implied, as was to become apparent after 2016, that the sovereignty of Parliament would, in due course, come to be trumped by the sovereignty of the people; the referendum, as we have seen, provoked another constitutional innovation, the suspension of collective responsibility under a single-party government. Entry into the European Community, therefore, established precedents which could be followed on other issues. Although Europe was held to be a unique issue to which alone the referendum was relevant, the 1975 referendum was to be followed shortly after by referendums on devolution in 1979. Since then, the referendum has come to be established as an accepted part of the British constitution. The agreement to differ in 1975 was to be followed in 1977 by agreements to differ on direct elections to the European Assembly and then, after

2010, in the coalition government, on a host of other issues. Indeed, the device came to be given official recognition in the coalition agreement, the ministerial code and the Cabinet Manual. So, in consequence of British membership of the European Community, both the sovereignty of Parliament and the principle of collective responsibility seemed to have become freely adjustable commodities rather than permanent principles of the constitution.

British entry into the European Community had even further constitutional consequences of a major kind. It exposed Britain for the first time in its history to a bill of rights, the European Charter of Fundamental Rights and to the judicial review of primary legislation for compatibility with those rights. In consequence of the Charter, judges now had the power to disapply legislation which contravened the human rights guaranteed in it. This was a further revolutionary development in the British constitution, which had always been uneasy with the assertion of rights against Parliament. The Human Rights Act 1998 had not given judges this power. It had required them to construe all legislation to make it compatible with the European Convention of Human Rights, a Convention drawn up by the Council of Europe, a body quite separate from the European Union. If legislation could not be so construed, all that the judges could do was to issue a declaration of incompatibility. This declaration, however, had no legal effect and it remained for Parliament to amend the legislation if it so chose. The Human Rights Act had, all the same, brought the language of rights into the British constitution.

Some philosophical traditions, however, find it difficult to come to terms with the concept of rights against the state. Majoritarians argue that our rights should be determined by the majority in the legislature, not by the judges. Relativists argue that the rights we enjoy should depend upon the norms of the society in which we live; legislators are much more likely to be able to determine what these norms actually are than judges, who, inevitably, must be somewhat insulated from society. Utilitarians such as Dicey argue that to assert a right other than a legal right is merely to claim that the general welfare would be increased if a new legal right were to be created. That, of course, is a matter for government and the legislature. So, the utilitarian comes to agree with the majoritarian that it is the majority in the legislature, not the judges, who should determine what our rights should be.

Majoritarians argue that in a democracy the majority should rule and that judges should not entrench upon decisions which are the province of representative institutions. In a lecture in 2011, entitled 'Judicial and Political Decision-Making: The Uncertain Boundary', Jonathan Sumption QC, shortly to become a judge of the Supreme Court, claimed in a discussion of the Human Rights Act that decisions by the courts on the abuse of discretionary powers were coming to entrench upon the political domain. 'By this', he argued, 'I do not mean that the judges who decided them were politically partisan, but simply that they were dealing with matters (namely the merits of policy decisions) which in a democracy are the proper function of Parliament and of ministers answerable to Parliament and the electorate'. In his view, the Human Rights Act had:

> significantly shifted the boundaries between political and legal decision-making in areas some of which raise major political issues, such as immigration, penal policy, security and policing, privacy and freedom of expression ... By giving legal effect to the Convention [i.e. the European Convention of Human Rights] ... we have transferred it out of the political arena altogether, and into the domain of judicial decision-making where public accountability has no place.

The fallacy of this view is that it assumes that in a democracy a majority that has won power in a free election has the right to govern in any way that it chooses. That, however, would lead to a tyranny of the majority. A well-functioning democracy requires respect for human rights, particularly the rights of minorities, as well as rule by the majority. Some minorities, of course, can and do ensure that their rights are respected through the electoral process. That is true of large ethnic and religious minorities. Many of them have sufficient leverage to ensure that their views are taken account of by policy makers. However, some of the minorities protected by the Human Rights Act are very small, unpopular and vulnerable, such as asylum-seekers, prisoners and suspected terrorists. They do not constitute pressure groups able to influence policy makers. There is no pressure group ensuring that the arguments in favour of prisoners obtaining the vote are heard in the electoral arena; there is no pressure group ensuring that the arguments in favour of sex offenders being allowed to have their position on the sex offenders register reviewed after a certain period of time are heard. Only the courts can ensure that the rights of such unpopular and vulnerable minorities are protected. It is worth pointing out that the Human Rights Act protects *human* rights (i.e. the rights of everyone). Indeed, any of us may, at any time, become vulnerable individuals whose rights are infringed, yet we may be unable to secure redress through the electoral process and therefore require rights protection. As the constitutional lawyer Conor Gearty has eloquently written:

> The human rights insight is that none of us has a guaranteed space among the fortunate, that the border between affluence and misfortune is more porous than we assume. Human rights are for us all but likely to be called upon only when we need them. And rich and fortunate though we might seem, these are not guaranteed

conditions: we will grow old, we may be visited unexpectedly by the police, an onset of mental ill-health may leave us vulnerable; our lives may change suddenly for the worst.[1]

Sumption added to the majoritarian criticism of human rights a criticism based on relativism. He attacked what he called 'one of the most striking features of modern human rights theory' namely 'its claim to universal validity'. 'The European Convention', he complained, 'has been construed as attributing rights to humans simply by virtue of their humanity, irrespective of their membership of any particular legal or national community'. Sumption echoed Burke in his argument that 'rights are necessarily claims against the claimant's own community, and in a democracy, they depend for their legitimacy on a measure of recognition by that community'. And 'extremes apart, political communities may and do legitimately differ on what rights should be recognised'.

The European Convention of Human Rights and the European Union's Charter of Fundamental Rights were, of course, promulgated as a protest against this sort of relativism which is as inimical to the protection of human rights as the doctrine that the majority, after a free election, can govern in any way that it chooses. Rights depend, as the Human Rights Act and the European Charter recognize, upon our common humanity rather than on whether they happen to be congruent with the norms of the community in which we happen to live. It is, therefore, a mistake to say that rights 'depend for their legitimacy on a measure of recognition' by the community. Their basis is more fundamental than that.

---

[1] Conor Gearty, *On Fantasy Island: Britain, European and Human Rights*, Oxford University Press, 2016, p. 8.

Therefore, neither the doctrine of majoritarianism nor the doctrine of cultural relativism can be used to deny the importance of human rights, rights which may be better protected by judges rather than by majoritarian institutions such as the House of Commons.

But the utilitarian tradition of which Dicey was a part finds it as difficult as the majoritarian tradition championed by Sumption to accommodate rights. For the great utilitarian, Jeremy Bentham, the claim of rights against the state was a mere claim that it would be in accordance with the value of utility, the greatest happiness of the greatest number, if the particular claim were to be embodied in the law. But it is by no means obvious that it is for the general good, in utilitarian terms, to give rights to small and unpopular minorities. It is perfectly possible that the greatest happiness of the greatest number would be better secured by denying the rights of such small minorities. But individuals have rights, surely, whether or not they are able to contribute to the general good of the community. Rights are owed to individuals irrespective of utilitarian considerations.

A system based on the sovereignty of Parliament finds it difficult to accommodate the notion of rights against the state. Indeed, the whole logic of the idea of the sovereignty of Parliament is that there can be no rights against Parliament. Under such a system it is Parliament which creates the rights of the citizen, Parliament which can at any time amend or abrogate them. Therefore, there can be no place for a Charter of Fundamental Rights or a Bill of Rights such as exists, for example, in the United States in the shape of the first ten amendments to the United States constitution and in many other democracies. 'Most foreign constitution-makers', Dicey wrote, 'have begun with declarations of rights'. 'For this', he adds ironically, 'they have often been in no way to blame'.[2] There is, admittedly, an English Bill of

---

[2] Dicey, *Law of the Constitution*, p. 198.

Rights enacted in 1689, but that is a quite different sort of animal from the American. For, while the American Bill of Rights limits the power of Congress and the executive, granting rights against the state, the English Bill of Rights, by contrast, emphasized the sovereignty of Parliament. Passed at the end of a period of struggle between the King and Parliament, it sought to limit the power of the monarch, who would, in future, be required to obtain the consent of Parliament for all legislation. The Bill of Rights set out in statutory form the rights of Parliament, including the requirements of regular parliaments and freedom of speech in Parliament. The Bill did, admittedly, provide for certain rights, such as the right of Protestants to bear arms and the right not to undergo a cruel or unusual punishment. But these rights were to remain at the mercy of Parliament which could at any time modify or abrogate them by the same procedure – a simple majority in both Houses – as would be needed to modify or abrogate any other statute. The main purpose of the Bill of Rights was to redistribute power between the monarch and Parliament. The power of the King in Parliament, however, remained supreme. The Bill of Rights, therefore, confirmed the sovereignty of the legislature rather than limiting it as is normally the case with bills of rights.[3]

Until the Second World War and, perhaps, for some time afterwards, the lack of any restriction on the sovereign legislature requiring it to respect human rights was seen not as a weakness in the British system of government but as a strength. That was certainly Dicey's view. He was, indeed, proud of the fact that Britain had no bill of rights. 'There is', Dicey declares, 'in the English constitution (*sic!*) an absence of those declarations or definitions of rights so dear to foreign constitutionalists'. Instead, the principles defining our civil liberties

---

[3] The Bill applied only to England and Wales, though Scotland passed not dissimilar legislation in 1689. There is uncertainty as to whether the Bill applies to Northern Ireland.

were, he said, 'like all maxims established by judicial legislation, mere generalizations drawn either from the decisions or dicta of judges, or from statutes'. 'With us', he says, 'the law of the constitution, the rules which in foreign countries naturally form part of a constitutional code are not the source but the consequence of the rights of individuals, as defined and enforced by the courts'.

The result, however, was, as Dicey appreciated, that:

> the relation of the rights of individuals to the principles of the constitution is not quite the same in countries, like Belgium, where the constitution is the result of a legislative act, as in England, where the constitution itself is based on legal decisions – the difference in this matter between the constitutions of Belgium and the English constitution may be described by the statement that in Belgium individual rights are deductions drawn from the principles of the constitution, whilst in England the so-called principles of the constitution are inductions or generalisations based upon particular decisions pronounced by the courts as to the rights of given individuals.[4]

Following the Second World War, however, many on the Continent came to believe that it was no longer sufficient to rely on legislatures to protect human rights. A majoritarian democracy, based on the doctrine that a majority which had been victorious in a free election, could pass whatever legislation it liked, was seen, in the light of the experience of Nazism and the failure of human rights in most of the European continent, as inadequate. It was primarily for this reason that the Council of Europe, an intergovernmental organization quite separate from the European Community and comprising most of the democracies in Europe, drew up a Convention of Human Rights. A

---

[4] Dicey, *Law of the Constitution*, 10th edn, pp. 144, 203.

leading role in drawing up this Convention was played by a British lawyer and politician, the future Conservative Home Secretary, Sir David Maxwell Fyfe, later, as Lord Chancellor, Lord Kilmuir. Maxwell Fyfe had the strong support of his party leader, Winston Churchill, who hoped to see a unified Europe based on the rule of law. Britain was one of the first countries to ratify the European Convention, in 1951, during the dying days of Attlee's Labour government; unlike some other European countries, it was agreed that it should also apply to colonies. From 1966, individuals were allowed to take cases against the United Kingdom to the European Court of Human Rights at Strasbourg. However, the Convention did not become part of British law until the Human Rights Act of 1998 passed by Tony Blair's Labour government.

The Human Rights Act altered the basis on which rights were to be understood in Britain. Following the Act, our rights would no longer be based on inductions or generalizations. They would, instead, be derived from 'principles of the constitution' (i.e. the substantive rights to be found in the European Convention on Human Rights). Under the Act, judges were to be charged with interpreting legislation in the light of a higher law, the European Convention. Dicey, however, had famously declared that there can be no such higher law in the British constitution: 'There is no law which Parliament cannot change. There is no fundamental or so-called constitutional law, and there is no person or body which can pronounce void any enactment passed by the British Parliament on the ground of such enactment being opposed to the constitution.'[5]

Formally these statements remained true. The European Convention was not fundamental law in the sense that it was a law which Parliament which could not change. The Human Rights Act formally preserved the

---

[5] Ibid, pp. 88, 91.

sovereignty of Parliament. But the Act implied a more active role for the courts which came under a duty to interpret all legislation, wherever that was possible, so that it conformed to the European Convention of Human Rights. It did not empower judges to strike down Acts of Parliament as is the case with most bills of rights. Nor did it permit executive action to be overridden where its sole purpose was to give effect to the violating primary legislation. All that judges were permitted to do, if they believed that legislation could not be construed to conform with the European Convention of Human Rights, was to issue a declaration of incompatibility. That declaration was a mere statement without legal effect. It would then be for Parliament to amend or repeal the offending statute or part of a statute if it wished to do so; the Act provided for a special fast-track procedure by which this might be done, a so-called 'Henry VIII' procedure by which secondary legislation in the form of an order could repeal primary legislation. The method of correcting a legal abuse of human rights would be through government or Parliament and, in theory, of course, Parliament could refuse to remedy a breach of human rights or vote down an order issued by the government correcting such a breach. The Act, then, did not provide for a judicial remedy against Acts of Parliament that violated Convention rights, even though Article 13 of the European Convention required such a remedy. Article 13, however, was not made part of the Human Rights Act. So far, however, ministers and Parliament have always taken remedial action following a declaration of incompatibility.[6] Nevertheless, by virtue of the Act all the courts can say to a successful litigant is, 'Your rights have been infringed but there is nothing further that we can do

---

[6] There is a seeming exception to this statement that Parliament has so far always taken remedial action in that it has not yet dealt with the issue of prisoners voting rights, the subject of a declaration in *Smith v Scott* 2007 SC 345, effectively approved by the Supreme Court in the *Chester* case [2013] UKSC 63, para. 39. But the government has promised to take such remedial action.

about it' or perhaps 'Your rights would have been infringed if you had any, but under a Diceyan constitution, your rights are dependent upon a sovereign parliament, and we have no further status in the matter'. In *Burden and Burden v The United Kingdom*,[7] heard by the European Court of Human Rights in December 2006, that Court declared that a declaration of incompatibility did *not* automatically provide an effective remedy – such as is required by Article 13 of the European Convention. The declaration of incompatibility was, the Court declared, 'dependent on the discretion of the executive and [one] which the Court has previously found to be ineffective on that ground'.[8] But the Court also declared it to be 'possible that at some future date evidence of a long-standing and established practice of ministers giving effect to the courts' declarations of incompatibility might be sufficient to persuade the Court [of Human Rights] of the effectiveness of the procedure. At the present time, however, there is insufficient material on which to base such a finding'.

Even so, the Human Rights Act made the European Convention part of the law of the land. In a lecture in 2005, the late Lord Steyn, a Law Lord, declared: 'In the development of our country towards becoming a true constitutional state the coming into force of the Human Rights Act 1998 … was a landmark … By the Human Rights Act Parliament transformed our country into a rights-based democracy. By the 1998 Act Parliament made the judiciary the guardians of the ethical values of our bill of rights.' Lord Steyn defined 'a true constitutional state' as one which has 'a wholly separate and independent Supreme Court which is the ultimate guardian of the *fundamental law* of the community'[9] (emphasis added). The idea of

---

[7] Application no. 13378/05 [2008] ECHR 357.

[8] Ibid, para. 40.

[9] Lord Steyn, '2000–2005: Laying the Foundations of Human Rights Law in the United Kingdom'. Lecture to The British Institute of International and Comparative Law, 10 June 2005.

fundamental law is, of course, something new in our constitutional experience and its being cited by Lord Steyn is a good indication that the Human Rights Act could prove the first step on what may prove a long and tortuous journey towards a codified constitution.

II

That journey and the transformation of Britain into a rights-based democracy was strengthened by the European Union's Charter of Fundamental Rights. This was adopted by the EU in 2000, but it did not become part of EU law until the Lisbon Treaty of 2008, which came into force in December 2009. The Charter draws on the European Convention of Human Rights, although it is, constitutionally, quite separate from the Convention and its fifty-four articles contain a number of rights which are not in the Convention. Amongst these rights are the Article 3 right to the integrity of the person, which prohibits eugenic practices and reproductive cloning; the Article 8 right providing for the protection of personal data and a right of access to such data; the Article 13 right to academic freedom; the Article 14 right to vocational and continual training; the very specific Article 21 right to non-discrimination on grounds 'such as sex, race, colour, ethnic or social origin, genetic features, language, religion or belief, political or any other opinion, membership of a national minority, property, birth, disability, age or sexual orientation' – this article, unlike the European Convention, provides explicit protection for members of the LGBT community; the Article 24 rights of the child, giving effect to a United Nations Convention on the rights of the child and specifically including a right of access on the part of the child to both parents; and the Article 25 rights of the elderly. There are, in addition, an Article 34 right to social security, an Article 35 right to health care and an Article 38 right to environmental protection. In some cases, a European Convention right is considerably widened in application, most notably the Article 47 right to a fair trial and an effective remedy, which in part replicates Article 6 of the European Convention, but also provides for a right to a fair hearing which would almost certainly apply, for example, to tribunals such as immigration tribunals, as well as to the courts.

The Charter, which only applies when member states are implementing EU law, is a part of EU law and in consequence its provisions can be used to justify a declaration to the effect that a challenged provision of a member state is illegal in substance or was illegally arrived at. So the protection given by the Charter is much stronger than the unenforceable declaration in the Human Rights Act. The institutions of the member states, including their courts, are under a duty to recognize the consequences of such a declaration of illegality. If they do not, various remedies are available. The European Court of Justice can perhaps now be compared to the United States Supreme Court in terms of the breadth of its powers; the national courts of the member states are also required to disapply primary legislation and quash secondary legislation if they find such legislation to be incompatible with a Charter provision that is directly effective where the national legislation lies within the scope of EU law.

Britain did not, however, incorporate the Charter into her domestic law and, together with Poland, secured what ministers believed was an opt-out or, to be more precise, a protocol – Protocol 30 – providing, first, that the Charter did not extend the ability either of Britain's domestic courts or of the European Court of Justice to find any British legal provision inconsistent with the Charter; secondly that the Charter would not create any new actionable rights in Britain or Poland; and thirdly that the Charter would only apply to Britain and Poland if the rights for which it provided were already recognized in domestic law. The then Prime Minister, Tony Blair, told the Commons in 2007, 'it is absolutely clear that we have an opt-out from the charter. ...' The then Foreign Secretary, David Miliband, told the Commons in 2008 that: 'The treaty records existing rights rather than creating new ones. A new legally binding protocol guarantees that nothing in the charter extends the ability of any court to strike down UK law.'[10] Much later, in 2014, the then Home Secretary, Theresa May, told the Commons that the Charter was 'declaratory only and we do not consider that it applies to the United Kingdom.'[11]

However, Protocol 30 did not have the effect envisaged of allowing Britain to enjoy a general opt-out from the Charter. In a case in December 2011, concerning the transfer of asylum seekers from one member state of the European Union to another – the *NS* case – the European Court of Justice ruled that the Protocol 'does not call in question the applicability of the Charter in the United Kingdom or Poland ... Thus ... the Charter must be applied and interpreted by the courts of Poland and of the United Kingdom.' The Protocol 'was not intended to exempt the Republic of Poland or the United Kingdom from the duty to comply with the provisions of the Charter, nor to prevent a court of one of those Member States from ensuring compliance with those provisions.'[12] From the point of view of the EU, it would indeed have appeared odd if an opt-out were possible from what was seen as a fundamental constitutional document so that fundamental rights came to be different from one member state to another. In the case of some rights, for example, the right to environmental protection, if a member state were able to ignore it, that member state might gain an unfair competitive advantage over those prepared to abide by it.

---

[10] House of Commons, 25 June 2007, vol. 462, col. 21; 21 January 2008, vol. 470, col. 1250.
[11] House of Commons, 19 November 2014, vol. 588, col. 342.
[12] Joined Cases C-411/10 and C 493/10, summary of the judgment, para. 4.

The Charter has been used by British judges to do what the Human Rights Act does not allow them to do, namely to disapply parts of Westminster statutes because they are in conflict with human rights. This was a revolutionary and little-noticed development in British government. This power was first used in a case, *Benkharbouche v Secretary of State for Foreign Affairs* in 2017.[13] Ms Benkharbouche was a Moroccan national who was employed by the Sudanese embassy in London. She claimed against the Sudanese embassy for unfair dismissal, failure to pay her the national minimum wage, unpaid wages and holiday pay, as well as breaches of the Working Time Regulations. The Sudanese embassy claimed that it was entitled to immunity under the provisions of the State Immunity Act 1978. But Lord Sumption, speaking for a unanimous Court, ruled that sections of the Act conferring immunity were incompatible with Article 6 of the European Convention providing for a fair trial and therefore a right of access to a court. The remedy for this would be a declaration of incompatibility which, as we have seen, is not a strictly legal remedy, since it has no legal effect. But Article 47 of the Charter of Fundamental Rights provides that anyone whose rights have been violated has 'the right to an effective remedy'. If the Convention had been violated, Lord Sumption held, so also had the Charter; he concluded, therefore, that 'a conflict between EU law and English domestic law must be resolved in favour of the former, and the latter must be disapplied'.[14]

In an earlier case, *Vidal-Hall v Google Inc*,[15] the claimant had argued that Google through its use of internet 'cookies' had misused private information, breaching her confidence and so infringing the Data

---

[13] [2017] UKSC 62.
[14] Ibid, at para. 78.
[15] [2015] 3 WLR 409.

Protection Act 1998. Part of that Act limited the right to compensation for distress. The Court of Appeal in its judgment declared that the exclusion of a right to compensation for distress in certain circumstances was contrary to Articles 7 and 8 of the Charter requiring respect for private and family life and a right to the protection of personal data, as well as Article 47 guaranteeing the right to an effective remedy. The Supreme Court granted Google permission to appeal to the Supreme Court, but the case was withdrawn following agreement between the parties. Here also, the Charter was held explicitly to trump an Act of Parliament. This case, although earlier than *Benkharbouche*, went further in that it showed that the Charter could be used 'horizontally' in a dispute between private persons, rather than, as with *Benkharbouche,* only in a dispute between a private person and a public body.

In an earlier case than *Benkharbouche* or *Vidal-Hall*, in 2014, two backbench MPs, Tom Watson, now deputy leader of the Labour Party and David Davis, later to become Secretary of State for Exiting the European Union, brought proceedings to secure the disapplication of the Data Retention and Investigatory Powers Act 2014 as contrary to the Charter, arguing that parts of the Act were incompatible with Articles 7, 8 and 11 of the Charter providing for respect for private and family life, protection of personal data and freedom of expression and information, since, in their view, the Act did not protect the rights of data protection of citizens against the police and public bodies. This Act was repealed in 2016 although those of its provisions which did not offend against the Charter were incorporated in the Investigatory Powers Act of 2016. The High Court found for Watson and Davis. The Court of Appeal referred the issue to the European Court of Justice, which held that parts of the Act were contrary to Articles 7, 8 and 11 of the Charter and that EU law precluded legislation such as the Data Protection Act. Watson and Davis had invoked the Charter, rather than the Human Rights Act, precisely because the Charter provided for greater protection than the European Convention. It seems ironic that a leading Brexiteer, David Davis, brought proceedings to question the validity of an Act of Parliament on the grounds that it offended against European Union principles! The effect of the Charter, however, was to empower the High Court to render invalid those parts of a Westminster statute that were inconsistent with EU law.[16] The Charter, then, had revolutionized the approach of British judges to the protection of rights. Presumably not even the strongest Brexiteer would seek to argue that any of the three judgments considered above ought to be reversed. Yet, on leaving the European Union, Britain will also abandon the protections offered by the Charter.

What is clear is that, far from Britain achieving an opt-out, the Charter provided stronger protection of human rights than those offered by the European Convention of Human Rights. In October 2017, in evidence to the Commons Exiting the EU Committee, Dr Charlotte O'Brien of the University of York Law School, detected 248 cases in the courts of England and Wales that had cited the Charter, seventeen in Northern Ireland and fourteen in Scotland.[17]

There was, therefore, until Brexit, a hierarchy of rights protection in Britain. The Charter provided for disapplication of conflicting domestic legislation, whilst the Human Rights Act provided only for a declaration of incompatibility, even though the rights protected in the European Convention are at least as fundamental as those in the Charter. The former limits Parliamentary sovereignty, the latter does not. The protection given by the Charter does, therefore, expose

---

[16] *Secretary of State for the Home Department v Davis & Watson* [2015] EWCA Civ 1185; *Tele2 Sverige v Post-och, Secretary of State v Watson* (2016) C-203/15 and C-698/15.
[17] HC 373, Oral Evidence, 11 October 2017, Q19.

the very limited protection in terms of enforceability in relation to primary legislation given by the Human Rights Act.

The Charter is not, however, to be incorporated into UK law as retained EU law after Brexit. The Solicitor General, Robert Buckland, in a parliamentary debate on the Charter, declared that: 'Allowing courts to overturn Acts of Parliament, outside of the context of EU law, on the basis of incompatibility with these principles [of the Charter] would be alien to our legal system and would offend against parliamentary sovereignty.'[18] The Charter, therefore, will no longer apply domestically in interpreting and applying retained EU law. Nevertheless, Article 5(5) of the Withdrawal Bill purports to provide for the preservation after Brexit of 'fundamental rights or principles which exist irrespective of the Charter', although the bill does not specify what these 'fundamental rights' are. It would, admittedly, be pointless to incorporate the whole of the Charter into domestic law. It is, after all, addressed to 'the institutions, bodies, offices and agencies of the Union ... and to Member States ... only when they are implementing Union law' (Article 51.1) and the preamble refers to the aspiration of 'ever closer union', an aspiration to which David Cameron, in his renegotiation, successfully argued Britain was not committed. Further, some of the Charter rights, such as the right to vote in European Parliament elections, become irrelevant after Brexit. Others, such as the right to free movement in the European Union, are opposed by the government. Indeed, one of the main motives for leaving the European Union on the part of many Brexiteers was precisely a desire to limit free movement.

There are, nevertheless, many rights in the Charter which would certainly remain relevant to Britain. Many would argue that such

---

[18] House of Commons, 21 November 2017, vol. 631, col. 971,

rights as the right to equality, the right to health care and the right to environmental protection as well as the right to a remedy, should become part of British law. In the case of some rights guaranteed by the Charter, such as the rights of the child, access is given to United Nations conventions which Britain has ratified but not incorporated into her system of law. But, of course, if provisions of the Charter were to become part of our domestic law, some would have to be rewritten and some would have to be adapted to suit specifically British conditions.

The government has promised that all EU-derived rights in domestic law – or some variant of them – will be preserved after Brexit and that it will present to Parliament a list of the rights in the Charter to show that they are all, in fact, being secured in domestic law. But a list of rights presented by a minister is hardly a substitute for a codification of rights protected by the judicial review of primary legislation such as is secured by the Charter. Even more important, the legal remedy provided by the Charter will be lost. The courts, therefore, will no longer be able to rule that a particular statute or part of a statute is unlawful or quash an action on the basis that legislation is not compatible either with Charter rights or with domestic provisions intended to replicate such rights. This means that there will no longer be a legal remedy for a breach of Charter rights. It will no longer be possible for the courts to enforce the provisions of the Charter. In addition, the rights guaranteed by the Charter will in future be at the mercy of a sovereign parliament which can, at any time, amend or delete them. The rights may be incorporated into our law, but their status will be radically different. They will no longer be protected rights, nor will there be a remedy if they are breached. Unless the rights in the Charter become part of an amended Human Rights Act, there will not even be the remedy of a declaration of incompatibility.

The Withdrawal Act does admittedly provide that retained EU law shall be supreme over domestic legislation enacted prior to exit day, though not after exit day, so that, until exit day, such domestic legislation can presumably be disapplied by the courts if it is in conflict with retained EU law. But after exit day, retained EU law can be amended, repealed or modified at any time by a sovereign parliament and nothing in the Act provides that primary legislation would be required to achieve this purpose.

What value, it might be asked, does a right have if it is dependent upon the whim of a sovereign parliament and if there is no legal remedy for a breach? There can be little doubt that an important protection given by the Charter will be lost upon Brexit and that the rights of all British citizens will be considerably diminished.

It would seem that, after Brexit, Britain will revert to the constitutional position before 1973, before joining the European Union, when the sovereignty of Parliament was the dominant, if not her only constitutional principle. Britain will be engaged in a process, not of entrenchment, as was the case in 1973, but a process of disentrenchment, quite unique in the democratic world. Just as Britain's entry into the European Community strengthened the courts at the expense of Parliament and the executive, so Brexit could reverse the process by strengthening Parliament and the executive at the expense of the courts. In practice, since British governments normally enjoy a majority in the House of Commons, the confidence principle means that that the view of the majority in the Commons normally coincides with that of the government. So, Brexit is likely to increase the power of government rather than Parliament. Restoring the sovereignty of Parliament was, of course, one of the major political aims of those who supported Brexit. But 'taking back control' will mean not only that Parliament will be taking back control from the EU and from the European Court of Justice. Parliament and, still more, the government, will also be 'taking back control' from British courts as well as from EU courts.

Indeed, some of the Brexiteers who sought to 'take back control' did so precisely because they wished to remove what they regard as burdensome regulations from our law, such as the Working Time Directive or the Temporary Agency Work Directive. In their view, the supremacy of EU law prevented the British public from being able to decide for themselves on employment law and to vote out those who had made laws which the public did not like. Theresa May has, admittedly, committed the government to retaining EU employment rights. Nevertheless, in the EU, so Brexiteers argued, because of the system of qualified majority voting in the Council of Ministers, laws could be imposed upon Britain to which the government and Parliament of the day were opposed. After Brexit, by contrast, all laws will be scrutinized by Parliament, which can, at least in theory, modify or reject them.

It follows, nevertheless, that, because the Charter of Fundamental Rights is not being retained, Brexit will mean a reduction in the rights of the citizen and in the means by which these rights can be enforced. Excluding the Charter means that individual citizens will no longer enjoy the protection which it provides. The rights of the citizen, therefore, will become entirely dependent upon Parliament. That trend goes very much against that in most democracies where rights protection is gradually being enlarged rather than abolished. In Britain, by contrast, rights are being deliberately withdrawn by a political decision on the part of the government. Brexit, therefore, will leave a huge gap in the British system of rights protection unless our judges become more creative. This could have momentous constitutional consequences. It could also affect the devolution settlement.

The Scottish government takes a different view of the Charter from the British government and in its European Union (Legal Continuity)

Bill, adjudicated by the Supreme Court in late 2018, provided for the incorporation of the Charter into Scots law from Brexit day insofar as it applies to devolved matters retained in Scots law. Even if this bill is judged by the Supreme Court to be outwith the powers of the Scottish Parliament, it may nevertheless be open to the Scottish Parliament to provide for parts of the Charter relating to devolved matters to be incorporated into Scots law in relation to devolved matters.

The problem in Northern Ireland is more serious, as the Belfast Agreement commits the signatories to achieving parity of rights in the whole island of Ireland. In December 2017, in the Joint Report of the British Government and the European Union, the British government committed itself in paragraph 53 to ensuring that there would be 'no diminution of rights' in Northern Ireland as a result of Brexit. The Irish Republic is, of course, remaining in the European Union so its citizens will continue to enjoy the protection of the Charter. Therefore, the only way to achieve parity is for the Charter to remain incorporated in the law of Northern Ireland. If that is not done, it may be possible for the Northern Ireland Assembly to incorporate the Charter into Northern Irish law insofar as devolved matters are concerned. But incorporation into Scottish or Northern Irish law would give rise to two problems. The first is that there would be different rights regimes in different parts of the United Kingdom. There would, for example, be a right to health care in Scotland and Northern Ireland but not in England. The second is that there would be different rights within Scotland and Northern Ireland in relation to devolved matters, which would be covered by the Charter, from rights in relation to non-devolved matters to which the Charter would no longer apply. Furthermore, in Northern Ireland, the Belfast Agreement made provision for those living in Northern Ireland to take up Irish citizenship in addition to, or as an alternative to, their British citizenship. Those who have, in fact, chosen to take up Irish citizenship remain citizens of the European Union after Brexit, but they lose the protection of the Charter, a protection which citizens of the Irish Republic living in the European Union will continue to enjoy. The implications for Northern Ireland and for the peace process are discussed in further detail in Chapter 6.

III

For Britain as a whole, the main consequence of losing the rights protection offered by the Charter could be pressure for further rights protection to achieve the same level of protection as we enjoyed while in the EU. Such protection could be secured by a home-grown Bill of Rights.

Those who favour such a Bill of Rights have various motives. Some Conservatives favoured replacing the Human Rights Act with a Bill of Rights to reduce, not to increase, the protection secured by the Human Rights Act which, so they believed, made it too difficult to apprehend and deport those guilty of serious offences, in particular terrorist offences. They wanted a Bill of Rights which would be a Human Rights Act 'minus'. But some other Conservatives favour a Bill of Rights for other reasons, as do several non-Conservatives. In 2012, seven out of nine members, including four Conservatives, of an official committee on a Bill of Rights, chaired by Sir Leigh Lewis, came out in favour of a British Bill of Rights primarily because they believed that the 'Europe' label prevented the Human Rights Act from acquiring the degree of popular support which constitutional rights enjoy in most other democracies.[19]

---

[19] Commission on a Bill of Rights: *The Choices Before Us*, 2012.

Brexit could lead to pressure for a British Bill of Rights which would be the Human Rights Act 'plus'. Of course, it would not be possible for so wide-ranging a legislative exercise to take place as a mere by-product of the process of withdrawing from the European Union. For it would be a highly complex and time-consuming exercise to rewrite relevant parts of the Charter of Fundamental Rights to render it applicable to post-Brexit Britain. It would require considerable public education, debate and consultation and this would have to include consultation with the devolved bodies in Scotland, Wales and Northern Ireland. There is, nevertheless, as the Charter shows, a strong case for increasing the number of rights which the courts can protect, over and above those protected by the European Convention and also for instituting a genuine judicial remedy for a breach of these rights. Indeed, the Convention was regarded by its signatories in 1950 not as a ceiling, as the maximum level of protection which member states of the Council of Europe should grant, but as a floor, as the very minimum which any state claiming to be governed by the rule of law should support.

One obvious path would be to take the relevant rights from the Charter and add them to those protected under the Human Rights Act so as to create a home-grown Bill of Rights. An alternative would be to follow the parliamentary Joint Committee on Human Rights which, in its report entitled *A Bill of Rights for the UK*, published in 2007–2008, before the Charter of Fundamental Rights came into force, proposed five types of rights for inclusion. These were:

1   Civil and political rights and freedoms, such as the right to life, freedom from torture, the right to family life and freedom of expression and association. The Joint Committee also proposed a new right to equality.

2   Fair process rights, such as the right to a fair trial and the right of access to a court. The Committee also proposed a right to fair and just administrative action.

3 Economic and social rights, including the right to a healthy and sustainable environment. The Joint Committee accepted that such rights could not easily be made justiciable, but declared that they would nevertheless impose a duty, on the part of government and other public bodies, of 'progressive realisation', the principle adopted in the post-apartheid South African constitution. This principle would require the government to take reasonable measures within available resources to achieve these rights and report annually to Parliament on progress, although individuals would not be able to enforce the rights against the government or any other public body.

4 Democratic rights, such as the right to free and fair elections, the right to participate in public life and the right to citizenship.

5 The rights of particular groups, such as children, minorities, people with disabilities and victims of crime.[20]

One argument for adding such rights to those already recognized in the Convention so as to constitute a home-grown Bill of Rights has been stressed by Dominic Grieve, a Conservative MP and former Attorney-General. It is that it would make it easier for the British people to feel that they, as it were, 'owned' the bill of rights. At present, many regard the Human Rights Act as an elite project, designed only to protect highly unpopular minorities, such as suspected terrorists and asylum seekers. The Act, therefore, is not grounded in strong popular support and is seen by some as a villains' charter. Rights that might be generally used by all, such as a right to health care, would give human rights legislation greater popular salience and might thus,

---

[20] HL165, HC 150, 2007–2008.

paradoxically, make it easier to protect the rights of unpopular minorities. In addition, the very title 'A Home-grown Bill of Rights' might help to secure public support for rights in that it will appear as something indigenous, rather than as a foreign import – even though, of course, so much of the impetus of the European Convention came from British lawyers and from Winston Churchill.

In addition to adding to the rights listed in the Convention, the Human Rights Act could be strengthened in another way by providing stronger protection for rights than is given by the Act. There are two ways in which this can be done. The first is by legislative entrenchment. The second is by judicial entrenchment.

In 2006, David Cameron, as Leader of the Opposition, called for a home-grown Bill of Rights which would be entrenched. He suggested that this could be achieved by its being made exempt from the provisions of the Parliament Act of 1949, which allows the Commons to override the Lords on all bills except a bill to extend the life of Parliament and requiring a general election to be held at least once every five years. The reason for this, of course, is to ensure that an unscrupulous government with a majority in the Commons cannot postpone the date of a general election beyond five years to keep itself in power. Cameron proposed that a Bill of Rights be similarly exempt, so that the Lords would have an absolute veto over attempts to amend or abrogate it.

An alternative might be to provide that the Act could be amended only by a special majority in the House of Commons, for example, two-thirds of those voting. Such provisions are common in relation to Bills of Rights. The American Bill of Rights can only be amended by a special majority of Congress and a special majority of the states; the same is true of the protection of rights in the South African constitution. The Canadian Charter of Rights and Freedoms can be amended only by two-thirds majorities in both houses. Israel, which, like Britain, lacks a codified constitution, has a set of Basic Laws protecting rights which can be amended only by an *absolute* majority in the single-chamber parliament, the Knesset. New Zealand, which also lacks a codified constitution and has a sovereign parliament, entrenches part of the 1993 Electoral Act by providing that it can be amended only by 75 per cent of the MPs in the single-chamber parliament or by referendum. Were Britain to adopt a similar provision providing that a special majority were needed to amend or abrogate the Bill of Rights, there would, of course, be a question as to whether such a provision would be effective on the part of those who believe that Parliament remains sovereign. If the argument in Chapter 2 is accepted, a provision of this kind would in fact be defended by the courts.

The second way of strengthening the protection offered by the Human Rights Act is by giving judges the power to do more than simply issue a declaration of incompatibility when, in their view, legislation infringes the European Convention. In most countries with a bill of rights, such as the United States, South Africa and Germany, judges can invalidate primary legislation which conflicts with the Act. In Canada, the government can override the judges by introducing primary legislation, accepting explicitly that it is not in accordance with the Charter of Fundamental Freedoms of 1982, but declaring that 'notwithstanding' this, it ought to be enacted. All primary legislation of this 'notwithstanding' type needs to be renewed every five years; but the political stigma attached to introducing primary legislation with such a clause is so great that the Federal government has never yet employed it – although it has been employed at sub-federal level by provincial governments. The Canadian government and Parliament can thus, like the British government and Parliament, decide to ignore the decision of a judge in a human rights case. It is, however, more difficult to take this course in Canada than it is in Britain, because if Westminster disagrees with a declaration of incompatibility, it needs to do nothing other than maintaining the status quo; whereas, the Canadian Parliament must act positively to override the Charter. Admittedly, Parliament in Britain has in the past always responded to a declaration of incompatibility by amending or repealing the offending statute or part of a statute. But the danger remains, especially since, as we have seen, many of the provisions in the Human Rights Act are used to protect highly unpopular minorities, such as suspected terrorists, prisoners and asylum seekers. How much easier it would be to protect human rights if that protection were only to be invoked by nice people such as ourselves! But rights are human rights, not just rights for nice people.

A further consequence of Brexit, therefore, could be pressure for a greater role for the judges in protecting human rights. The judges may themselves decide to fill the gap in what will be an unprotected British constitution after Brexit. In the White Paper, *Rights Brought Home*, accompanying the introduction of the Human Rights Bill into Parliament, the government declared of the proposal that judges be given the power to set aside Acts of Parliament that it 'would be likely on occasions to draw the judiciary into serious conflict with Parliament. There is no evidence to suggest they desire this power, nor that the public wish them to have it'.[21] Yet, some senior judges are coming to believe that they may need the power to disapply primary legislation if protection of human rights is to be effective. A natural consequence, so it may seem, of the Human Rights Act, is an erosion of the principle of the sovereignty of Parliament. Some judges believe that this principle is but a judicial construct, a creation of the common law. If the judges could create it, they can now supersede it. We may remind ourselves of the comment H.W.R. Wade, already quoted, to

---

[21] *Rights Brought Home: The Human Rights Bill Presented to Parliament* by The Secretary of State for the Home Department, HMSO, October 1997, para. 2:13.

the effect that 'The seat of sovereign power is not to be discovered by looking at the Acts of any Parliament but by looking at the courts and discovering to whom they give their obedience'.[22]

In *Jackson and others v Her Majesty's Attorney-General* in 2005, the Law Lords for the first time considered whether Acts of Parliament – the 1949 Parliament Act and the 2004 Hunting Act – were valid. Although the Court determined that these Acts were, in fact, valid, three Law Lords declared, for the first time, obiter, that Parliament's ability to pass primary legislation might be limited in substance. Lord Steyn declared that the principle of the sovereignty of Parliament, while still being the '*general* principle of our constitution', was:

a construct of the common law. The judges created this principle. If that is so, it is not unthinkable that circumstances could arise where the courts may have to qualify a principle established on a different hypothesis of constitutionalism.

Lord Steyn then went on to say, in words which were to be much quoted:

In exceptional circumstances involving an attempt to abolish judicial review of the ordinary role of the courts, the Appellate Committee of the House of Lords or a new Supreme Court may have to consider whether this is a constitutional fundamental which even a sovereign Parliament acting at the behest of a complaisant House of Commons cannot abolish.[23]

He later elaborated, saying that: 'For my part the dicta in *Jackson* are likely to prevail if the government tried to tamper with the fundamental principles of our constitutional democracy, such as

---

[22] 'The Basis of Legal Sovereignty', p. 196.
[23] [2005] UKHL 56, para. 102.

five-year Parliaments, the role of the ordinary courts, the rule of law, and other such fundamentals. In such exceptional cases the rule of law may trump parliamentary supremacy.[24]

In another obiter dictum in *Jackson*, Lady Hale, currently the President of the Supreme Court, declared: 'The courts will treat with particular suspicion (and might even reject) any attempt to subvert the rule of law by removing governmental action affecting the rights of the individual from all judicial powers.'[25]

In a third obiter dictum in the same case, Lord Hope declared:

> Parliamentary sovereignty is no longer, if it ever was, absolute. It is not uncontrolled ... It is no longer right to say that its freedom to legislate admits of no qualification whatever. Step by step, gradually but surely, the English principle of the absolute legislative sovereignty of Parliament ... is being qualified.

He then said: 'The rule of law enforced by the courts is the ultimate controlling factor on which our constitution is based.'[26]

Significantly, Lord Hope spoke of the *English* 'principle of the absolute legislative sovereignty of Parliament'. Lord Hope was a Scottish Law Lord and the Scots have always been somewhat more sceptical than the English of the doctrine of the absolute sovereignty of Parliament which they find difficult to reconcile with the Acts of Union of 1707. In these Acts, uniting the Scottish and English parliaments, the Scottish negotiators sought and believed that they had succeeded in preserving the Scottish legal system and the system of Presbyterian church government in Scotland from alteration by the English. The conflict between this interpretation of the Treaty of

---

[24] Attlee Foundation Lecture: 'Democracy, The Rule of Law and the Role of Judges', 11 April 2006, p. 20.
[25] UKHL, para. 159.
[26] Ibid, paras 107 and 120.

Union and the principle of the sovereignty of Parliament is further discussed in Chapter 6. Lord Hope's view was endorsed by two London University law professors, Jeffrey Jowell and Dawn Oliver in the sixth edition of their edited work, *The Changing Constitution*, in which they declared: 'It may now be that the rule of law has supplanted parliamentary sovereignty as our prime constitutional principle.' In the eighth edition, the editors, Jowell, Oliver and another London University law professor, Colm O'Cinneide, declared: that 'it may take some time, provocative legislation and considerable judicial courage for the courts to assert the primacy of the rule of law over parliamentary sovereignty, but it is no longer self-evident that a legislature in a modern democracy should be able with impunity to violate the structures of the rule of law'.[27]

It is, of course, a fundamental implication of the doctrine of the sovereignty of Parliament that Acts of Parliament are not subject to judicial review. But, in the last resort, that depends upon the acceptance of this situation by the judges. The implication of the obiter remarks by the three Law Lords is that the sovereignty of Parliament is a doctrine created by the judges which can also be superseded by them and that some senior judges would wish to see the sovereignty of Parliament supplanted by an alternative rule of recognition: the rule of law.

The Human Rights Act proposed a compromise between the doctrines of Parliamentary sovereignty and that of the rule of law. It sought to muffle the conflict between the two doctrines by proposing a dialogue between the judiciary, Parliament and government, all of which are required to observe human rights. It sought to avoid the question of what happens if there is a conflict between parliamentary

---

[27] 6th edn, 2007, p. xi; 8th edn, 2015, p. 34. Both editions are published by Oxford University Press.

sovereignty and the rule of law. When I put that very question to a senior judge – 'What happens if there is such a conflict?' – he replied with a smile, 'That is a question that ought not to be asked!'

Even so, there must always be a danger of conflict between these two constitutional principles, the sovereignty of Parliament and the rule of law. It is possible that the compromise embodied in the Human Rights Act will break down. There may be a difference of view between politicians and judges as to what the rule of recognition is or ought to be.

The government and most MPs believe that issues involving human rights should continue to be resolved by Parliament. In this they are supported by much of the popular press. The judges, however, are required by the Human Rights Act to review the actions of all public authorities for their compatibility with human rights, to quash secondary legislation where it cannot be found compatible and to issue a declaration of incompatibility where primary legislation cannot be found compatible. The judges no doubt also believe that such a declaration should always be respected by Parliament. But, despite the Human Rights Act, ministers and MPs tend to the view, that, on human rights issues, there is some danger of judges usurping power and thwarting the will of Parliament; they are, some ministers and MPs believe, misusing the power of judicial review so that it becomes a power of judicial supremacy over the nation's elected representatives. Tensions between law and government have been aggravated by the separation of the Supreme Court from Parliament, a reform that may have intensified judicial activism. Part of the purpose of Brexit, indeed, was to put an end to judicial supremacy. The judges, for their part, argue that ministers should not attack them for doing their job of reviewing legislation for its compatibility with the Human Rights Act. There is a danger, then, that the British constitution will come to mean different things to different people. It may come to mean something different to the judges from what it means to government, Parliament and the people. The argument from Parliamentary sovereignty points in one direction, the argument from the rule of law in another. It is too early to tell how the constitutional conflict will be resolved and what the shape of the final constitutional settlement is likely to be.

But what is clear is that Europe fundamentally altered the British constitution by empowering judges to quash legislation conflicting with human rights. Brexit will disempower them. But, once having enjoyed judicially protected rights, will British citizens be content to abandon them, to return to the status quo before 1973; or will they recognize a gap in the constitution; and will the judges fill that gap in the constitution? These issues will be further considered in Chapter 7.

6

Brexit and Devolution: The Future of the United Kingdom

I

The United Kingdom is a country comprising four territories – England, Scotland, Wales and Northern Ireland. In 1998 it was explicitly acknowledged that the United Kingdom is a multinational state. For it was in that year that legislation providing for devolution to the non-English parts of the United Kingdom – Scotland, Wales and Northern Ireland – was enacted. Devolution was an acknowledgement that there were separate political wills in Scotland, Wales and Northern Ireland. But, when Britain joined the European Community in 1973, she had done so as a unitary state. Even so, there had been concern in the first Europe referendum in 1975 that the different parts of the United Kingdom might vote in different ways and that this might threaten the unity of the Kingdom. But that concern, was, as we have seen, ironically, the opposite to what it was to be in 2016. At that time the SNP was opposed to British entry into

Europe. Indeed, it was the only major party in Scotland so opposed. The fear was that, while the United Kingdom as a whole would vote 'Yes' to continued membership, Scotland would vote 'No' and this would give Scottish nationalism a boost because the SNP would argue that Scotland was being forced into the European Community against her wishes. One Labour MP, Jim Sillars, later to defect to the nationalists, told Tony Benn in November 1974 'that if the English majority in the forthcoming Referendum was sufficient to overturn the Scottish and Welsh opposition, then the United Kingdom would split'.[1] In the event, however, all the parts of the United Kingdom voted 'Yes' with the exception of the Western Isles and Shetland Islands.

In 2016, the Brexit referendum provided stark evidence of the existence of these separate wills. While the United Kingdom, as a whole, voted to leave the European Union, Scotland and Northern Ireland voted to remain. The United Kingdom vote for Brexit was around 52 per cent to 48 per cent. England and Wales both voted to leave the European Union by around 53 per cent to 47 per cent. Scotland, however, voted to remain by around 62 per cent to 38 per cent, while Northern Ireland voted to remain by around 56 per cent to 44 per cent. The Brexit verdict, therefore, was determined by voters in England and Wales. Scotland and Northern Ireland were to be extruded from the European Union against the wishes of their voters. Brexit, therefore, is likely to pose severe strains on the cohesion and unity of the United Kingdom. Nationalists in Scotland and Northern Ireland see it as striking confirmation of their view that the United Kingdom is a union dominated by England. Were the United Kingdom a federal state, the consent of all four territories might well have been needed for Brexit. But for Scottish and Irish nationalists, Brexit represents primarily the will of England. Brexit, then, could threaten

---

[1] Tony Benn, *Against the Tide, Diaries 1973–1976*, Hutchinson, 1988, p. 263.

the unity of the United Kingdom, a country built up slowly and steadily over a long period of time. Certainly, Brexit will make the devolution settlement more vulnerable because it is likely to transform the relationship between the British government and the devolved bodies.

The United Kingdom was constructed not through any conscious plan, but pragmatically as a result of decisions made by Henry VIII in the sixteenth century, by the Whigs who negotiated the Anglo-Scottish union in 1707, and by Lloyd George, who negotiated a treaty with Irish nationalists in 1921. The United Kingdom came about, therefore, through a long historical process extending over many centuries. Wales was joined with England in an incorporating union by Acts of Parliament passed in 1536 and 1543. Scotland and England combined to form a new kingdom of Great Britain through a treaty of Union in 1707, following Acts of Union in the English and Scottish parliaments. Ireland joined Great Britain in 1800 following Acts of Union in the British and Irish parliaments. However, in 1921, when the current boundary of the United Kingdom was determined, twenty-six Irish counties seceded from the Union to form the Irish Free State, now the Irish Republic, leaving the six Irish counties in the north east which constitute Northern Ireland and remain a part of the United Kingdom. Unlike Scotland, therefore, Northern Ireland did not join the United Kingdom as a separate unity, but as an entity carved out of the island of Ireland.

The Union between Scotland and England posed a constitutional dilemma. The Parliament of this new state of Great Britain was to be, like the English Parliament which it superseded, located at Westminster; like the English Parliament, the new Parliament of Great Britain was, on most orthodox interpretations of the constitution, intended to be a sovereign Parliament. The Scottish Parliament, however, was quite unlike the English parliament which is generally assumed to have been a sovereign Parliament. The Scottish Parliament had only been sovereign since 1689, but the Scottish executive was not responsible to it. It is not by any means clear why the new Parliament of Great Britain should have shared a main characteristic of the English Parliament as a sovereign Parliament rather than the characteristics of the Scottish Parliament. Indeed, the Scottish negotiators of Union insisted on provisions in the treaty which seemed incompatible with sovereignty. Articles 18 and 19 of the treaty provided for the preservation of the Scottish legal system. Article 18 in addition provided that Scottish private law was to remain unaltered 'except for evident utility of the subjects within Scotland', while Article 19 provided that the Scottish Court of Session would 'after the Union and notwithstanding thereof, remain *in all time* coming within Scotland as it is now, constituted by the Laws of that Kingdom, and with the same Authority and Privileges as before the Union' (emphasis added). Furthermore, shortly before the Union, an Act was passed by the Scottish Parliament to secure the Protestant religion and Presbyterian church government in Scotland, which was to be 'held and observed *in all time* as a fundamental and essential condition of any Treaty of Union to be concluded between the two Kingdoms without any alteration thereof, or derogation thereto in any sort *for ever*' (emphasis added). It is not clear how such commitments can be reconciled with the concept of the sovereignty of Parliament. Shortly after the Union, in 1712, Westminster altered the powers of lay patrons within the Scottish church and no one suggested that this was unconstitutional. In 1800, the Acts of Union with Ireland provided that the united churches of England and Ireland would remain established 'for ever'. But, in 1869, Gladstone's Irish Church Act disestablished the Irish church and the courts in *Ex parte Canon Selwyn*[2], refused to rule it unlawful.

---

[2] (1872) 36 JP 54.

In *The Law of the Constitution*, Dicey had gone so far as to claim that 'neither the Act of Union with Scotland, nor the Dentists Act 1878, has more claim than any other to be considered a supreme law'.[3] He would probably have believed that the European Communities Act had no more claim than the Dentists Act to be considered a supreme law. As we have seen, the judges in *Factortame* were to take a different view; following the *Thoburn* case, the Treaty of Union has come to be thought of as 'constitutional' and so, unlike the Dentists Act, not subject to implied repeal.

The first edition of Dicey's *Law of the Constitution*, in which he claimed that the Act of Union was of no more constitutional significance than the Dentists Act, was published in 1885. He therein claimed that 'the Parliaments both of England and of Scotland did, at the time of the Union, each transfer sovereign power to a new sovereign body, namely the Parliament of Great Britain'.[4] The Acts of the English and Scottish Parliament were, however, constituent Acts which, of course, the Dentists Act was not. Towards the end of his life, Dicey came to modify somewhat his view of these two Acts of Union. He faced the conundrum of how it was that the Scots could have believed that their church and their legal system could be preserved if the new Parliament was to be a sovereign one. But he never answered the conundrum of why it was that the new Parliament of Great Britain was to take on one of the main characteristics of the English parliament rather than the Scottish parliament. In a book he wrote in 1920, towards the end of his life, with the Scottish Historiographer Royal, R.S. Rait, entitled *Thoughts on the Union Between England and Scotland*, he tried to elucidate the significance of phrases such as 'for all time' and 'for ever',

---

[3] A.V. Dicey, *Introduction to the Study of the Law of the Constitution*, 10th edn, Macmillan, 1959, p. 145.
[4] Ibid, p. 69.

given that they could not bind a sovereign Parliament. Dicey and Rait argued that:

> the enactment of laws which are described as unchallengeable, immutable or the like, is not necessarily futile … A sovereign Parliament … although it cannot be logically bound to abstain from changing any given law, may, by the fact that when an Act when it was passed had been declared to be unchangeable, receive a warning that it cannot be changed without grave danger to the Constitution of the country.[5]

Dicey was perhaps suggesting that the relevant articles in the Acts of Union and the accompanying legislation made for a constitutional convention. If a convention were to be broken – as was to be the case in 1909 when the House of Lords broke the convention that it should not interfere with financial legislation, by rejecting Lloyd George's 'People's Budget' – there would be a constitutional crisis.

The view that the Acts of Union created a sovereign Parliament is not by any means accepted by Scottish writers on the constitution. In 1957, T.B. Smith, perhaps the pre-eminent Scottish constitutional lawyer of his generation, declared that he was 'quite unable to accept the view of those English constitutional lawyers who hold that the terms of Union have no more ordinary force than an Act of Parliament'. He believed that the Union had the character of 'fundamental law' and was, indeed, in effect the 'fundamental written constitution' of the British state.[6] It was, so he was to declare in his Hamlyn lectures of 1961, 'the prototype of written constitutions which expressly limit the

---

[5] A.V. Dicey and R.S. Rait, *Thoughts on the Union Between England and Scotland*, Macmillan, 1920, p. 253.
[6] Quoted in Colin Kidd, *Union and Unionisms, Political Thought in Scotland, 1500–2000*, Cambridge University Press, 2008, pp. 121–22. This book provides an admirably succinct account of Scottish constitutional debates over the past 500 years.

powers of organs of government in relation to each other so as to "protect the interests of a permanent minority from the danger of their interests being overridden by a permanent majority". He went on to add, rather ruefully, that only 'the very Uncommon Man indeed ... in South Britain' seemed to appreciate this![7] On this view, Dicey was wrong to regard the British constitution as 'historical', a product of evolution and custom, for the constitution, if Smith is right, had been enacted by the Acts of Union of 1707.

In a case in 1953, *MacCormick v Lord Advocate*, the Scottish nationalist leader, John MacCormick, challenged the assumption by the Queen of the title, Elizabeth II, since she was clearly Elizabeth I of Great Britain, the Union with Scotland having occurred over 100 years after the death of Elizabeth 1 of England. In dismissing MacCormick's case, Lord Cooper of Culross, Lord President of the Court of Session, the supreme civil court of Scotland, nevertheless made the following comments obiter.

> The principle of the unlimited sovereignty of Parliament is a distinctively English principle which has no counterpart in Scottish constitutional law ... Considering that the Union legislation extinguished the Parliaments of Scotland and England and replaced them by a new Parliament, I have difficulty seeing why it should have supposed that the new Parliament of Great Britain must inherit all the peculiar characteristics of the English Parliament but none of the Scottish Parliament ... The Treaty, and the associated legislation by which the Parliament of Great Britain was brought into being as the successor of the separate Parliaments of Scotland and England, contain some clauses which expressly reserve to the Parliament of Great Britain powers of subsequent

---

[7] Smith, *British Justice: The Scottish Contribution*, Stevens, 1961, p. 202.

modification, and other clauses which either contain no such power or emphatically exclude subsequent alteration by declarations that the provisions shall be fundamental and unalterable in all time coming, or declarations of a like effect. I have never been able to understand how it is possible to reconcile with elementary canons of construction the adoption by English constitutional theorists of the same attitude to these markedly different provisions.[8]

Lord Cooper, it should be added, was a Unionist not a nationalist. Indeed, he had been a Conservative MP from 1935 to 1942 and had served the Conservative-dominated National Government during the 1930s first as Solicitor-General and then as Lord Advocate.

John MacCormick's son, Sir Neil MacCormick, a distinguished jurist, holder of the Regius Chair of Public Law at the University of Edinburgh and then an SNP member of the European Parliament, reflecting in 1978 on the case brought by his father, was to argue that the British constitution comprised more than the eight words: 'Whatever the Queen in Parliament enacts is law.' Instead. the constitution declared that: 'Whatever the Queen in Parliament enacts, unless in derogation from the justiciable limits set by the Articles of Union, is law.'[9] But the difficulty with this position is that these Articles seem not to be justiciable. No court has ever ruled an Act of Parliament invalid because contrary to the terms of Union, nor is it currently likely to do so. The Acts of Union did not provide for machinery such as a federal type of upper house or judicial review to ensure that the interests of Scotland as a permanent minority within Great Britain

---

[8] Ibid, p. 411.

[9] Neil MacCormick, 'Does the United Kingdom have a Constitution? Reflections on MacCormick v Lord Advocate' (1978) 29 *Northern Ireland Legal Quarterly*, 1–20 at 11.

would be preserved. In consequence, England through weight of numbers would always be the dominant nation in the Union.

Nevertheless, the terms of Union do suggest that it is misleading simply to regard the United Kingdom as a standard unitary state. J.D.B. Mitchell, the first English lawyer to be appointed Professor of Constitutional Law at Edinburgh, declared in 1964 in his book, *Constitutional Law*, an interpretation of the British constitution as seen from Scotland, that Britain's constitution was 'neither federal nor strictly unitary'.[10] For, although no British government has been prepared to federalize the United Kingdom, there has been no undue pressure for standardization, a result in part no doubt of beneficent indifference and there has been considerable scope for institutional variation in the non-English parts of the kingdom, culminating in devolution. Until the post-war years, political elites were happy to rule over a 'dual polity', being prepared to allow divergence in such domestic matters as education and health care as long as they could remain in untrammelled charge of the 'high politics' of foreign affairs, defence and the economy.[11] Unity, therefore, has never meant uniformity.

Political scientists refer to the United Kingdom not as a unitary state but as a union state. The distinction between the two has been drawn in the following way:

The unitary state [is] built around one unambiguous political centre which ... pursues a more-or-less undeviating policy of administrative standardisation. All areas of the state are treated alike and all institutions are directly under the control of the centre.

---

[10] J.D.B. Mitchell, *Constitutional Law*, Green, 2nd edn 1968, cited in Kidd, *Union and Unionisms*, p. 127.

[11] This is the theme of Jim Bulpitt, *Territory and Power in the United Kingdom: An Interpretation*, Manchester University Press, 1983.

In contrast:

> The union state [is] not the result of straightforward dynastic
> conquest. Incorporation of at least parts of its territory ...
> [is] through personal dynastic union, for example, by treaty,
> marriage or inheritance. Integration is less than perfect. While
> administrative standardisation prevails over most of the territory,
> the consequences of personal union entail survival of pre-union
> rights and institutional infrastructures which preserve some degree
> of regional autonomy and serve as agencies of indigenous elite
> recruitment.[12]

The United Kingdom, one authority has argued, is based on 'Union
without Uniformity'.[13]

The United Kingdom contains, in addition to England, Wales and
Scotland, a fourth territory, Northern Ireland. But Northern Ireland,
unlike England, Wales and Scotland is not a nation. The United
Kingdom is often mistakenly characterized as being composed of
four nations – indeed critics of devolution were wont to speak of it as
four nations and a funeral for the United Kingdom! But Northern
Ireland is a province containing two conflicting national communities.
The majority Unionist community regards itself as being British and
belonging to the British nation, just as Scots who do not support
separatism regard themselves as Scottish but also British. The minority
Nationalist community in Northern Ireland, by contrast, claims that
being Irish is incompatible with being British and regards itself as

---

[12] Stein Rokkan and Derek Urwin, 'Introduction: Centres and Peripheries in Western
Europe' in Rokkan and Urwin, (eds), *The Politics of Territorial Identity: Studies in European
Regionalism*, Sage, 1982, p. 11.
[13] Richard Rose, *Understanding the United Kingdom: The Territorial Dimension in
Government*, Longman, 1982, p. 35. Although written some time before the advent of
devolution or the Brexit referendum, this book offers a penetrating account of the
relationships between the different parts of the United Kingdom.

belonging to the Irish nation. Neither of the two communities regards Northern Ireland as a nation. A Unionist cannot, by definition, regard Northern Ireland as a nation. She must, by definition, regard herself as a member of the British nation, while a Nationalist regards herself as part of the Irish nation, illegitimately separated, in her view, from the rest of the Irish nation when the island of Ireland was partitioned.

In addition to the three nations, England, Wales and Scotland, there is, of course, a fourth nation, the over-arching British nation. The United Kingdom therefore is a multinational state. While the Welsh and Scots have always been conscious of this and conscious also of their nationality, it is only comparatively recently that such awareness has struck the English. In 1973, the report of the Royal Commission on the Constitution declared that 'what many Scots and Welshmen consider a partnership of nations, the average Englishman tends to regard as one nation comprising different kinds of people'. In addition, the English, irritatingly, so the report declared, 'use the terms England and English when they mean Britain and British, often to the annoyance of the Scots and the Welsh'.[14] 'An Englishman', James Bryce had declared in the nineteenth century, 'has but one patriotism because England and the United Kingdom are to him practically the same thing'.[15] Perhaps Scotland, Wales and Northern Ireland were seen as mere appendages of England. In 1924, Stanley Baldwin, speaking at the annual dinner of the Royal Society of St George, had confessed to 'a feeling of satisfaction and profound thankfulness that I may use the word "England" without some fellow at the back of the room shouting out "Britain"'.[16]

---

[14] Report of the Royal Commission on the Constitution, Cmnd 5460, 1973, pp. 102–58.
[15] Quoted in Michael Kenny, *The Politics of English Nationhood*, Oxford University Press, 2014, p. 37.
[16] Arthur Aughey, *Nationalism, Devolution and the Challenge to the United Kingdom State*, Pluto Press, 2001, p. 65.

For most of those living in Britain, however, national identities are not exclusive but multiple. Most Scots, Welsh and Northern Irish Unionists find no difficulty in being Scottish, Welsh, Irish as well as British. Further, the existence of national feeling in Scotland and Wales does not by any means necessarily imply voting for nationalist parties. While most Scots are proud of their Scottish identity, it was only in 2015 that the SNP approached 50 per cent of the vote in a Westminster election. Its next highest scores have been 37 per cent in 2017 and 30 per cent in October 1974. Although it has been in power in the Scottish Parliament in Edinburgh either alone or in coalition since 2007, the SNP has never won a majority of votes in an election for the Scottish Parliament. For almost the whole of its existence, therefore, the SNP has been a distinctly minority party in Scotland. Plaid Cymru has been even more of a minority party in Wales. Its highest vote in a Westminster election was 14 per cent in 2001 and in elections for the National Assembly for Wales 31 per cent in 1999. In Northern Ireland, politics is dominated by the community division and since most Protestants are Unionists and the Protestants are the majority in the province, Unionists normally win a majority of the vote, both in Westminster elections and in elections for the Northern Ireland Assembly. However, by the provisions of the Belfast Agreement of 1998, the government of Northern Ireland must be shared between representatives of both communities.

II

Nationalism in Scotland and Wales found its main outlet in the past, not in voting for nationalist parties, but in seeking its own distinctive institutions of government through which national feeling could be expressed. The first stage in this process was executive devolution, the creation of a separate executive layer of government. A Scottish Secretaryship was created by Gladstone's Liberal government in 1886 and the office became a Secretaryship of State in 1926. A Welsh Secretaryship was created by Harold Wilson's Labour government in 1964. The next stage was legislative devolution, the creation of a separate legislative layer of government. This was achieved following referendums in 1998. Scotland voted by a three to one majority for devolution, while Wales voted for it a week later by the narrowest of margins – 50.1 to 49.9 per cent. The devolution legislation of 1998 was, however, but the beginning of the devolution process; since then, further legislation has extended the powers both of the Scottish Parliament and of the National Assembly for Wales.

In 2012, a Scotland Act extended the competences of the Scottish Parliament and extended devolution of tax powers to it. In 2016, in accordance with a promise made shortly before the 2014 independence referendum, a further Scotland Act was passed providing for further devolution in areas such as onshore oil and gas extraction and rail franchising. More importantly, it also devolved almost complete control over income tax rates and bands to the Scottish Parliament. That Parliament was in future to be responsible for setting rates and thresholds of income tax on earned income for Scottish taxpayers. This was a wider fiscal devolution than in many federal states, including Switzerland, often thought of as the most decentralized federal democracy in the world where federal income tax accounts for no more than around one-eighth of total tax revenues. The Scottish Parliament would also receive half of the VAT revenues raised in Scotland and it was given control over a few other minor taxes. In consequence, the Scottish Parliament would in future be responsible for raising over 50 per cent of the money it spends. Various welfare provisions were also devolved to Scotland. In addition, the Scottish Parliament was given the power to legislate for Scottish Parliament elections, including the electoral system to be used and the size of the Parliament, although use of these powers would require a two-thirds majority at Holyrood, rather than a simple majority. Finally, the Act declared that 'the Scottish Parliament and the Scottish Government are a permanent part of the United Kingdom's constitutional arrangements' and that it was not to be abolished except by means of a decision of the Scottish people through a referendum; the Act also put into statute the so-called Sewel convention, which had been operating since the Parliament had been set up, to the effect that 'the Parliament of the United Kingdom will not normally legislate with regard to devolved matters without the consent of the Scottish parliament'. The House of Lords' Constitution Committee declared that these extensions of devolution made it somewhat akin to federalism in that the constitutional powers of the constituent units are coming to be protected 'beyond the unilateral competence of the central legislature'.[17] As will be seen, that may have been an optimistic judgment, for the convention is not justiciable.

Devolution in Wales has also proved to be a process rather than an event. Acts passed in 2006, 2011, 2014 and 2017 gave Wales powers over primary legislation, rather than just secondary legislation as in the original Government of Wales Act establishing devolution in 1998, as well as taxing powers. In 2011, a referendum was held in Wales on extending the legislative powers of the Assembly which resulted in a 63 to 37 per cent vote in favour, showing that devolution was more firmly embedded in Wales than it had been in 1997 when the margin for victory for the devolutionists had been so very narrow. In 2017, a further Government of Wales Act imitated the 2016 Scotland Act in recognizing the National Assembly for Wales and the

---

[17] House of Lords: Select Committee on the Constitution, 6th Report, 2015–2016, *Scotland Bill*, HL 29, 2015, para. 41.

Welsh Government as being permanent in the constitutional arrangements of the United Kingdom, with a referendum needed before either could be abolished; it put into statutory form the convention that Parliament would not normally legislate for Wales on devolved matters without the approval of the Welsh Assembly and government. More fundamentally, it altered the model of Welsh devolution. As originally established in 1998, specific powers had been conferred on the Assembly and all powers not specifically conferred had been reserved to Westminster. The Scottish system, by contrast, was a reserved powers model, in which the Scottish Parliament could exercise all powers except those reserved to Westminster. Such a system is regarded as more favourable to a devolved body. The 2017 Government of Wales Act replaced the 1998 conferred powers model with a reserved powers model of the sort used in Scotland since 1998. There have, therefore, been four amendments – in 2006, 2011, 2014 and 2017 – to the original devolution legislation for Wales.

Devolution in Northern Ireland has been modified just twice – first in the St Andrews Agreement of 2006 which devolved policing and criminal justice powers to the Assembly and secondly in the Stormont House Agreement of 2014 which was the prelude to Northern Ireland being given the power to alter the rate of corporation tax in the province. But the main problem, which devolution has not yet resolved, is, of course, the community problem; the inability of Unionists and Nationalist to agree has led to periodic suspensions of the Assembly. The Assembly has, in fact, been suspended on five occasions following inter-communal disagreements since it was established in 1999, twice for just twenty-four hours. The last suspension, the longest, was in January 2017 and, at the time of writing in September 2018, it has not since been reconvened.

The extension of devolution has occurred in a disjointed and ad hoc manner. That was particularly noticeable with regard to the 2016 Scotland Act. This Act was based on the report of a Scottish Devolution Commission chaired by a Scottish cross-bench peer, Lord Smith of Kelvin. Shortly before the 2014 referendum, Prime Minister David Cameron, together with the leaders of the Labour and Liberal Democrat parties had made a 'vow' that if Scotland rejected independence, she would be given much wider powers. When, after the referendum, Cameron established the Smith Commission, he pledged to deliver whatever it decided. In fact, he devolved the power to decide on the future government of Scotland to the Smith Commission. Summarizing the various extensions of devolution, the Institute for Government, an independent think tank, concluded in 2015, that: 'The overall impression is of upheaval at a rapid pace, without a great deal of consideration about how the various proposed changes relate to one another, or how they should be implemented ... Insufficient attention is paid to the big picture.'[18] This was written before Brexit.

The prime purpose of devolution to a Scottish Parliament was to contain the rise of Scottish nationalism. Devolution, declared George Robertson, as Shadow Secretary of State for Scotland, in 1995, 'will kill nationalism stone dead'. But, of course, nationalism has certainly not been killed 'stone dead'. Indeed, in the 2011 elections for the Scottish Parliament, the SNP achieved what Labour had never succeeded in doing, achieving an overall majority in the Scottish Parliament, albeit on just 44 per cent of the vote. In consequence, Westminster legislated to make provision for an independence referendum, which was duly held in September 2014. Independence was rejected by 55 to 45 per cent of the Scottish vote.

---

[18] Institute of Government (2015) 'Governing in an Ever-looser Union: How the Four Governments of the UK Co-operate, Negotiate and Compete' p. 8.

Devolution is not the same as federalism. It is to be distinguished from federalism in two respects. The first is that it is asymmetrical. There has been devolution to the non-English parts of the United Kingdom, but not to England, by far the largest part of the United Kingdom containing around 84 per cent of its population. There are some who propose an English Parliament with legislative powers, parallel to the devolved bodies in Scotland, Wales and Northern Ireland and it constitutes part of the UKIP programme, which bears some resemblance to that of an English nationalist party. But there is no federal system in the world in which one of the units represents over 80 per cent of the population. The nearest equivalent is Canada, where 39 per cent of the population live in Ontario.

The case against an English parliament was well summed up by the Royal Commission on the Constitution in 1973:

A federation consisting of four units – England, Scotland, Wales and Northern Ireland – would be so unbalanced as to be unworkable. It would be dominated by the overwhelming political importance and wealth of England. The English Parliament would rival the United Kingdom federal Parliament; and in the federal Parliament itself the representation of England could hardly be scaled down in such a way as to enable it to be outvoted by Scotland, Wales and Northern Ireland, together representing less than one-fifth of the population. A United Kingdom federation of four countries, with a federal Parliament and provincial Parliaments in the four national capitals, is therefore not a realistic proposition.[19]

---

[19] Cmnd 5460, 1973, para. 531.

This conclusion was to be endorsed by the Constitution Committee of the House of Lords in 2017. It concluded that:

'Given the relative size of England within the UK, the creation of an English Parliament would introduce a destabilizing asymmetry of power to the Union. Meanwhile, enacting a new legislature and administration covering 84 per cent of the population that the UK institutions currently serve would not bring decision-making significantly closer to the people and communities of England. An English parliament is not a viable option for the future of the governance of England'.

One witness, Adam Tomkins, Professor of Public Law at Glasgow University, told the Committee: 'If you had an English First Minister with the powers of the Scottish First Minister, that English First Minister would have a bigger budget and would be more powerful and important than the United Kingdom Prime Minister. That is a recipe for collapsing the union rather than strengthening the Union.'[20]

Federal systems in which the largest unit dominates seem to have little chance of survival. That is the lesson of the former USSR, dominated by Russia, of the former Czechoslovakia, dominated by the Czechs and the former Yugoslavia, dominated by Serbia.

Symmetrical federalism, therefore, with an English parliament is a highly unlikely development.

An alternative would be legislative devolution to the regions of England. But few believe that it would be sensible to fragment the English legal system by providing for different laws in different parts of England (e.g. different laws in Newcastle from those in Bristol) and, in any case, there seems little support for regional devolution in any

---

[20] House of Lords Select Committee on the Constitution, 'The Union and Devolution' HL 149, para. 376.

form. In 2004, voters in the north east, thought to be the region most sympathetic to devolution, rejected a proposal for non-legislative, executive devolution to a regional assembly by four to one in a referendum. It is doubtful if opinion has altered very much since then. The Royal Commission concluded in 1973 that 'no advocate of federalism in the United Kingdom has succeeded in producing a federal scheme satisfactorily tailored to fit the circumstances of England' and that 'there is no satisfactory way of fitting England into a fully federal system'.[21] In England, by contrast with many countries on the Continent and with federal states such as the United States and Canada, there is little regional feeling. If one asked someone in Bristol or in Canterbury which region they belong to, they would be likely to respond with a blank look. Most people in England feel that they belong to a town and a county but not to a region. In England, the regions are little more than ghosts.

In any case, the dynamic behind legislative devolution to the non-English parts of the United Kingdom was not the same as the dynamic, such as it was, behind regional devolution in England. Those who favoured the latter sought decentralization. But those who favoured devolution in Scotland and Wales based their argument on a national claim, a claim whose logic is quite different from that of the decentralizers. Nationalists and devolutionists in Scotland and Wales sought separate treatment for their nations. Those who call for a federal system do not seek separate treatment or exceptional rights for Scotland and Wales, while nationalists and devolutionists most certainly do not equate Scotland and Wales with regions of England. The logic of nationalism, therefore, is quite contrary to the logic of regionalism and the logic of federalism.

---

[21] Ibid, paras 531 and 534.

The truth is that any form of symmetrical federalism is inimical to the nature of the United Kingdom. The nationalists and most devolutionists do not want it, while England, although it has always resisted integration and is prepared to accept devolution for the non-English parts of the United Kingdom, does not want it for herself and has always resisted it. Therefore, the United Kingdom is likely to remain asymmetrical for the foreseeable future.

There is a second fundamental reason why devolution is to be distinguished from federalism. In his classic work on federalism, *Federal Government*, K.C. Wheare defines the federal principle as follows: 'By the federal principle I mean the method of dividing powers so that the general and regional governments are each within a sphere co-ordinate and independent.'[22] But the devolution legislation sought to preserve the sovereignty of Westminster. Although, by convention, Westminster agreed not normally to legislate on matters devolved to Scotland, Wales or Northern Ireland, it could always lawfully do so; indeed, it could, if it so wished, abolish the devolved bodies as it abolished the Unionist-dominated Northern Ireland Parliament in 1972. In a federal government, by contrast, the constitution of the states comprising the federation cannot be altered unilaterally, the states are generally represented at the centre, often in an upper house and there is almost always a constitutional court to act as an umpire resolving disputes. In Britain, the courts are empowered to determine the competence of legislation from the devolved bodies, but not legislation from Westminster which may entrench on the functions of the devolved bodies. Federalism is based on a compact in which the partners are often juridically equal. In the British system, by contrast, Westminster can be both judge and jury in

---

[22] K.C. Wheare, *Federal Government*, 4th edn, Oxford University Press, 1964, p. 10.

its own case. Were the Scots, for example, to believe that Westminster had illegitimately entrenched on a devolved area, they would almost certainly be told by the courts that their complaints were not justiciable. Westminster would not have broken any compact, since no compact had been made. Westminster, as Tocqueville noticed over 150 years ago, is both a legislative assembly and a constituent one.

Under normal circumstances, these differences between federalism and devolution do not matter very much. Devolution, like federalism, so it has been argued by Lady Justice Arden, then a member of the Court of Appeal of England and Wales, but now a member of the Supreme Court, 'means a stable relationship under which, in fact, two sets of political institutions exercise mutually exclusive powers in the same territory. The doctrines used by the courts to interpret the powers of the devolved bodies are very similar to those used to interpret the powers of states in federal systems. Devolution, therefore, 'can be analysed a as form of federalism'.[23]

But, under abnormal situations, the difference is an important one since devolution by contrast with federalism enables Westminster to exercise its supreme authority. That is precisely what Westminster did in 1972 when it abolished the Unionist-dominated Parliament of Northern Ireland. Brexit also has, in the government's view, created an abnormal situation, since it raises the issue of whether powers to be taken back from the European Union are to be returned to Westminster or to the devolved bodies. The government is determined to retain the supremacy of Westminster, while the devolved bodies are equally determined to ensure that powers transferred in the devolution legislation, but hitherto exercised primarily by the European Union, are now returned to them.

---

[23] Mary Arden, 'What is the Safeguard for Welsh Devolution?' in *Common Law and Modern Society: Keeping Pace with Change*. Oxford University Press, 2015, pp. 120, 133.

III

Politics in Northern Ireland is quite different from politics in Scotland, Wales or indeed any other part of the United Kingdom. Indeed, Northern Ireland is often seen as somewhat un-British in its politics. Paradoxically, that is because 'the principal political division in the province is about whether it should remain British, that is, part of the United Kingdom'.[24] In most of the rest of country, there is what has been called 'unthinking Unionism', a tacit acceptance of the current borders of the United Kingdom and of allegiance to the state.[25] The major parties have in the past performed an integrative role dividing opinion along sociological, ideological and generational lines, but uniting citizens in terms of identity. Northern Ireland politics, however, is primarily about identity. There, Unionism is an articulate philosophy but held by only one of the two communities in the province; and, by contrast to England, it is a highly contentious philosophy. Since the Unionists seem to enjoy a permanent majority, there is little chance of any alternation of power such as is normally achieved in democratic systems. Therefore, the Westminster Model can hardly work in the province as it would in Scotland or Wales. So devolution in Northern Ireland has been constructed on a quite different basis. It was re-established in 1998 as part of the provisions of the Belfast Agreement, an agreement between the British and Irish governments as well as the main political parties in Northern Ireland. The Agreement was endorsed by a treaty signed by the British and Irish governments and also by massive majorities in parallel referendums in Northern Ireland and Ireland. In the Republic the figure was 94 per cent; in Northern Ireland it was 78 per cent. This

---

[24] Richard Rose, *Understanding the United Kingdom*, p. 76.
[25] Ibid, p. 209.

latter figure concealed a considerable divergence between the two communities, with Nationalist support for it being far higher than Unionist support which was just 57 per cent. The Agreement was given effect in British law by the Northern Ireland Act of 1998. This Act required the executive in Northern Ireland to be on a cross-community basis and for all contentious legislation to be based upon the principle of power-sharing between the two communities. The executive was to be chosen by the Assembly. Following the St Andrews Agreement of 2006, which modified the provisions of the Northern Ireland Act, members of the Assembly are required to register themselves as 'Unionist' 'Nationalist' or 'Other'. The largest party in the Assembly, which is elected by the single transferable method of proportional representation, nominates a first minister and the second party nominates a deputy first minister. The first minister and the deputy are required to act jointly. The first minister, therefore, is in no sense a prime minister and his deputy is in no sense a subordinate. The first minister is not the leader of the executive, but co-equal with the deputy. A cabinet is chosen in proportion to representation in the Assembly. The executive, in consequence, is required to be a coalition representing the main parties in the Assembly. No single party can rule alone. Coalition government in Northern Ireland is not, as is normally the case in parliamentary systems, a voluntary choice, but is required by statute. The first minister so far has always been a Unionist, representing the majority community, the deputy a Nationalist, representing the minority community. Key legislation and decisions require cross-community support – either a parallel majority of 50 per cent of Unionists present and voting and 50 per cent of Nationalists present and voting, as well as 50 per cent of members of the Assembly as a whole present and voting; or a weighted majority – at least 60 per cent of those present and voting and at least 40 per cent of those present and voting of Nationalists and Unionists as well as a majority of those present and voting in the Assembly. Each community, therefore, enjoys a veto on contentious legislation. The situation in Northern Ireland is as if, at Westminster, Theresa May and Jeremy Corbyn were to be required to form a coalition – though the differences between Unionists and Nationalists are even greater than those between Theresa May and Jeremy Corbyn since they are based on a difference of view as to the very legitimacy of the Northern Ireland state. The Unionists believe that they are required to share power with those who, in the past, have been involved in heinous crimes. In the Republic, the two main parties, Fianna Fáil and Fine Gael, both refuse at the time of writing to share power with Sinn Féin, yet the Unionists in Northern Ireland are required to share power with that party.

The Assembly's legislation was required, like that of the other devolved bodies, to be in accordance with the European Convention of Human Rights, but it was also required to develop extra rights 'to reflect the particular circumstances of Northern Ireland', such as the need to ensure parity of esteem between the two communities. It was hoped that, first a Bill of Rights for Northern Ireland and then a common Charter of Rights for the whole island of Ireland, would be developed so that those living in both parts of the island would enjoy equivalent rights. In 2006, under the St Andrews Agreement, a Forum on a Bill of Rights was established which included representatives from the voluntary and community sectors as well as the main political parties. Nevertheless, neither a Bill of Rights for Northern Ireland nor a Charter of Rights have yet been achieved.

The provisions for devolution form only one of the three strands of the Belfast Agreement. The second strand recognized the Irish dimension to the Northern Ireland problem and the legitimate interest of the Irish government in developments there. The second strand provides for a consultative North/South Ministerial Council which is tasked with achieving common all-Ireland policies in areas of mutual benefit especially areas involving the application of European Union policies to the island of Ireland. One practical example of such cooperation is the development of a single electricity market for the island of Ireland. The North/South Ministerial Council enjoys executive powers but can exercise them only when there is agreement between the power-sharing Assembly in Northern Ireland and the parliament of the Irish Republic.

The Belfast Agreement recognized the Irish identity of the minority community in Northern Ireland. All those born in Northern Ireland were given the right to hold either British or Irish citizenship or, alternatively, dual citizenship of both countries. Northern Ireland is the only part of the United Kingdom whose people can choose to be and to remain, after Brexit, citizens of a European Union state and the only jurisdiction outside the European Union whose citizens will be entitled to European Union citizenship. In 2016, the year of the Brexit referendum, the number of Irish passport applications submitted from Northern Ireland was 27 per cent larger than in 2015.[26] Dual citizenship caused no problems as long as both Britain and the Irish Republic were member states of the European Union. But one consequence of Brexit will be that there will be a jurisdiction outside the European Union, the United Kingdom, some of whose citizens will remain entitled to European Union citizenship as citizens of the Irish Republic, with all the rights that this entails, but with no means of realizing those rights. There will, therefore, be a greater inequality of rights between citizens of Northern Ireland and citizens of the Republic. Those who identify as Irish would, as European Union citizens, in theory be entitled to the protections offered by the European Union's Charter of Fundamental Rights. But that protection

---

[26] Siobhán Fenton, *The Good Friday Agreement*, Biteback Publishing, 2018, p. 273.

will not be available in Northern Ireland unless either the Charter comes to be incorporated into British law or there is a Charter of Rights in Northern Ireland providing similar rights protection to that in the Republic. Perhaps, therefore, Brexit might prove an incentive to achieve that all-Ireland Charter of Rights prefigured in the Belfast Agreement. Otherwise, it will result in a greater inequality of rights between the two parts of the island of Ireland.

While the first two strands of the Belfast Agreement seek to acknowledge the unique status of Northern Ireland and the Irish dimension, the third strand seeks to acknowledge the interconnectedness of Britain and Ireland and of Britain's Crown Dependencies. This third strand provides for a British/Irish consultative Inter-Governmental Conference and a British/Irish Council, comprising not only the British and Irish governments, but the governments of the Scottish Parliament and Welsh National Assembly and of the three Crown Dependencies – the Isle of Man, Jersey and Guernsey. The purpose of this Council is, in the words of the Agreement, 'to promote the harmonious and mutually beneficial development of the totality of relationships among the people of these islands'.[27] This Council has, since 2016, provided a forum for intergovernmental discussions on Brexit matters.

The Belfast Agreement was predicated on the inter-connectedness of Britain and the Irish Republic. Since Brexit is likely to draw the two countries apart, it will make both the North/South and East/West dimensions more difficult to maintain.

Although the Belfast Agreement recognized the interest of the Irish Republic in the government of Northern Ireland, it confirmed the sovereignty of Britain over Northern Ireland. It did not provide for joint authority of the British and Irish governments in the province.

---

[27] Cm 3883, 1998.

The role of the Irish government in Northern Ireland is purely consultative. But the position of Northern Ireland in the United Kingdom was made conditional upon the continuing consent of a majority of the population in the province. Provision was made for regular referendums to be held in Northern Ireland to test whether that consent remained whenever the Secretary of State of Northern Ireland believed that there might be a majority for joining with the Republic. Were there to be a majority in Northern Ireland for joining with the Republic and a concurrent majority in the Republic for Irish unity, as shown in referendums, the British government laid itself under a duty to facilitate the transfer. The future constitutional status of Northern Ireland depends, therefore, on the consent of its people.

The main aim of the Agreement was to bridge the tensions between the two communities in Northern Ireland. That has hardly been achieved. Indeed, ironically the two moderate parties which played the primary role in negotiating the agreement – the Ulster Unionist Party and the Social Democratic and Labour Party – have been replaced by parties which had either opposed power-sharing – the DUP – or, while accepting it, had for many years been sceptical of it – Sinn Féin. These parties now dominate not only in elections for the Northern Ireland Assembly but also Westminster elections. In the general election of 2017, the two parties won all but one of Northern Ireland's eighteen seats, although, since Sinn Féin refuses to take its seats at Westminster, it is only the Unionist community that is currently represented there; since the Northern Ireland Assembly has, at the time of writing, been suspended since January 2017, Northern Ireland's voice is not being fully heard during the Brexit process.

Nevertheless, the Agreement has achieved its prime aim which was to ensure that tensions are resolved peacefully. While there are still some dissident groups in the province who do not accept the Agreement, almost all the parties representing the two communities have committed themselves to the peaceful resolution of conflict. In consequence, terrorism and armed paramilitary gangs have almost completely disappeared from the province. So, even though there has not been reconciliation between the two communities, the Northern Ireland of today is quite unrecognizable from the Northern Ireland of the Troubles. That is because the Agreement has contained or institutionalized the conflict, requiring it to be managed within an agreed peaceful and democratic process. Moreover, the Belfast Agreement was not intended as a final settlement, but as a first step, albeit an important one, in a *process*. That process was continued after the Belfast Agreement with reforms of the Northern Ireland policing system, the decommissioning of weapons held by terrorist organizations and effective demobilization of paramilitary organizations. Further measures are certainly necessary if reconciliation between the two communities is to be achieved, particularly in securing integrated housing and education systems and removing the so-called 'peace walls' dividing the two communities. Nevertheless, the Belfast Agreement remains the cornerstone of the peace process and the British and Irish governments are firmly committed to maintaining it.

Until devolution, as we have seen, many believed that the non-English parts of the United Kingdom formed part of a single British nation. Devolution has converted the United Kingdom into a new union of nations, each with its own identity and institutions, a multinational state. Devolution has created, therefore, a new constitutional settlement among the various parts of the United Kingdom. But the Belfast Agreement provided, in addition to this settlement, a new settlement between the United Kingdom and the other nation in these islands, the Irish nation. The Agreement, therefore, while recognizing and acknowledging the various distinctive national identities within these islands, also acknowledged the close and complex links between them and their overall unity. In 1979, the Fine Gael Party in the Republic issued a document entitled 'Ireland – Our Future Together', with an introduction by Garret Fitzgerald, later to be Taoiseach of the Republic, which declared:

> 'It would be as well to face the fact that the actual relationship between Northern Ireland and the Republic, and between both areas and Great Britain, is of such historical complexity, and has carried into modern times such overtures of past inter-relationships between all three, that to try to define them in traditional terms of international relations is to attempt the impossible. There **is** no precedent for a situation where a State (the Republic) and a part of another State (Northern Ireland as part of the United Kingdom), are linked together by religious, trade union, banking and sporting bonds which do *not* exist in the same form between the part of the United Kingdom involved and the rest of that State. There *is* no precedent for the situation in which all citizens of the Republic are automatically endowed with the same rights as citizens of the United Kingdom … Nothing in the North–South–Britain relationship fits into any known model of relationships between States, and it has been a mistake made by politicians in all three areas to try to find solutions which are based on standard models that find no relevant application in this unique situation' (emphasis in the original).

John Whyte, Professor of Irish Politics at Queen's University, Belfast, has similarly stated: 'Anglo-Irish relations are more complex than the more strident simplifiers on either side are aware. Unionists are not irrevocably opposed to any kind of all-Ireland framework: in some fields they adopt it already. Nationalists do not inevitably perceive an all-archipelago framework as a throwback to tyranny;

they accept it for some purposes already.'[28] In the nineteenth century, the Irish nationalist, Henry Grattan, an opponent of the 1800 Act of Union, had declared that: 'The Channel forbids Union, the Ocean forbids separation.' The Belfast Agreement gives effect to that insight. The Agreement constituted a recognition by both Britain and the Irish Republic that the manifold links between the two countries could not be contained within a framework which would make the two countries as foreign to each other as, for example, Chile and Nigeria.

IV

In his poem, *The Secret People*, G.K. Chesterton wrote of the English, 'Smile at us, pay us, pass us, but do not quite forget; for we are the people of England that never have spoken yet'. But how, constitutionally, is England to speak? England, by far the largest part of the United Kingdom, is the anomaly in the devolution settlement, the only part of the United Kingdom not to enjoy a representative devolved government and legislature. It is the only nation not represented in the British–Irish Council for membership of the Council depends on constitutional status and England seems to have no constitutional status.

In 1741, the Scottish philosopher, David Hume in his essay 'Of National Character' declared: 'The English, of any people in the universe, have the least of a national character, unless this very singularity may pass for such.' In his novel, *The Tragic Muse*, the American novelist, Henry James described his hero, Nick Dormer,

---

[28] John Whyte, 'The Permeability of the United Kingdom-Irish Border: A Preliminary Reconaissance' (1983) 31(3) *Administration* 313.

surveying a landed estate which he will never inherit and feeling 'the sense of England – a sort of apprehended revelation of his country' which 'laid on him a hand that was too ghostly to press, and yet somehow too urgent to be light'. Traditionally, it mattered little that the sense of Englishness was so difficult to express, since England was by far the dominant nation in the United Kingdom. She had no need to beat the drum or blow the bugle. English views are never likely to be overlooked at Westminster and, when one is dominant, it is perhaps best not to remind others of the fact too often or too insistently. The raucous assertion of English identity might indeed have threatened the existence of the United Kingdom by reminding the Scots and the Welsh of their subordinate status. In more recent times some in England have felt that dominance to be threatened by devolution and, even more, by the European Union.

England had no place in the devolution settlement of 1998, yet she is, in many respects, the key to the success of devolution. The purpose of devolution was to ensure that the non-English parts of the United Kingdom do not follow the Irish in seceding from it. Devolution therefore required a generous cession of powers from Westminster. But it also seemed to require acceptance by the English of the justice of an asymmetrical settlement. England, therefore, must be persuaded that she is not disadvantaged by devolution to the non-English parts of the United Kingdom. Some critics argued that the devolution settlement imposed so much injustice on the English that they can no longer be expected to submerge their identity to hold the United Kingdom together. Devolution, on this view, means that the English will no longer be able to express their Englishness within the United Kingdom. So, if they wish to retain their identity, it is they who will need to burst the bounds of Union and establish an independent English state. The English, it is suggested can remain truly English only if they come home from Britain. The devolution settlement appears to have strengthened the feeling of Englishness which, until then, seemed somewhat dormant. It has not, admittedly, led the English to reject devolution for the non-English parts of the kingdom. Indeed, remarkably perhaps, support in England for Scottish devolution is, at around 55 per cent, almost exactly the same as it was in 1998.[29] Nevertheless, Englishness has caught up with the English, many of whom are now turning the mirror on to themselves and asking basic questions about English identity. What does it mean to be English and how can that Englishness be expressed politically? How in the multinational state that Britain has become can England defend her interests?

Perhaps the reason why England has never spoken is that, constitutionally, England does not seem to exist. Constitutionally, it appears to be a void. 'England', it has been said, 'is a state of mind, not a consciously organised political institution'.[30] There has always been politics *in* England, but there does not seem to be a politics *of* England; although devolution may have strengthened the sense of Englishness, it does not seem, as yet at least, to have led to a strong English backlash against devolution. English identity, however, may have been more strongly formed by resistance to Europe than by devolution to the non-English parts of the United Kingdom. In a lecture at Chatham House in 2018, the psephologist, Matthew Goodwin, noted that in 2016, 64 per cent of those who felt 'English not British' believed that European Union membership was a bad thing, but only 28 per cent of those who felt 'British not English' believed it to be a bad thing. Brexit, therefore, was made in England. The greater the sense of Englishness, the greater the support for Brexit. In recent years, Euroscepticism has

---

[29] Curtice and Montague, *Scotland: How Brexit has Created a new Divide in the Nationalist Movement*, p. 2.
[30] Rose, *Understanding the United Kingdom*, p. 29.

been far stronger in England than in Scotland or Northern Ireland. For, while in Scotland the European Union is widely regarded as an enabler of independence and by nationalists in Northern Ireland as an enabler of Irish unity, in England it has been seen as a threat.[31] Since the Scots had for so long learned to share power with England, they did not find it difficult to believe that it could also be shared with the European Union. The English sense of identity, by contrast, is Hobbesian, something that is difficult to share with anyone. The Scottish response to a threat to its national identity was devolution. The English response has been Brexit. For in England, the notion that the sovereignty of Parliament is a guarantor of liberty has been felt more strongly than in other parts of the United Kingdom. England, therefore, found herself less sympathetic to the European project whose leitmotif is the transcending of sovereignty. But England, unlike the other parts of the United Kingdom has no nationalist party. The Conservatives, who might have seemed best suited to that role and are sometimes characterized as an 'English' party are, in fact, a Unionist party, seeking to win back support in Scotland and Wales, even though Scottish and Welsh independence would almost certainly make the Conservatives the permanent majority party at Westminster. Perhaps UKIP is the nearest there is to an English nationalist party. Of its fourteen members of the European Parliament elected in 2014, twelve represent English constituencies, one a Welsh constituency and one a Scottish constituency. The party, as we have seen, favours an English parliament. Brexit is likely to resurrect the English Question in British politics, strengthening the sense of Englishness but also the resentment of the non-English parts of the United Kingdom to the predominance of England which the Brexit referendum has emphasized.

---

[31] This is the theme of Wellings, *English Nationalism and Euroscepticism.*

The Scottish referendum in 2014 resurrected the English Question. For, just before it, the three British party leaders – David Cameron, Ed Miliband and Nick Clegg – promised the Scots more devolution and, in particular, extra powers over taxation and welfare if only they would reject independence. That promise was fulfilled in the Scotland Act of 2016, but it seemed to increase the constitutional imbalance between England and Scotland. Therefore, the English Question needed to be confronted. The day after the referendum, David Cameron insisted that: 'We have heard the voice of Scotland – and now the millions of voices in England must also be heard ... Just as the people of Scotland will have more powers over their affairs, so it follows that the people of England, Wales and Northern Ireland must have a bigger say over theirs....' He proposed that a 'new and fair settlement for Scotland should be accompanied by a new and fair settlement that applies to all parts of our United Kingdom', and declared 'I have long believed that a crucial part missing from this national discussion is England'.

The English Question comprises two elements. The first is the West Lothian Question, named after the MP who first raised it, the late Tam Dalyell, who was for many years MP for West Lothian. The West Lothian Question asks whether it is fair that, while English MPs can no longer in practice vote on domestic matters such as health, education and housing affecting West Lothian in Scotland, because these matters have been devolved to the Scottish Parliament, Scottish MPs can continue to vote on matters affecting West Bromwich in England. This means that legislation affecting the health service, schools or housing in England can be put on the statute book as a result of the votes of Scottish MPs, even though English MPs no longer have responsibility for these matters in Scotland.

The response of the government to the West Lothian Question in 2015 was to alter the Standing Orders of the House of Commons to provide for English Votes for English Laws at Westminster. The Speaker is now required to certify at the outset of a bill's career in the Commons those parts which relate only to England (or to England and Wales) and where its provisions would be within the power of the devolved bodies. With such bills there is, following the report stage, a new stage in the legislative process before the bill can proceed to its Third Reading. This stage, called the 'Consent Stage', requires that any 'certified' portion of a bill, including new material added at committee or report stage, must be agreed in one of three new 'legislative grand committees' – for England, England and Wales or, very occasionally, for finance bills, England, Wales and Northern Ireland. These Grand Committees can exercise a veto at the Consent Stage in which case the relevant provisions are struck from the bill which is presented for Third Reading with those parts excluded. A similar system is applied by the standing orders to delegated legislation. In consequence, MPs for England (or England and Wales) have a veto over legislation applying to their countries even if that legislation is supported by the House as a whole.

This policy, however, whatever its merits, can hardly be sufficient to assuage popular concerns that England is disadvantaged by the devolution settlement. Few of those who are concerned that Englishness is unrecognized will be mollified by being told that Parliament had agreed to a special procedure for English legislation.[32] England remains different from the other parts of the United Kingdom in that it does not possess a separate executive, even though those ministers in departments, such as health and education, whose functions have been devolved in Scotland, Wales and Northern Ireland, are, in practice, ministers for England, not for the United Kingdom as a whole.

---

[32] I have criticized the idea of English Votes for English Laws in 'The Crisis of the Constitution' (2106) 2nd edn, Constitution Society, January 2016.

But, if the English Question cannot be answered in strict constitutional terms, perhaps it can be answered politically. The day after the Scottish referendum in 2016, Prime Minister, David Cameron, declared: 'It is also important we have wider civic engagement about how to improve governance in our United Kingdom, including how to empower our great cities.' That promise was implemented in the Cities and Local Government Devolution Act 2015, part of the Northern Powerhouse project, the brainchild of George Osborne, the first Chancellor of the Exchequer to represent a Northern constituency since Denis Healey in the 1970s.

This Act, an enabling measure, established a legislative framework providing for devolution to combined local authorities following agreement between central government and these authorities. They would not enjoy legislative devolution as with Scotland, Wales and Northern Ireland so devolution will still be far from symmetrical. Nevertheless, the combined authorities will enjoy substantial new powers. To secure these new powers, the combined local authorities must agree to a directly elected mayor.[33] In consequence of devolution deals, the local elections of May 2017 saw a quiet revolution in local government when voters in six metropolitan areas – Greater Manchester, Liverpool, Peterborough and Cambridge, Tees Valley, the West of England and the West Midlands – elected metro-mayors. A seventh metropolitan area – the Sheffield city region – elected a mayor in 2018. Further deals are under negotiation.

---

[33] One unitary county council, however, Cornwall, was granted devolved powers without being required to provide for a directly elected mayor as long as its governance arrangements satisfied the government's criteria of being both accountable and transparent. Cornwall proposed a Leader-Cabinet model, and this proved sufficient to satisfy the government. But the deal with Cornwall devolved much more limited powers than in other areas. It is not yet clear whether Cornwall is to prove an exception, or a model for other unitary counties.

Currently, the metro-mayors currently represent around 6.7 million people; if one includes the London mayoralty and the local authority mayors, around one-third of the population of England now live under mayoral regimes. The powers of the new authorities are divided between the metro-mayors and the combined authorities. While each devolution settlement is different, in general the metro-mayors are responsible for infrastructure issues crossing local authority boundaries such as transport and strategic planning, while the combined authorities are responsible for public services – skills, employment and, in some cases, the integration of health and social care – though there is to be no devolution of any functions relating to the core duties of the Secretary of State for Health, nor of health-related regulatory functions vested in national bodies. The combined authorities are funded through their constituent councils by a levy and are not allowed to raise additional resources. Metro-mayors can, however, make a precept on local council tax bills where there has been an order allowing them to do so. They may also increase business rates by up to 2p in the pound provided that the relevant Local Enterprise Partnership agrees. Further devolution of business rates is likely in the future.

The most important power enjoyed by the new mayors is not, however, on the statute book at all. For these mayors, like the mayor of London, will be regarded as spokespersons for their areas even over matters for which they have no statutory responsibility. With an electoral mandate behind them, mayors can mobilize public opinion and speak for local electors in a way in which a traditional council leader could not. That has certainly proved to be the case since 2000 with the mayor of London, the first directly elected mayor in British history. He is responsible for no more than around 10 per cent of public spending in London and has no power to raise his own taxes. Yet he is regarded by most Londoners as their spokesman on a very wide range of policies, whether or not he is statutorily responsible for them. After the terrorist atrocity at Westminster in March 2017, it was Sadiq Khan, the mayor, not the Home Secretary, who spoke for London; while few can name the leader of an old-style local authority, most Londoners know the name of their mayor. Areas with directly elected mayors are likely to be in a better position to defend their interests in Brexit negotiations than local authorities without mayors. In this sense, the mayor of London and the metro-mayors can be said to be representatives of their areas in a manner not too dissimilar to the manner in which the first ministers of Scotland and Wales are able to represent their nations. The metro-mayors, therefore, may well give English city regions a voice which they have hitherto lacked, thereby helping to correct the imbalance between London and the rest of England and acting as a counterweight to the devolved bodies in Scotland and Wales. But the metro-mayors do not have the powers of the devolved bodies. They have neither legislative powers, nor extensive taxing powers and there is no likelihood of them being given such powers in the foreseeable future; the metro-mayors can speak only for some of the larger parts of urban England, not for England as a whole. In addition, the role of the metro-mayors, by contrast with that of the devolved bodies, is not at present institutionalized. There is no body representing them, so the voices of the English regions are not heard as loudly in Whitehall as those of the devolved bodies.

V

The outcome of the 2016 Brexit referendum seemed at first to provide encouragement for Scottish nationalists. For they could claim that Scotland was being forced out of the European Union against her will by England. One of the arguments that had been used by Unionists in the 2014 Scottish independence referendum was that only by voting to reject independence could the Scots be assured of retaining their membership of the European Union. An independent Scotland, so Unionists argued, would have to renegotiate its way back into the European Union through the procedure laid down in Article 49 of the treaty and probably on less advantageous terms than she currently enjoyed as part of the United Kingdom. But, having duly rejected independence, the Scots were nevertheless to lose their membership of the European Union against their wishes. Therefore, so nationalists argued, the Scots had been induced to support the Union under false pretences. In the immediate aftermath of the Brexit referendum, the leader of the SNP, Nicola Sturgeon, called for a second referendum on independence precisely to preserve Scottish membership of the European Union.

But the brute facts of electoral behaviour were to offer little encouragement to the nationalist cause. In the 2017 general election, the SNP sought to corral Remain voters to the nationalist cause. But they lost both votes and seats as compared to their electoral performance in 2015. In 2015, the SNP won fifty-six of the fifty-nine Scottish seats on around 50 per cent of the vote. In 2017, they won just thirty-five seats on around 36 per cent of the vote.

The difficulty faced by the SNP was that around one-third of the 1.6 million people who had voted for independence in 2014 were also Brexiteers. Some of them were not prepared to support a Remain party in 2017. For them, Brexit was more important than Scottish independence. In the 2017 general election, the SNP retained 78 per cent of those who had voted for them in 2015 and who had voted Remain in the 2016 referendum; but only 58 per cent of those who had voted to Leave in 2016. Twenty per cent of SNP Leave voters in 2016 switched their vote to Labour, while 19 per cent switched their vote to the Conservatives.[34]

---

[34] Ailsa Henderson and James Mitchell, 'Referendums as Critical Junctures? Scottish Voting in British Elections' in Jonathan Tonge, Cristina Leston-Bandeira and Stuart Wilks-Heeg, *Britain Votes 2017*, Oxford University Press and the Hansard Society, p. 122.

The Brexit referendum had exposed a fissure in the SNP. A nationalist party faces electoral problems whenever it advocates a policy in addition to separation (e.g. membership of the European Union). For there are bound to be nationalists who are, in fact, opposed to the European Union; while, conversely, a Unionist supporter of the European cause who might be attracted by the SNP's commitment to the cause might be repelled by its separatist aspirations.

In any case, Brexit is likely to make the cause of Scottish independence more difficult to argue, not less. Admittedly, an independent Scotland would face no constitutional difficulty in re-joining the European Union, under the provisions of Article 49 of the Treaty. For the European Union is required, under Article 2 of the Treaty, to admit any well-ordered European country adhering to democracy, human rights and the rule of law. However, the European Union is not anxious to encourage separatism, as was shown by its hostile reaction to the declaration of independence in Catalonia in 2017. It might well, as it has done with all new member states in the twenty-first century, insist that Scotland join the eurozone. That would entail Scotland complying with the Maastricht budget criteria which require member states to reduce their budget deficit to no more than 3 per cent of GDP. Scotland's current budget deficit is currently nearly 8 per cent of GDP. In addition, Scotland would probably not be granted its proportionate share of the United Kingdom budget rebate negotiated, with great difficulty, by Margaret Thatcher at Fontainebleau in 1984. Therefore, an independent Scottish government seeking to join the European Union would have to adopt radical policies of austerity, cutting public spending and raising taxation. Such a government would make the British austerity Chancellor, George Osborne, appear to be Santa Claus!

If, as the British government currently intends, Brexit leads to Britain being outside the customs union and internal market of the

European Union, then Scotland would be confronted with a hard border with England, by far her largest market. She would be excluded from the internal market of the rest of the United Kingdom, which might well adopt regulations and quality standards different from those of the European Union. Were Scotland to seek to keep the pound, perhaps temporarily, until it was fit to join the Eurozone, she would be faced with a position whereby its monetary policy would be determined in London. So there would be severe restrictions on an independent Scotland's fiscal and monetary policies. Scotland would be in a similar position to those Mediterranean members of the eurozone such as Greece and Italy who are required to implement drastic policies of economic austerity. The likelihood, therefore, is that calls for Scottish independence will become muted for the foreseeable future; indeed, Nicola Sturgeon, the SNP leader, has not recently reiterated her call for a second independence referendum.

In place of independence, some in Scotland have argued for a special status, a differentiated relationship with the European Union and one which respects the wishes of the Scottish people as expressed in the Brexit referendum. That would entail either Scotland alone remaining in the European Union or Scotland alone remaining in the internal market of the European Union by joining the European Economic Area.

The European Union certainly has provisions for differential relationships. Gibraltar, for example, although not part of the United Kingdom but a British Overseas territory, is, nevertheless, a full part of the European Union. British Crown dependencies – the Channel Islands and the Isle of Man – are not part of the European Union, but, under Protocol 3 of the United Kingdom's Treaty of Accession, they have trading rights with the European Union, there is free movement of goods between them and the European Union and they are not subject to the EU's common external tariff. There are also differential relationships applying to various small islands which were once part of the French and Dutch empires. The Faroe islands, which are part of Denmark, are not part of the European Union, but can negotiate trade agreements with all countries that are members of the European Free Trade Association, which includes all European Union member states, while Greenland, which is also part of Denmark, left the European Union in 1985. This seems to provide a precedent for part of a state to secede from the European Union.

It is doubtful, however, whether these differential arrangements could be used to justify Scotland alone remaining in the European Union after Brexit. For the Channel Islands, the Isle of Man, the Faroe islands and Greenland are all small islands with no land borders. The various provisions providing for differential treatment of these islands did not alter the relationship between the European Union and the member state of which they are a part. When, for example, Greenland, with a population of around 55,000, left the European Union, the sovereign state of Denmark, with its population of around 5.5 million, remained the continuing member and its relationship to the European Union did not change. But, were Scotland able to remain in the European Union after Brexit, the relationship between a member state and the European Union would most certainly have been affected, since the continuing member would be Scotland, which has only around 10 per cent of the population of the United Kingdom. The other European Union members might be worried about an arrangement which they would see as an encouragement to separatism in other member states (e.g. Spain, facing serious separatist problems in Catalonia). Even more important, the British government would be unlikely to agree to an arrangement which it would see as encouraging Scottish nationalism. The Danish government gave the Faroe islands power to negotiate independent trade agreements with European Free Trade Association countries.

The British government would be unlikely to extend similar generosity to Scotland for a policy which it would regard as a move towards separation.

In December 2016, the Scottish government proposed, as a second best, in a policy document, *Scotland's Place in Europe*, that Scotland remain in the single market of the European Union even if the rest of the UK were to leave it. That would entail remaining on the outer rim of the European Union by becoming a member of the European Economic Area, together with Norway, Iceland and Liechtenstein. Scotland would thereby retain the benefits of the internal market. However, in return for this benefit, members of the European Economic Area are required to make a large financial contribution to the European Union budget – Norway currently pays around 83 per cent per head of the British per head contribution, although that includes contributions towards the Schengen passport-free area to which Britain does not belong – they are required to accept the jurisdiction of the European Free Trade Area Court which normally follows the rulings of the European Court of Justice and also required to accept free movement. This last requirement would not be a particular problem for Scotland, since immigration is not a serious issue there. Indeed, the Scottish economy has suffered in recent years from emigration, not immigration. But, if, as is likely, the British government decided to restrict immigration from the European Union, there would be different rules on immigration between a Scotland committed to free movement and the rest of the United Kingdom. Immigration, moreover, is a reserved function, retained by Westminster in the devolution legislation. There would, therefore, have to be a further instalment of devolution to Scotland – and not only in immigration but in other areas such as employment and social policy – so that it could remain aligned with the European Union. The British government would be very unlikely to provide for such further devolution which it would regard as an encouragement to separatism. In addition, Scotland would be faced with the same basic problem as the other members of the European Economic Area in that she would suffer regulation without representation, being required to accept the acquis of the European Union – not just the current acquis but future additions to it – without having a vote since she would not be a member of the European Community. Indeed, Norway is often known as a fax democracy since conclusions of the European Council are faxed to her for comments, but there are few examples of these comments actually influencing legislation; nor has the European Economic Area so far made any provision to allow a part of a state to become a member. Article 56 of the European Free Trade Area Convention, which regulates membership of the European Economic Area, provides that the member states may negotiate agreements between them and 'any other State, union of States, or international organisation'. It makes no provision for an agreement with a part of a state.

Any form of special status for Scotland – or for Northern Ireland – would also involve a special status for Scotland or Northern Ireland within the United Kingdom, a form of exceptionalism. It is for that reason unacceptable both to the British government and to Unionists in Scotland and Ireland.[35] It is, therefore, unlikely, that there will be a differential arrangement for Scotland when Britain leaves the European Union. Scotland is likely to leave the European Union on the same basis as the rest of the United Kingdom. Nevertheless, the process of Brexit is likely to put serious strain on the devolution settlement.

---

[35] This point is made in relation to Northern Ireland in Cathy Gormley-Heenan and Arthur Aughey, 'Northern Ireland and Brexit: Three Effects on "the Border in the Mind"' (2017) *British Journal of Politics and International Relations* 1–15.

VI

In Scotland, Brexit has led to a constitutional dispute concerning whether powers repatriated from the European Union should be located at Westminster or at Holyrood. The devolution legislation for Scotland and, as amended, for Wales, provides for certain powers to be reserved to Westminster – primarily foreign affairs, defence and macro-economic management. All powers not specifically reserved are devolved. Amongst the devolved powers are some – primarily agriculture, fisheries and environmental protection – where devolution has, until now, been largely illusory since policy in these areas has been made by the European Union leaving the devolved bodies with little real discretion. For the devolved bodies were under a legal obligation not to legislate contrary to European law. Clearly Brexit removes that obligation. After Brexit, by the terms of the devolution legislation, real powers in areas such as agriculture and fisheries would, unless Westminster takes countervailing action, return to the devolved bodies which could then decide upon their own policies in regard to such matters as agricultural subsidies and protection of the fishing industry. But that, in the government's view, would threaten the internal market of the United Kingdom, a market which, until Brexit, had been regulated by the European Union, and it could lead to a harmful divergence of standards. It would, for example, make little sense to have four entirely different systems of agricultural protection in the four parts of the United Kingdom. Therefore, so the government believes, there must be common minimum trading standards as well as limits on the degree of variation of state aid, business support and environmental requirements. In addition, the United Kingdom government might wish to use, for example, the level of agricultural subsidies, as a bargaining chip in trade negotiations. Indeed, a trade agreement could hardly avoid concerning itself with agriculture. But any agreement on agriculture would have implications for the devolved bodies. Indeed, it would impact more heavily on the economies of the devolved territories than on that of England since they have larger agricultural sectors. But Britain would have to convince the country with which it was negotiating that it was able to implement the agreement across the whole of its territory. For these reasons, a common framework was needed. While Britain remained a member of the European Union, there was no need for it, since EU law and the interpretation of it by the European Court of Justice would ensure consistency of legal and regulatory standards in all parts of the United Kingdom, including devolved policy areas, such as food safety, environmental protection, agricultural subsidies and fisheries. There was a UK-wide single market deriving from EU rules. Perhaps, if Britain had not been a member of the European Union when devolution was enacted, the whole of agriculture and fisheries would not have been devolved and some matters would have been retained by Westminster to ensure the integrity of the United Kingdom internal market. But, for as long as Britain remained a member of the European Union, the internal market was upheld by the EU's internal market rules. So, from this point of view, in the words of the European Union Select Committee of the House of Lords, the European Union was 'in effect, part of the glue holding the United Kingdom together since 1997'.[36] That glue is now becoming unstuck.

In the European Union Withdrawal bill as originally published, clause 11 proposed that all powers repatriated from the European Union be repatriated to Westminster. The government would then decide which powers needed to be retained. It would then return the remainder to the devolved bodies. While there was general agreement on the part of the devolved bodies that there needed to be a nationwide

---

[36] HL 9, 2017–18, *Brexit: Devolution*, p. 12.

United Kingdom framework, there was widespread condemnation in Scotland and Wales of what was seen as a unilateral power grab, a radical, albeit tacit, amendment of the devolution legislation.

During the parliamentary proceedings of the European Union Withdrawal bill the government modified clause 11 in response to criticism. It now proposed, in what became section 12 of the European Union Withdrawal Act 2018, to pass most of the repatriated powers to the devolved bodies. It would retain only those powers needed to ensure the integrity of the United Kingdom single market. It proposed to consult with the devolved bodies on what powers should be retained, but, if agreement could not be reached, the government would make the final decision. The government sought to retain the power to make regulations freezing the ability of the devolved bodies to alter repatriated European Union law in twenty-four specific areas out of 153 areas of EU law that intersect with devolved competences. These comprised primarily agricultural support, animal health and welfare, elements of reciprocal healthcare, environmental quality, fisheries management and support, food safety and hygiene law and plant health. In these areas it would not, so the government believes, be in the general interest to develop separate and possibly incompatible regulatory regimes in the four parts of the United Kingdom. Under the original clause 11, the default position had been that all repatriated powers would be returned to the British government. Under section 12, the default position was that powers would be returned to the devolved bodies unless the British government decided otherwise. There will, in addition, be a sunset clause. The government will lose the power to make regulations freezing the temporary arrangements two years after Brexit day and the regulations themselves will last no longer than five years. The government has also promised not to legislate for England in the twenty-four frozen areas while common frameworks are being implemented, so that England will not be able to take advantage of the freezing process to secure a competitive advantage for herself.

But, despite these important concessions, the government remains in control of the process and, while it hoped to proceed by agreement of the devolved bodies, it would, if that agreement was not forthcoming, act unilaterally. The National Assembly of Wales accepted the agreement, with only Plaid Cymru dissenting. The Scottish Parliament did not, however, accept it and declared that it would refuse legislative consent. The SNP government was joined in its opposition by every party represented in the Parliament, except the Scottish Conservatives, in rejecting the government's proposal. This gave the objections of the Scottish Parliament greater political legitimacy than if it had only been the SNP which had objected.

The Scottish Parliament argued that, while the constraints on the Scottish government would be legal and binding, the constraints on the British government would be merely voluntary and dependent on the promises of politicians. Indeed, for as long as Westminster regarded itself as sovereign, they could not be anything else since, according to this view, Westminster could not bind itself.

The National Assembly for Wales took a different view from the Scottish Parliament. By contrast with Holyrood, Cardiff Bay, is dominated by the Labour Party, a strongly Unionist party as are the Welsh Liberal Democrats and the Welsh Conservatives. There is little pressure for independence in Wales and the main concern of the National Assembly has been to protect the status of Wales in the United Kingdom. It seeks to achieve this by transforming the devolution settlement into a quasi-federal relationship. It wants the Joint Ministerial Committee, established at the time of devolution to coordinate relationships between the devolved bodies and the British government, to be transformed into an annual Heads of Government Summit and then into a Council of Ministers. The Welsh government believes that the Council of Ministers should have procedures for independent dispute resolution, arbitration and adjudication mechanisms. But, how should decisions in such a Council be made? Voting based purely on population share would allow the United Kingdom government permanently to dictate outcomes, so obviating the need for that government to secure consensus. But it would hardly be constitutionally appropriate for the three devolved administrations to be able to outvote the United Kingdom government. The Welsh government therefore suggested that decisions should require the agreement of the United Kingdom government and at least one of the devolved administrations. But this would allow the devolved bodies acting together to veto the United Kingdom government and that would hardly be compatible with the Westminster view of the sovereignty of Parliament. It could also prevent the British government from signing a trade agreement with another country because the three devolved bodies, representing 16 per cent of the population of the country were against it, just as the Walloon sub-national government in Belgium was able to hold up the EU's trade agreement with Canada, an agreement requiring ratification by a number of regional parliaments as well as all national parliaments. Nevertheless, Wales, in contrast with Scotland, has sought to use Brexit not to confront the British government, but as a means of transforming the British constitution so as to give greater weight to the devolved bodies.

The Scottish government, in contrast, took the view that its consent was essential for the freezing of powers. It invoked against the British government the Sewel convention which provided that Westminster would not normally legislate in the area of devolved competences without the consent of the devolved bodies. Whenever Westminster had in the past wanted to do so, it had sought a legislative consent motion from the devolved body or bodies in question. Between 1999, when the devolved bodies were established and May 2018, there were 173 such motions in Scotland, seventy-nine in Northern Ireland and eighty-eight in Wales. On only nine occasions had consent been denied. The Northern Ireland Assembly had denied consent only once, but the Welsh National Assembly has denied consent on seven occasions. Before the disagreement on the repatriation of powers, the Scottish Parliament had, despite being governed by the SNP since 2007, denied consent only once, on aspects of the Welfare Reform bill of 2011; on that occasion it had reconsidered and granted consent after the bill had been amended at Westminster to meet Scottish concerns. The SNP could claim, therefore, that it had not sought to oppose British governments in a contumacious spirit but had sincerely sought to operate the devolution settlement. The government, however, maintains that it cannot allow the Scottish Parliament to veto a measure which it believes necessary for the integrity of the United Kingdom. All the same, it is unprecedented for it to press ahead with legislation affecting a devolved area without the consent of the Scottish Parliament.

The Sewel convention had been put into statute in section 2 of the Scotland Act 2016 and section 2 of the Wales Act of 2017; in principle, the convention applies equally to Northern Ireland. In the *Miller* case in 2017, the Supreme Court unanimously took the view that, although embodied in statute, the convention was not justiciable and not enforceable by the courts, declaring that, while 'the Sewel Convention has an important role in facilitating harmonious relationships between the UK Parliament and the devolved legislatures', nevertheless 'the policing of its scope and the manner of its operation does not lie within the constitutional remit of the judiciary, which is to protect the rule of law'. 'Judges', the court added, '. . . are neither the parents nor the guardians of political conventions; they are mere observers' and 'cannot give legal rulings on operation or scope, because these matters are determined within the political world'. The fact that the convention had been written into legislation merely recognised 'the convention for what it is, namely a political convention … the purpose of the legislative recognition of the convention was to entrench it as a convention'.[37] While, therefore, the consent of the Scottish Parliament might be required by convention, it could not be enforced in law. It is, however, by no means clear what it means to 'entrench' a convention if, as the *Miller* case implies, it is still subject to the untrammelled supremacy of Parliament. Furthermore, the Sewel convention does not state that Westminster can *never* legislate in the devolved areas, only that it will not *normally* do so. A proposed amendment to the Scotland bill in 2015 to substitute for the word 'normally' the words 'save in times of war or national emergency' was rejected. The government can claim that Brexit is far from being a normal situation. But, in a debate in the Scottish Parliament in April 2018, Mike Russell, Minister for United Kingdom Negotiations on Scotland's Place in Europe, quoted from the *Miller* judgment, that 'whether circumstances are "normal" is a quintessential matter for political judgment for the Westminster Parliament'.[38] There is a strong case at least for specifying in legislation the precise circumstances in which the British government would think it justifiable to proceed with legislation entrenching on the powers of the devolved bodies without consent. The government should need to justify its decision to Parliament on the circumstances; legislating without consent should always be subject to sunset provisions (i.e. they should last only for a specific period of time and be subject to specific renewal should a government wish to extend them). Such measures would end the unlimited

---

[37] *R(Miller) v Secretary of State for Exiting the European Union* [2017] UKSC 5, paras 146, 148–9, 150, 151.

[38] Scottish Parliament, Official Report, 29 April 2018, col. 14.

discretion which Parliament now enjoys over the interpretation of the Sewel convention.

In response to the British government, the Scottish Parliament passed a Withdrawal from the European Union (Legal Continuity) (Scotland) bill, which provided for the retention of all European Union law in Scotland pending negotiations with the British government. When introduced, the presiding officer of the Scottish Parliament, roughly equivalent to the Speaker at Westminster, declared that this bill was beyond the competence of the Scottish Parliament, but the Lord Advocate, the chief legal officer of the Scottish government, told the Parliament that, in his view, it was within its competence. The bill was not, however, presented for Royal Assent after being passed by the Scottish Parliament since the British government referred it to the Supreme Court to determine whether it was in fact within the powers of the Scottish Parliament. In the panel of seven judges appointed to adjudicate the claim, the English judges were in the minority.

Whatever the outcome of this constitutional case, a constitutional convention is not lightly to be discarded. Such conventions generally reflect important values. They constitute, Dicey declared, 'the constitutional morality of the day'.[39] A convention was defined by Wheare, in his book *Modern Constitutions*, as 'a rule of behaviour accepted as obligatory by those concerned in the working of the constitution'. Though not part of the law, Wheare believed, they 'are accepted as binding'.[40] They reflect fundamental constitutional principles and, often, when conventions are ignored, major political consequences follow. For example, when in 1909, the Conservative-dominated House of Lords rejected Lloyd George's 'People's Budget', the response of the Liberal government was to pass legislation

---

[39] *Law of the Constitution*, p. 422.
[40] K.C. Wheare, *Modern Constitutions*, Oxford University Press, 1951, pp. 179, 178.

enshrining the convention in legislation, the 1911 Parliament Act. For the Lords had broken a fundamental principle of representative government; not being an elected chamber, they had rejected a money bill, so flouting the principle of no taxation without representation. Were the Queen to break the convention that she assents to government legislation, this convention too would no doubt be put into statutory form. For, in these circumstances she too would be ignoring a fundamental principle of representative government. This example shows that an action may be legal without being constitutional. So, although, as *Miller* shows, it would be lawful for the government to ignore the Sewel convention, it does not follow that it would be constitutional; to ignore a constitutional convention on such a sensitive matter could be de-stabilizing. States can be broken up not only through the activities of secessionists but also through a unilateral repudiation by central government of what is seen by the units as part of a contractual settlement. When in 1982, the Canadian Prime Minister, Pierre Trudeau, patriated the Canadian constitution without the consent of the government of Quebec, he destabilized relations between Canada and Quebec for many years. This convention was not 'entrenched' as the Sewel convention is entrenched; nor had it been put into statute. The moral sanction against breaking an 'entrenched' convention is perhaps even stronger than that involved in breaking a convention which is not entrenched.

Whatever the outcome of the Scottish constitutional case, it is clear that the devolved powers to be repatriated in areas such as agriculture and fisheries will, in practice, be shared between Westminster and the devolved bodies within a common framework. The key question remains – how is that common framework to be established? How are the interests of the devolved bodies to be protected in international trade negotiations which may affect their powers such as, for example, agriculture? Are these matters to be decided unilaterally by the British government or through a shared process of negotiation between the British government and the devolved bodies? A similar problem will arise with the distribution of state aids, for example monies under the Common Agricultural Policy and structural funds, formerly provided by the European Union. After Brexit, there will have to be a new regime of state aids. But, again, the issue arises – should the rules of that state aid regime be drawn up by a British government which might well prioritize English interests; or, unilaterally by negotiation between the British government and the devolved bodies? If devolution is to work successfully, many former European Union matters will undoubtedly require joint consideration. It will no longer be possible, therefore, to understand devolution solely in terms of dividing and separating powers into separate boxes. In a number of areas, powers will have to be shared between the devolved bodies and the British government.

What is clear is that Brexit not only raises issues concerning Britain's relationship with the Continent. It also raises profound issues concerning relationships between the British government and the devolved bodies. Indeed, the Brexit process is showing that the basic premise of devolution – that the sovereignty of Parliament could be reconciled with recognition of the Scottish claim to autonomy – was now in doubt. Perhaps it is the very principle of the sovereignty of Parliament, a principle hardly appropriate to the government of a multinational state, which renders the devolution settlement insecure.

VII

Post-Brexit financial arrangements are also likely to disturb the relationship between the government of the United Kingdom and the devolved bodies. Britain receives around €8 billion gross each year from the EU, primarily these monies that sustain agriculture under the EU's Common Agricultural Policy and help to sustain less-developed regions under the Structural Funds programme. Scotland, Wales and Northern Ireland benefit disproportionately as compared to England from European Union policies as the tables below show.

The relative size of agriculture in the economy and the type of agriculture are quite different in the different parts of the United Kingdom and this is reflected in the distribution of European Union funding. England is less dependent on agricultural support than other parts of the United Kingdom, while Scotland, Wales and Northern Ireland receive nearly double their population share owing primarily to the larger relative size of the agricultural industry in those parts of the United Kingdom.

Table 6.1 *Agricultural Funding under the Structural Funds Programme*

	Share of European Union agricultural funding	Population share
England	58.9	84
Scotland	18.5	8
Wales	13.8	5
Northern Ireland	8.8	3

Table 6.2 *Structural funds per capita, 2014–2010 budget round*

England	£13
Northern Ireland	£30
Scotland	£18
Wales	£83

The distribution of structural funding is determined by European Union rules and is greatest for regions with incomes below 75 per cent of the European Union average.

With Brexit, monies from the European Union will, of course, no longer be available. The British government has promised to guarantee replacement funding until at least 2020 and, in regard to agricultural support until at least 2022, when, under the Fixed-term Parliaments Act, the next general election is due. After that, however, there will be a new spending review to determine whether and how European Union spending should be replaced. It will then seemingly be for the United Kingdom government to determine how much replacement spending there should be and how it should be allocated. In place of European Union rules, monies will be distributed within the United Kingdom on a discretionary basis.

Public spending distribution within the United Kingdom is currently determined by the Barnett formula, a formula named after Joel Barnett, Chief Secretary to the Treasury when it was introduced

Table 6.3 *Average annual net payments to the European Union, 2014–2020 budget round*

Net contribution per capita	
UK	117
England	140
Northern Ireland	94
Scotland	64
Wales	90[41]

---

[41] David Bell, *Brexit, EU-Area Policies and the Devolved Governments*, Centre for Constitutional Change, University of Edinburgh, 2017, pp. 5, 8, 9,

in 1979, some years before the enactment of devolution. The formula was not, however, designed to deal with the overall level of public spending in the different parts of the United Kingdom, which was inherited and reflected past negotiations and somewhat rough and ready historic estimates of the needs of England, Scotland, Wales and Northern Ireland. But what Barnett provided was a formula based on relative levels of population change for incremental alterations in public expenditure. It provides that there should be an equivalent alteration in funding in Scotland, Wales and Northern Ireland to any alteration in funding in England. It was designed to avoid an annual squabble between the Treasury and those representing Scotland, Wales and Northern Ireland over the distribution of public spending. Originally designed as a mechanism internal to government, it became after devolution a mechanism used to transfer monies from one tier of government to another. It has no statutory basis and can at any time be altered by Westminster. No doubt devolved bodies would be consulted before any alteration in the formula, although their consent is not statutorily required. On occasion, the British government ignores the formula, distributing money outside its framework, for example, after the 2017 general election, yielding a hung parliament, when the Conservative government gave £1 billion to Northern Ireland to secure the support of the Democratic Unionist Party in a 'confidence and supply' agreement.

The formula entails that public expenditure is driven by the needs of England, since it is the change in the English level, determined by a Cabinet in which ministers for spending departments whose remit extends only to England, predominate. How much is available, therefore, to the non-English parts of the United Kingdom depends upon the political skills of ministers heading English spending departments such as health and education in defending their budgets against both the Treasury and against ministers heading departments dealing with reserved matters such as foreign affairs and defence. Sometimes this can work to the benefit of the non-English parts of the United Kingdom. For example, currently, tuition fees for university students in England serve to increase public expenditure in England, since the monies derived from tuition fees are spent on the universities. This means that the non-English parts of the United Kingdom, including Scotland, which does not charge tuition fees, benefit from the increased public spending in England.

Following Brexit, however, it is more likely that public expenditure comes to be reduced in England with knock-on effects in Scotland, Wales and Northern Ireland, even though the devolved administrations in those areas may not wish to cut their own public spending. A future Conservative government might decide, after 2022, to reduce the level of agricultural subsidy in England. This would entail equivalent reductions in the other parts of the United Kingdom, even though the patterns of agriculture in these areas are quite different and even though the devolved bodies might not be sympathetic to a policy of reducing agricultural subsidies. It is probable that the devolved bodies would be consulted before any radical changes were made in the English pattern of public expenditure, but their consent would not be statutorily required. The non-English parts of the United Kingdom are tied to the tail of England and that perhaps is inevitable with any formula approach given the relative disparity of size between England and the other parts of the United Kingdom. But the devolved bodies suffer from a lack of constitutional protection and this will become even more apparent when the British government comes to decide upon the level and distribution of replacement funds after Brexit.

The British government gave a commitment shortly before the 2014 independence referendum in Scotland that the Barnett formula would not be abandoned. But does Brexit make for a material change of circumstances? Should the Barnett formula continue to be used to

Table 6.4 *Spending on public services*

England	97%
Scotland	116%
Wales	110%
Northern Ireland	121%

regulate the distribution of monies? This formula is by no means universally accepted as a fair method of distributing public spending. Spending on public services in the different parts of the country is currently, in terms of the United Kingdom average of 100, as shown in the table above.

The Welsh argue that, even though they secure more than the English average, they have been disadvantaged under the formula, because, so they believe, the initial basis of need on which the formula was based took insufficient account of Welsh concerns; nor does it take account of relative taxation levels. The devolved government in Wales has argued for a new needs assessment. The British government responded to Welsh concerns by agreeing that from 2015 there would be a funding floor in Wales; in 2017, it was agreed that from 2018–2019 a needs-based factor would be added to the formula to make it more equitable. But there are also concerns that the formula does nothing to secure equity for the English regions. Under-privileged regions in England argue that the formula masks differences between the English regions and that London benefits disproportionately from public spending. They claim that the under-privileged regions of England have needs which are just as great as the needs of Scotland and that, under the formula, England is subsidizing Scotland to the detriment of the under-privileged regions. The complaints of the English regions came to be supported by Joel Barnett himself, who had represented a north of England constituency in the House of

Commons. He told the *Scotsman* newspaper in January 2004 that his formula had become 'increasingly unfair to the regions of England'. 'I didn't create this formula', he went on, 'to give Scotland an advantage over the rest of the country when it comes to public funding. . . .' In his unsuccessful campaign to become metro-mayor of the West Midlands in 2017, the Labour candidate, Sion Simon, declared that Scotland received £10,536 per head in public spending, London £10,129 but the West Midlands just £8,750. Parliamentary committees have, from time to time, suggested that Barnett be replaced with a needs-based formula. The difficulty, however, is that it is not easy, even if it is possible, to discover an objective measurement of need. Further, even if a statistically satisfactory measurement of need were to be secured, those areas of the country which suffered losses in funding as a result might well cry that they were disadvantaged and refuse to accept its legitimacy. What devolution has done is to make explicit the territorial distribution of public expenditure, offering fertile material for territorial grievances. It has also highlighted the fact that neither the devolved bodies nor the English regions have constitutional protection against decisions made by a British government with a majority in the House of Commons. These problems will become more serious after Brexit.

If there are to be negotiations on the distribution of monies after Brexit between the United Kingdom government and the devolved bodies, England and, in particular, the English regions will wish to ensure that their views are heard. England, after all, was, with Wales, the driving force behind Brexit and the sense of Englishness was strongly associated with a Brexit vote. But, as we have seen, the political system finds it difficult to accommodate Englishness. How could England be represented in the Welsh government's proposed Council of Ministers? It is true that United Kingdom government departments dealing with matters wholly devolved to the non-English parts of the United Kingdom are, in practice, English departments. For the British government has a dual status. It is both the quasi-federal government of the United Kingdom but also, in devolved matters, the government of England. It is difficult, therefore, for the Scots, Welsh and Northern Irish to accept the British government as representatives of England as well as arbiters. How can the devolved bodies be confident that the British government will not prioritize the interests of England in the negotiations? The British government, for example, will be in charge of allocating fishing quotas after Brexit when Britain will no longer be bound by the Common Fisheries Policy. It could, if it wished, prioritize the interests of England in their allocation of fishing quotas. Moreover, while the governments of the devolved bodies are legally constrained in how they use the devolved powers repatriated to them by section 12 of the European Union Withdrawal Act 2018, the British government are under only a voluntary constraint with regard to England. Westminster has the legal power to alter retained EU law on, for example, agriculture and fisheries, for England in any way it wants. The devolved bodies do not enjoy this power. The problem is compounded since there is no guarantee that the United Kingdom government will represent the majority of constituencies in England. It did not do so in the case of the Labour governments of 1964–1966 and 1974–1979. Perhaps a solution might be found along the lines of seeking representatives for England to be chosen by the metro-mayors, the mayor of London and by the English local government association. But what is needed are binding conventions regulating how the British government acts in its capacity as the government of England in devolved matters. What is clear is that the distribution of replacement monies to the various parts of the United Kingdom following Brexit will strain the relationship between the government of the United Kingdom and the devolved bodies and it is also likely to resurrect the English question.

VIII

In the 1975 referendum, Northern Ireland had delivered the slimmest majority – 52 per cent – in favour of maintaining Britain's membership in Europe of any of the four parts of the UK – England 69 per cent, Wales 65 per cent and Scotland 59 per cent. But, in 2016, Northern Ireland proved more favourable to Britain's membership than any part of the United Kingdom except Scotland: 56 per cent voted to Remain and 44 per cent to leave. In Northern Ireland, as in Scotland, the Brexit referendum seemed to offer encouragement to nationalists, and, with the Irish Republic remaining an enthusiastic member of the European Union, there was clearly a large majority on the island of Ireland for continued membership. The Brexit referendum, therefore, seemed to tilt Northern Ireland towards the Republic and increase the chances for Irish unity.

The Brexit campaign in Northern Ireland had been quite different from that in England. Whereas in England, the main issues were control of immigration, and 'taking back control' from the EU, such issues played almost no part in Northern Ireland. Instead, the referendum campaign was dominated by the community conflict and by the possible consequences of Brexit for the peace process and the prospects of economic and constitutional cooperation with the Irish Republic. The referendum proved to be yet another battleground for the struggle between the two communities. The main nationalist party in Northern Ireland, Sinn Féin, had traditionally been opposed to engagement with Europe. It had advised a 'No' vote in 1975 and had recommended voters in the Republic to vote 'No' in the referendum on the Lisbon treaty in 2008. More recently, however, it has come to favour membership of the European Union, though it is opposed to further integration. The other main representative of the nationalist community, the Social Democratic and Labour Party was also in favour of Remain. So also were two of the Unionist parties – the Ulster Unionist Party, sometimes referred to in the past as the Official Unionist party and, from the time of partition in 1920 until 2003, when it was overtaken by the Rev Ian Paisley's Democratic Unionist Party, the dominant Unionist party in Northern Ireland – and also the bi-confessional Alliance Party of Northern Ireland, a sister party of the Liberal Democrats and a member of the Liberal International. But the currently dominant representative of the Unionist community and majority party in the province, the Democratic Unionist Party recommended a Leave vote. It appears that an overwhelming majority of self-defined Nationalist voters – around 88 per cent – voted to remain – while, the Unionist parties being split in their recommendation, a smaller majority of self-defined Unionist voters – 66 per cent – voted to leave.[42] The referendum, therefore, served to intensify the community division and had a polarizing effect.

After the referendum, one commentator went so far as to suggest that 'for the first time in my life, the prospect of a united Ireland is not only credible but inevitable'.[43] Those in Northern Ireland who identified as British could argue that the decision for Brexit was a sovereign decision of the British people. Those who identified as Irish could argue that, despite the majority in the island of Ireland for remaining in the European Union, the province was being extruded from it against the wishes of a majority of its people. They objected to the fact that the assertion of British nationality was trumping Irish nationality. In the minds of nationalists, the Brexit decision undermined parity of esteem in the sense of equal respect for the two communities in Northern Ireland, by rendering Irish nationalism

---

[42] John Doyle and Eileen Connolly, 'Brexit and the Northern Ireland Question' in Federico Fabbini, *The Law & Politics of Brexit*, Oxford University Press, 2017, p. 142.
[43] Siobhán Fenton, *Independent*, 27 March 2017.

subordinate to British nationalism. However, it would be a mistake to believe that all of the 56 per cent who voted Remain were also supporters of Irish unity. It is highly unlikely that the 34 per cent of self-designated Unionists who voted Remain were also voting to join with the Irish Republic.

The Belfast Agreement had not altered the formal constitutional status of Northern Ireland. All the parties to it, including the nationalist community in Northern Ireland and the Irish Republic, recognized that, in law, it remained legitimately part of the United Kingdom and that Westminster remained sovereign over Northern Ireland. But Nationalists saw it as giving the Irish government a constitutional role in Northern Ireland, albeit one that could not be enforced by law, as a co-guarantor of the Agreement and as a protector of the rights of the minority in the province. And, while Unionists saw the Agreement as providing a stable end-point for Northern Ireland, Nationalists argued that it expressly recognized the legitimacy of the search for reunification, as long as that objective was pursued by peaceful and democratic means designed to secure the consent of the majority in the province. Far from being an end-point, therefore, the Agreement was, in the nationalist view, the beginning of a process of peaceful constitutional change. The Agreement also provided a constitutional mechanism by means of which reunification could be achieved. Nationalists believed that the settlement embodied in the Belfast Agreement, which, in their view, was predicated on British membership of the European Union, ought not to be unilaterally altered by one of the parties to it. Therefore there was, as in Scotland, a conflict between the strict letter of the law and what was believed, by nationalists, to be the conventions which should govern the application of that law. While Northern Ireland remained within the European Union, these different interpretations hardly seemed to matter. For, with the island of Ireland's membership of the European Union and the development of the single market, there was free movement of people and goods between Northern Ireland and the Republic. All-Ireland institutions could develop in such areas as electricity and agriculture without threatening British rule in Northern Ireland. This meant that the border came to be of much less significance. Indeed, Nationalists hoped that the growing practice of consultation, together with the obvious advantages of economic cooperation between the two parts of the island, would strengthen the case for Irish unity. The nationalists, after all, felt that they had made significant sacrifices in the Belfast Agreement. The Irish Republic had amended its constitution, abandoning its territorial claim to Northern Ireland, while Sinn Féin had agreed to take its place in a six-county parliament, something that it had hitherto resisted as illegitimate. In return, the Nationalists had secured cross-border institutions and recognition of the fluidity of the constitutional situation, encouraging them to hope that Irish unity could be achieved through peaceful and democratic methods. The European Union, after all, exemplified the principle of power sharing and showed that the sovereignty of Westminster could be qualified. If it could be qualified with reference to Brussels, why not also with reference to Dublin? But the fluidity embodied in the Belfast Agreement appeared to Nationalists to be threatened by Brexit since Brexit seemed to entail re-establishing a border between the Republic which would remain inside the European Union and Northern Ireland which would be outside. While the European Union was in no sense a guarantor of the Belfast Agreement, nevertheless, at the time the Agreement was signed, it was assumed that both parts of Ireland would continue to remain in the European Union; the European Union seemed to offer a beneficial underpinning to the peace process. The Annex to the Belfast Agreement, although not legally binding, speaks of the two countries 'wishing to develop still further the unique relationship between their peoples and the close cooperation between their countries as friendly neighbours and as partners in the European Union'.

The European Union had also, in the view of Nationalists, helped to improve the relationship between Britain and the Republic. Membership of the European Union gave a tremendous psychological boost to the Republic. For the Irish, membership of the European Union, which she had joined at the same time as Britain in 1973, transformed what had seemed to them a highly unequal bilateral relationship dominated by Britain into a relationship mediated by the European Union. This new relationship made Ireland far less dependent on Britain and decoupled her from what she saw as British tutelage, replacing it with what the Irish government saw as a partnership based on equality of membership of the European Union. The Annex to the Belfast Agreement, as we have seen, describes the United Kingdom and Ireland as 'friendly neighbours and partners in the European Union'. In addition, the European Union gave Ireland a new forum in which to pursue her interests.

In the minds of nationalists, Brexit seemed a unilateral repudiation by Unionists, both in Great Britain and in Northern Ireland, of that compromise and it would serve to embed Northern Ireland more firmly into the United Kingdom. That unilateral repudiation was, for Nationalists, emphasized by the outcome of the 2017 general election which destroyed the Conservative majority at Westminster and made them dependent on the Democratic Unionist Party of Northern Ireland, a party which had, in 1998, opposed the Belfast Agreement. The DUP rapidly agreed a 'confidence and supply' agreement with the Conservatives to maintain them in office. This, for Nationalists, unbalanced the political situation in Northern Ireland and prevented the United Kingdom from remaining a neutral guarantor of the Belfast Agreement. Unionists did not accept this interpretation and argued that Northern Ireland Unionists had as much right to participate in the government of Britain as did Sinn Féin in the government of Ireland. In their view, the 'confidence and supply' agreement at Westminster was in no way contrary to the Belfast Agreement. Nevertheless, this difference in interpretation is itself a sign of the strains which Brexit is likely to cause to prospects of reconciliation in Northern Ireland.

The referendum, then, seemed to Nationalists to strengthen the case for Irish unity. The Belfast Agreement had provided that it was for the people of the island of Ireland alone, both North and South, to determine, by agreement and without external impediment, whether they wished to remain in the United Kingdom or to join with the Republic of Ireland. To Nationalists, it appeared that Brexit was imposing an additional external impediment. For it might appear at first sight that a Northern Ireland joined with the Republic would be a new state and, as such, required, as with Scotland, to re-join the European Union under the provisions of Article 49.

There was, however, a seeming analogy with the reunification of Germany in 1990 whereby East Germany, the German Democratic Republic, automatically became a member of the European Union when it chose to join with West Germany, the Federal Republic, even though East Germany was far from qualifying under the terms of the European Union's normal accession criteria. By chance, but beneficially for the Irish nationalist cause, the accession of East Germany was agreed during the Irish presidency of the European Union. The accession of East Germany had been agreed because Article 23 of West Germany's Basic Law held that it extended to the whole of Germany, not just to West Germany. There had been similar clauses in Ireland's 1937 constitution Articles 2 and 3 of which had claimed that 'the national territory consists of the whole island of Ireland' and that the Parliament and government established by the constitution had the right 'to exercise jurisdiction on the whole of that territory'. But, following the Belfast Agreement, these Articles, a rough equivalent of West Germany's Article 23, had been deleted and replaced by articles claiming that 'It is the entitlement and birthright of every person born in the island of Ireland ... to be part of the Irish nation' and that 'It is the firm will of the Irish Nation, in harmony and friendship, to unite all the people who share the territory of the island of Ireland ... recognising that a united Ireland shall be brought about only by peaceful means with the consent of a majority of the people, democratically expressed, in both jurisdictions in the island'. The removal of the territorial claim, as required by the Belfast Agreement, also seemed to remove the possibility of Northern Ireland automatically becoming or remaining a member of the European Union after joining with the Republic.

The Irish government, together with Mark Durkan MP, leader of the nationalist SDLP and one of the negotiators of the Belfast Agreement, lobbied strenuously, both in Brussels and in London, that, in the event of Irish unity, Northern Ireland would be in the position of becoming part of an existing member state of the European Union, as with Germany, rather than needing to join as a new member state. That interpretation was accepted by the House of Commons Select Committee on Exiting the European Union in its report on 29 March 2017, ironically the very day on which the British government triggered Article 50, requiring Britain to leave the European Union two years later. One month after the Select Committee's report, on 29 April 2017, the twenty-seven members of the European Council, accepted this view, setting out its guidelines for the negotiations with Britain and agreeing the following text:

> The European Council acknowledges that the Belfast Agreement expressly provides for an agreed mechanism whereby a united Ireland may be brought about by peaceful and democratic means, and, in this regard, the European Council acknowledges that, in

accordance with international law, the entire territory of such a united Ireland would thus be part of the European Union.[44]

That makes Northern Ireland unique in the United Kingdom as the only part of it that could re-join the European Union without needing to re-negotiate entry.

Nevertheless, at the time of writing, a united Ireland seems a distant prospect since current evidence indicates that this option is supported by, according to an Ipsos MORI survey of May 2018, only around 21 per cent of those living in Northern Ireland and by a minority, 46 per cent, of the Catholic population. Part of the reason for this is that survey evidence also shows that the Catholic community has, since 1998, come to see devolution under the terms of the Belfast Agreement as their preferred status for Northern Ireland. For the foreseeable future, therefore, Northern Ireland is likely to remain part of the United Kingdom.

Sinn Féin, appreciating that Irish unity is not immediately possible, has argued for an interim solution, that Northern Ireland should remain in the European Union after Brexit. The Social Democratic and Labour Party has also sought special status for the North, while the Alliance Party, in its manifesto for the 2017 Northern Ireland Assembly election, argued for special status either in terms of 'continued associate membership of the European Union or a bespoke relationship with it'. None of these arrangements are, however, acceptable to the British government or to Unionists in Northern Ireland. Unionists also reject the idea of a customs border or immigration border in the Irish Sea as opposed to the current land border between Northern Ireland and the Republic. It would mean

---

[44] Chapter 14 of Tony Connelly, *Brexit & Ireland: The Dangers, the Opportunities and the Inside Story of the Irish Response*, Penguin Ireland, 2017, gives a succinct and informed account of how this issue was resolved.

that Northern Ireland would be a rule-taker, subject to the rules of an organization, the European Union, in which the Republic was represented but not the British government. Special status for Northern Ireland was also rejected by the Northern Ireland Assembly in October 2016, though by only one vote. Unionists regard such a 'special status' for Northern Ireland as weakening her ties to the rest of the United Kingdom, indeed a step towards extruding her from it altogether and therefore contrary to the Belfast Agreement, which preserves her right to continued membership of the United Kingdom for as long as that is the wish of the majority in Northern Ireland. In September 2017, the leader of the DUP, Arlene Foster, issued a statement declaring that: 'Northern Ireland must leave the EU on the same terms as the rest of the UK. We will not accept any form of regulatory divergence which separates Northern Ireland economically or politically from the rest of the UK.' A government whose parliamentary support depends upon the DUP is unlikely to ignore that view.

Brexit, therefore, imposes serious strains on the Belfast Agreement. It appears likely to re-emphasize the border between Northern Ireland and the Republic, both in terms of free movement of goods and free movement of people. For Brexit is likely to entail that the British government follows a different commercial policy and adopts different regulatory standards from those of the European Union and the government is also likely to restrict immigration from the European Union.

Northern Ireland is the only part of the United Kingdom which has a land border with another country, the Irish Republic, a country intending to remain in the European Union. But that border was never intended to be an international border. It was first established in 1920, when the whole of Ireland was part of the United Kingdom, under the Government of Ireland Act which provided for two Home

Rule parliaments in the island of Ireland, one in the twenty-six counties which now comprise the Irish Republic, the other in the six counties which now comprise Northern Ireland. It was then assumed that both parts of the island of Ireland would remain in the United Kingdom. There was, therefore, little consideration of whether the border was suited to be an international border with customs and immigration controls. But the twenty-six counties rejected Home Rule and fought a guerrilla war to secure independence, which was enacted for the whole of Ireland in the Irish Free State (Agreement) Act of 1922. This Act provided a right for the six counties to opt out if they wished, a right of which they took immediate advantage. In this way the border became an international frontier. It covers around 300 miles and cuts across parishes, farms and even private homes. It is permeable at very many points and almost impossible to police. After Brexit, however, there is a danger that there will be once again a real border both for goods and for people.

Immigration controls have been minimal for most of the period since Irish independence. Since 1923 there has been a common travel area, originally an informal arrangement rather than a legal framework, which, despite different visa and immigration policies in Britain and Ireland, is a border-free zone. The common travel area, therefore, is not dependent upon membership of the European Union. But it has never existed between Britain and Ireland when one jurisdiction was inside the European Union and the other outside it. However, the Crown Dependencies – the Channel Islands and the Isle of Man – which are not in the European Union are, nevertheless, also members of the common travel area. The common travel area has been suspended only during the wartime and immediate post-war period from 1939 to 1952 when there were immigration controls from the island of Ireland into Great Britain, not on the Irish border but at British ports and airports. When Ireland left the Commonwealth in 1949, Parliament decided not to treat her as a 'foreign country' for legal purposes and to treat her citizens not as foreign, but as Commonwealth citizens, who at that time enjoyed the right of free entry into the United Kingdom. When, in 1962, restrictions were, for the first time, imposed on immigration from the Commonwealth, the restriction was not applied to what had become the Irish Republic; Ireland was also excluded from later statutes restricting immigration. Ireland, therefore, was not treated as a foreign country in United Kingdom law and this special status precedes the entry of Britain and the Republic into the European Union. The common travel area was put on a statutory footing in 1971 in the Immigration Act of that year; neither Britain nor the Republic have signed the Schengen Agreement abolishing nearly all border controls between European countries. The common travel area is recognized by the European Union in Protocol 20 of the treaty which accepts that the two countries have the right to maintain special bilateral arrangements outside the Schengen area. These rights include reciprocal rights to work, study, access social welfare benefits, health services and the right to vote in local and parliamentary elections. The common travel area plays a particularly important part in facilitating mobility of travel between Northern Ireland and the Republic so encouraging on a reciprocal basis the freedom of British and Irish nationals to work across the border. It is supported in Northern Ireland not only by Nationalists but also by Unionists because of the considerable benefits that it brings, economic but also psychological, for those who have links with both parts of Ireland.

Currently around 30,000 people are said to cross the Irish border every day, but the only sign that they are in fact doing so is the existence of different road signs and speed limits, weights and measures, currency (since the Republic is part of the eurozone) and in their school systems. Nevertheless, the border, while both Britain and

Ireland were in the European Union, was frictionless. Both the British and Irish governments seek to preserve as much of the frictionless border as is possible after Brexit. Nationalists seek to replicate the 1939–1952 situation following Brexit, with the effective border being in the Irish Sea rather than between Northern Ireland and the Republic. But that solution is unacceptable to Unionists. The British government proposes to introduce new immigration legislation restricting the right of European Union citizens to immigrate into the United Kingdom. This means that there will be a divergence between the immigration policies of Britain and the Irish Republic in relation to immigration from the EU. But immigration controls at the Irish border are hardly practical. In the European Union's negotiating directives of 22 May 2017 endorsed by the European Council, it was agreed that the European Union should seek to avoid a hard border and that 'existing bilateral agreements and arrangements between Ireland and the United Kingdom such as the Common Travel Area which are in conformity with European Union law, should be recognised'. The Irish border would, however, then be the only land border of the European Union with physical controls; European Union citizens could, in theory, use Northern Ireland as a backdoor means to enter the United Kingdom illegally. But the numbers seeking to take advantage of this loophole might be quite small and United Kingdom legislation is reducing the ability of illegal immigrants to live and work in the country by regulating access to social security and the job market. A greater difficulty would be faced by the Republic, which would be required to treat United Kingdom citizens more favourably than those of other non-European Union member states if the common travel area is to be preserved. That would not be easy to reconcile with the rules of the European Union. There is no reason, in principle, however, why the European Union should not agree to the continuation of the special bilateral relationship between Britain and the Irish Republic after Britain leaves the European Union, by analogy with the European Union's relationship with the Crown Dependencies.

The problem of customs is even more difficult since customs, by contrast with immigration from outside the European Union, is an exclusive responsibility of the European Union and not of the member states. Customs borders in Ireland were removed in 1993 when the European Union's single market came into existence and before the Belfast Agreement, which had the effect of removing the security border. Before that, despite the common travel area, there were still long delays, security checks and customs checks on the border. While there is still a border for excise duties, currency and illegal immigration and ad hoc controls, for example, to prevent the spread of foot and mouth disease, these matters are handled without any need for border posts. Removal of the customs border has benefited the economy in both parts of Ireland very considerably and the two economies have come to be increasingly integrated. Following Brexit, however, Northern Ireland, like the rest of the United Kingdom, will be subject to the common external tariff of the European Union and also exclusion from the internal market of the European Union by which regulations on such matters as food standards, health and safety and environmental protection are aligned. Such divergence could be avoided were Britain to remain in both the customs union and the internal market. The Labour Party has indeed proposed that Britain remains in some sort of customs arrangement with the European Union. But the example of Turkey shows that this is far from sufficient to secure a frictionless border. This is shown by the queue of Turkish lorries at the Bulgarian border, which sometimes extends to ten miles – a two-mile queue is considered a good day. Indeed, it can take up to thirty hours for lorries to cross the border. Moreover, the 60,000 lorries sent from Turkey to the EU every year are required to carry a host of documents, including an export declaration, invoices for the products they are carrying, insurance certificates and a transport permit for each EU nation that they intend to drive through. These permits, which are set by agreement with individual countries, can be made subject to quotas. The EU has so far agreed to frictionless trade and open-access road transport only for countries accepting free movement and belonging to the internal market. The policy of the British government, however, is to remain outside both the customs union and the internal market. It is difficult, therefore, to see how border controls can be avoided after Brexit, though these need not necessarily be administered at the border itself. But border controls would damage both parts of Ireland economically and appear to Nationalists in both parts of Ireland as a tilt against the parity of esteem for both communities which was promised by the Belfast Agreement. For perhaps the most important effect of the re-establishment of border controls would be not economic nor even constitutional, but psychological. Such controls could threaten the huge psychological gains secured by the Agreement in improving relations between Britain and the Irish Republic, an improvement which both sides recognize as crucial to resolving the community problem in Northern Ireland. For the real border in Ireland is not a line on the map but a border in the mind. The great danger of Brexit is that it leads to a resurrection of the border in the mind which existed before the Belfast Agreement.[45]

Resolving the Irish problem after Brexit requires two things. The first is creative and flexible thinking from the European Union, which, as we have seen, has been prepared to adopt a policy of differentiation in certain areas. We have already noticed the position of Greenland. In fact, a total of twenty-five Overseas Countries and Territories

---

[45] Cathy Gormley-Heenan and Arthur Aughey, *Northern Ireland and Brexit*, pp. 497–511. The phrase 'border in the mind' was originally used by the Anglo-Irish historian, J.C. Beckett.

linked with Britain have associated arrangements with the European Union. There are also special arrangements on the border dividing independent Cyprus from the Turkish-occupied part of the island, which is temporarily outside the European Union, to facilitate trade and free movement and also on the border between Croatia, which is in the European Union and Bosnia, which is not. Secondly, there must be, as proposed by the European Union Committee of the House of Lords in its report 'Brexit: UK-Irish Relations' in 2017, a UK-Irish bilateral agreement to deal with the problems of the land border and the common travel area. These agreements are, of course, likely to impinge on European Union competences and so will require the agreement of the European Union. Even on the most beneficent scenario, however, Brexit is likely to impose severe strains on the Belfast Agreement and it will need all the resources of statesmanship to ensure that they do not polarize relationships between the two communities in Northern Ireland. In May 1886, at the time of the introduction of the abortive first Home Rule bill in the House of Commons, Gladstone declared that: 'The long, vexed and troubled relations between Great Britain and Ireland exhibit to us the one and only conspicuous failure of the political genius of our race to confront and master difficulty, and to obtain in a reasonable degree the main ends of civilised life.'[46] Dealing with the strains of Brexit will require the political genius both of Britain and Ireland in equal measure.

IX

Brexit and the strains that it is imposing upon the devolution settlement are likely to increase the pressure for Britain to follow

---

[46] Gladstone papers, May 1886, BL Add. Ms. 44772 f 82, quoted in Vernon Bogdanor, *Devolution in the United Kingdom*, Oxford University Press, revised edn, 2001, p. 19.

almost every other democracy by enacting a codified constitution. Indeed, the idea of such a constitution seems implicit in the logic of devolution. For the process of devolution, which now extends to England as well as to the non-English parts of the United Kingdom, raises in a very profound form the issue of the extent of territorial divergence which is tolerable within a state and how best to balance the conflict between a system of benefits and burdens based on geography with the basic principle of the welfare state, that benefits and burdens should be determined by need. That balance is best expressed in a codified constitution.

At present, many are confused as to how the balance between geography and need should be struck. Some of those who speak warmly of the virtues of devolution and decentralization, often also object, without perceiving the inconsistency, to the 'postcode lottery', whereby some areas enjoy better welfare services than others. But the postcode lottery is, of course, a logical consequence of devolution. The greater the freedom granted to devolved bodies, the greater the likelihood of divergence in public service standards. It is, therefore, inconsistent to support devolution while objecting to the inevitable divergences which are bound to arise from such a policy. But the public are ambivalent about devolution, supporting it in principle, but then blaming central government for deficiencies in local services and for the postcode lottery. It is the people as much as the politicians who are to blame if Britain still retains a centralist political culture.

But some politicians too are ambivalent about devolution, including even some of those responsible for implementing it. There is a revealing passage in the diaries of Paddy Ashdown, the former leader of the Liberal Party. Shortly after the devolution legislation was enacted in 1998, Prime Minister, Tony Blair, its architect, complained to Ashdown that the Liberal Democrats were pressing for a more generous policy in Scotland on student support than was being implemented in England.

'You can't have Scotland doing something different from the rest of Britain', said Blair.

'Then you shouldn't have given the Scots devolution', Ashdown retorted, 'specifically, the power to be different on this issue. You put yourself in a ridiculous position if, having produced the legislation to give power to the Scottish Parliament, you then say it is a matter of principle they can't use it'.

'Tony Blair (laughing), 'Yes, that is a problem. I am beginning to see the defects in all this devolution stuff'.[47]

Blair seems to have assumed that the devolved bodies in Scotland and elsewhere would follow broadly the same policies as the government in London. But were they to do so, what would be the point of devolution?

Blair's complaint to Ashdown draws attention to a fundamental conflict between devolution and the principle of territorial equity, the principle that benefits and burdens should depend upon need and not on geography. It was for reasons of territorial equity that, in 1946, Aneurin Bevan, creator of the National Health Service, insisted that, instead of creating separate English, Scottish, Welsh and Northern Irish health services, there should be a single *National* Health Service. For an individual's need for health care depended not on where she lived, but on the degree of illness from which she was suffering. The right to health care, therefore, should be the same in all parts of the country and not one qualified by geography.

---

[47] *The Ashdown Diaries*, vol. 2, 1997–1999, Allen Lane, The Penguin Press, 2001, p. 446: entry for 7 May 1999.

Devolution, of course, has already begun to undermine the principle of territorial equity, though so far only in a limited way. There are, however, now divergences in welfare provisions in the various parts of the United Kingdom. Few object to one part of the country supplementing basic provision. That is the rationale for free university tuition and free long-term residential care for the elderly in Scotland, as well as freedom from prescription charges in the three devolved areas. There might, however, be objections were one part of the country to abandon a fundamental principle of the welfare state by, for example, charging for a visit to a GP. But devolution could easily mean an erosion of national standards. Indeed, on 25 November 2015, Lord Porter, the Conservative chairman of the Local Government Association warned that devolution of health care would mean an end to national standards: 'it won't be a national service. It will be a range of local services'.[48]

The principle of territorial equity, therefore, is bound to constrain the extent of devolution. But, if we are to preserve that principle, we need a clear statement of what functions are so fundamental to the welfare state, so much a part of the social contract, a part of the social union, that they cannot be devolved. For Unionism has a social and economic dimension as well as a constitutional one. If devolution is to be compatible with fairness to all of the citizens of the United Kingdom, we must be clear about those basic social and economic rights which all citizens of the United Kingdom, wherever they live, are entitled to enjoy. Ideally, a basic statement of those rights should be embodied in a constitution defining those powers that need to remain at the centre as embodying the fundamental social and economic as well as the constitutional and political rights of the citizen. But, short of that, a Charter should be enacted laying down

---

[48] *Financial Times*, 25 November 2015.

the basic principles which should govern the territorial division of powers between central government and the devolved bodies. So far, much of devolution has consisted of responding to pressures from the devolved bodies for further powers. It has been ad hoc and unplanned. But, if the United Kingdom is to survive, devolution has to be understood in terms of the needs of the country as a whole, not just its component parts.

X

In 1973, when Britain entered the European Community, the future of the United Kingdom seemed assured, even though discerning eyes could detect the rise of Scottish nationalism fuelled by the discovery of oil in the North Sea – 'It's Scotland's oil' was the SNP's slogan in the 1970s. In 2019, despite the outcome of the 2014 referendum in Scotland and despite the fall in oil and gas production in the North Sea, the future of the United Kingdom is no longer assured but has become a question mark. The borders of the country in its current form date only from 1922. These borders are contingent. The independence referendum in Scotland and nationalist pressures in Northern Ireland show that there is no guarantee that the United Kingdom as currently defined must necessarily persist indefinitely.

'The unitary state', one authority declared in 2000, 'is parasitic upon the doctrine of parliamentary sovereignty'.[49] The submerged conflict between the two concepts – parliamentary sovereignty and devolution – was masked for twenty years by Britain's membership of the European Union which, like devolution, seemed to show that Westminster was

---

[49] Neil Walker, 'Beyond the Unitary Conception of the United Kingdom Constitution?' (2000) *Public Law*, 384 at 387.

capable of sharing power with other bodies. While the state in its traditional form would survive, its shape was being altered by the pressures of globalization, which, in the words of the sociologist, Anthony Giddens, '"pulls away" from the nation state in the sense that some powers nations used to possess . . . have been weakened. However, globalisation also "pushes down" – It creates new demands and also new possibilities for regenerating local identities. . . .' [50] But, with Brexit, the conflict between parliamentary sovereignty and devolution appears once again in stark form. What Brexit has revealed is that the United Kingdom, a multinational state comprising four territories, has not one constitution but four different constitutions, or perhaps four different interpretations of the constitution depending on whether it is viewed from Westminster, from Holyrood, from Cardiff Bay or from Stormont.

Seen from Stormont and indeed from Dublin, Irish Nationalists believe that the system of power-sharing enacted in the Belfast Agreement, together with the provisions for North–South cooperation and the consultative role for the government of the Republic, amount to a convention by which the British government is required not to make constitutional changes such as are involved in Brexit without the agreement of both communities in Northern Ireland. For there can be little doubt that Brexit will have consequences for North–South collaboration and for the border between Northern Ireland and the Republic. Nationalists took the view that, by convention, the Belfast Agreement had established a system of shared sovereignty in Northern Ireland. Indeed, Sinn Féin argued after the Brexit referendum that the Belfast Agreement had yielded a system of 'shared sovereignty relating to the North/South institutional and cross-border bodies'. [51] The

---

[50] Anthony Giddens, *The Third Way: The Renewal of Social Democracy*, Polity Press, 2000, p. 31.
[51] Sinn Féin, 'The Case for the North to Achieve Designated Special Status within the European Union'. Available at: www.sinnfein.ie/files/2017/BrexitMiniDocs-April 2017.

British government, however, stands by the legal position that the Belfast Agreement, which confirms United Kingdom sovereignty in Northern Ireland, does not provide for joint authority and that the Republic has no more than a consultative role in the affairs of the province. Northern Ireland Unionists too have a different view of the constitution from that held at Westminster. Traditionally, Unionists have held that their loyalty to Westminster is contractual rather than unconditional. It is conditional upon Westminster not taking measures which, in the view of Unionists, would serve to extrude them from the United Kingdom. That was why Unionists used what the rest of the United Kingdom regarded as unconstitutional methods, including the threat of civil disobedience, to defeat Irish Home Rule between 1912 and 1914, and why, in 1974, through a strike by power workers in Northern Ireland, they forced the British government to abolish the power-sharing institutions in the province established by the Sunningdale Agreement.[52] So, from both the Unionist as well as the Nationalist perspective, the Stormont view of the constitution is very different from that of Westminster.

The view from Holyrood is also very different from that from Westminster. The British government's conception of devolution is that it is a delegation of power from Westminster and subject to the continuing sovereignty of Parliament. The Scottish conception, by contrast, is that devolution was a response to the sovereign will of the Scottish people. That principle of the sovereign will of the Scottish people was renewed by the Scottish Constitutional Convention in 1989 when it reaffirmed the Claim of Right for Scotland, a claim first made in 1689. The Convention of 1989 comprised the Scottish Labour, Liberal Democrat and Green Parties, the Scottish Trades Union

---

[52] David W. Miller, *Queen's Rebels: Ulster Loyalism in Historical Perspective* (1978) University College Dublin Press, 2007 provides a good statement of the Unionist view that loyalty to the state is contractual rather than unconditional.

Congress and various bodies representing Scottish civil society. The SNP joined it at the beginning, but then left when it was decided that its terms of reference would not include Scottish independence. The Claim of Right issued by the Assembly declared: 'We, gathered together as the Scottish Constitutional Convention, do hereby acknowledge the sovereign right of the Scottish people to determine the form of government suited to their needs.' The Claim reflected, so it has been argued, 'an historical, if submerged, Scottish constitutional tradition of popular sovereignty.'[53] On this view, the Union between Scotland and the rest of the United Kingdom was a voluntary one which Scotland could at any time choose to leave if that was the view of the majority of her electors, even if a majority of MPs at Westminster were opposed. When David Cameron provided for a referendum in 2014, this seemed to show that the British government now accepted that view.

The reaffirmation of the Claim of Right in 1989 showed that the principle of the 'sovereign right of the Scottish people' was supported not only by Scottish nationalists, but also by a large swathe of Scottish opinion, probably the vast majority of the Scottish people. In terms of logic, however, the Claim would seem to provide for Scottish independence if that was the will of the Scottish people, but not devolution, for that would involve a re-negotiation of the Treaty of Union, something which could not be unilaterally altered by one signatory to it. From that point of view, ironically, the Claim justified the position of the SNP but not of the Convention which sought to design legislation providing for devolution; the SNP accordingly soon came to support the Claim of Right even though it had left the Convention.

Although in logic, the Claim seemed to allow independence but not devolution, it seemed nevertheless to have been tacitly endorsed

---

[53] Kidd, *Union and Unionisms*, p. 128.

by the decision of the Labour government in 1997 to provide for a pre-legislative referendum in Scotland rather than in the United Kingdom as a whole. The political justification of this, of course, was that devolution was designed to meet Scottish and Welsh grievances. Were there to be a Scottish majority for devolution which was outvoted by an English majority against it, that would intensify Scottish grievances rather than assuaging them. Therefore non-Scottish voters through their MPs may be regarded as having tacitly waived their right to a vote in the interests of maintaining the Union. The claim of popular sovereignty seemed to be further endorsed by the 2014 referendum. Some Westminster politicians seem to have supported the Scottish claim. In May 1997, shortly after the election of the Labour government led by Tony Blair committed to devolution, a Conservative back-bencher, Bernard Jenkin, referred to 'the ultimate sovereignty of the Scottish and Welsh peoples' as 'a fact'. 'Whatever the niceties of international law', Jenkin continued, 'Scotland and Wales can claim the right of self-determination if that is what they want'.[54] In July 1996, the Earl of Mar and Kellie, a Liberal Democrat peer, declared that 'sovereignty lies with the people of Scotland rather than with any Parliament'.[55] But the conflict over the Sewel convention and the Scottish Continuity bill polarizes a Westminster conception of the constitution, based on parliamentary sovereignty, against the view of the Scottish Parliament, all of whose members, except the Scottish Conservatives, believed that devolution had limited that sovereignty and that the Scottish people, not Westminster, are the sovereign authority in Scotland.

The view from Cardiff Bay is also different from that at Westminster, though less starkly perhaps than the view from Stormont or from

---

[54] House of Commons, 22 May 1997, vol. 294, col. 872.
[55] House of Lords, 3 July 1996, vol. 573, col. 1514.

Holyrood. For the Welsh government has pressed for a constitutional convention to determine the future relations between the different parts of the United Kingdom and then to produce a codified constitution so as to entrench that relationship. It believes indeed that the logic of devolution implies evolution towards a quasi-federal state, in which the rights of the various parts are protected by the requirement in its proposed Council of Ministers for the British government to secure the consent of at least one of the devolved bodies for policies affecting the territorial distribution of power. The Welsh government therefore seeks a new constitutional settlement for the United Kingdom in which Parliament would explicitly abandon its claim to sovereignty.

There is apparently an American saying to the effect that in politics where you stand depends upon where you sit. That may also be said of the British constitution following devolution and Brexit. For the meaning of the British constitution seems to depend upon where one views it from, whether one views it from London, Belfast, Edinburgh or Cardiff. Seen from Westminster, devolution is conceived as a delegation of power, a delegation which allows the sovereignty of Parliament to be retained intact. But, in all three of the non-English parts of the United Kingdom, the view is quite different. There it is felt that the devolution legislation was constitutional in nature, putting an end to the unitary state based on unconstrained parliamentary sovereignty, even though in law it did not do so. While no doubt in law there is still one constitution, what is lawful is, as we have seen, not necessarily constitutional. The Queen could lawfully refuse assent to government legislation, but that would not be constitutional. In terms of what is constitutional, however, there is no longer an agreed and shared understanding of what the British constitution actually is in the four parts of the United Kingdom. Instead, there is a profound difference of view on what is the fundamental rule of recognition of the British constitution and, in particular, whether a multinational state in which the rights and responsibilities of the various parts are defined in law is compatible with a situation in which the government can at any time overrule the various devolved bodies through the principle of the sovereignty of Parliament. That cannot be good for the cohesion and unity of the state.

Tocqueville famously said that there was no British constitution. Earlier in this book it has been said that the British constitution can be summarized in just eight words: 'whatever the Queen in Parliament enacts is law'. But there are now, in effect, four different constitutions, a different constitution in each of the territories of the United Kingdom. In consequence, many are unsure what our constitution actually is and, more particularly, what the conventions of the constitution actually are and to what extent they bind. The system of tacit understandings on which Sidney Low suggested in 1904 that the British system of government was based is perhaps less well understood than at any time in the recent past. The late Lord Bingham, regarded by many as the greatest judge of his generation, declared that 'constitutionally speaking, we now find ourselves in a trackless desert without any map or compass'. A constitution, by contrast, would enable 'any citizen to ascertain the cardinal rules regulating the government of the state of which he or she is a member'.[56] In a letter to *The Times* on 8 February 2006, the then Chairman of the Bar Council for England and Wales, Stephen Hockman, QC, argued that, following a period of constitutional reform, which of course included devolution, 'the vast majority of us lack a clear and comprehensive understanding of what the terms of our constitution actually are'.

---

[56] Quoted in *A Constitutional Crossroads: Ways Forward for the United Kingdom: Report of an Independent Commission*, Bingham Centre for the Rule of Law, 2015, p. 18. Notably, even before the 2016 European Union referendum, the members of this independent commission felt that Britain had reached a 'constitutional crossroads'.

It was, he suggested, difficult to discuss our constitution intelligently unless we were first clear on what it was. Hockman went on to suggest enacting

> a codifying measure, which would contain in a single piece of legislation all the key constitutional principles and procedures which underpin the governance of the country. Such a measure would enable every citizen to know and to understand how the British Constitution works, and above all would provide a clear framework against which to judge not only the decisions and actions of those who govern us, but also any proposal which they may make for reform.

More recently, a Constitution Reform Group under the chairmanship of Lord Salisbury, who, as Lord Cranborne, was a Cabinet minister in the government of John Major in the 1990s, has championed, not a constitution but an Act of Union defining the rights and responsibilities of the different parts of the United Kingdom and creating a 'broadly federal' system of government.

To refashion a new form of Union, a single British constitution which all four territories of the United Kingdom can accept, is the task which now faces a post-Brexit British government. It will require statesmanship of the highest order to bring it about.

7

Brexit: A Constitutional Moment?

I

It would seem, at first sight that, after Brexit, Britain will revert to the constitutional position it enjoyed before 1973, when the country joined the EU. In that year, the sovereignty of Parliament was the dominant, if not the only, principle of the British constitution. But, with hindsight, it can be seen that entry into Europe re-fashioned the British constitution, although in an inadvertent and unintended way. Devolution and the Human Rights Act also re-fashioned the British constitution, albeit in an ad hoc way.

The European Communities Act of 1972 abrogated the sovereignty of Parliament. Brexit, so it seems, will restore it. The European Communities Act entrenched European law into the British constitution. Brexit, so it seems, will disentrench it. The European Communities Act strengthened the courts at the expense of Parliament and the executive. Brexit, so it seems, will reverse this process by strengthening Parliament and the executive at the expense of the courts. Restoring the sovereignty of Parliament was, of course, one of the major aims of those who supported Brexit. But 'taking back control' will mean not only that Parliament will be taking back control from the European Union and the European Court of Justice. Parliament and, still more, the government, will also be 'taking back control' from our own national courts as well as from the European Court of Justice.

Nevertheless a return to the status quo ante is unlikely. For the world of 2016 is a very different world from that of 1972. In 1972, there was no Human Rights Act on the statute book, no devolution legislation and no Belfast Agreement. There were no directly elected mayors. Britain at that time was a unitary and centralized state. The Human Rights Act and devolution have, in effect if not in form, undermined the sovereignty of Parliament. The Human Rights Act has brought the principle of the rule of law into the constitution; the Belfast Agreement has qualified the sovereignty of Parliament by recognizing the sovereign right of the people of Northern Ireland alone to determine their own constitutional future, even against the wishes of Parliament; and the independence referendum qualified the sovereignty of Parliament by recognizing a similar sovereign right on the part of the Scottish people.

Brexit will present Britain with a whole series of constitutional conundrums. For it is, as we have seen, interlinked with major constitutional issues – in particular human rights, the Scottish problem and the Northern Irish problem.

Brexit comes in the wake of a long period of constitutional reform which began with Tony Blair's government in 1997, but continued with David Cameron's coalition government in 2010. The main reforms have been:

1   Devolution to Scotland, Wales and Northern Ireland in 1998, following referendums.

2   A new partnership form of government in Northern Ireland.

3   A new Greater London Authority in 2000, following a
referendum.

4   Britain's first directly elected mayor in London, followed by
directly elected mayors in some other local authorities.

5   The use of proportional representation for elections to the
devolved bodies in Scotland, Wales, Northern Ireland, the
London Assembly and the European Parliament.

6   The Human Rights Act 1998, requiring government and all
other public bodies to comply with the provisions of the
European Convention of Human Rights.

7   The House of Lords Act 1999, providing for the removal of
all but ninety-two of the hereditary peers from the House of
Lords.

8   The Freedom of Information Act 2000, providing for a
statutory right of access to government information.

9   The Political Parties, Elections and Referendums Act 2000,
requiring the registration of political parties, controlling
donations to political parties and national campaign
expenditures and providing for the establishment of an
Electoral Commission to oversee elections and to advise on
improvements in electoral procedure.

10 The Constitutional Reform Act 2005, providing for the Lord
Chief Justice, rather than the Lord Chancellor, to become
head of the judiciary, removing the Lord Chancellor from
his role as presiding officer of the House of Lords and
establishing a new Supreme Court, whose members, unlike
the Law Lords whom they replace, are not members of the
House of Lords.

11 The Fixed-term Parliaments Act 2011, ending the Queen's discretion to agree to or to refuse a dissolution of Parliament.

12 The European Union Act 2011, providing for referendums before any further transfers of powers to the European Union.

13 The introduction of English Votes for English Laws in the House of Commons in 2016.

14 The introduction of directly elected metro-mayors for combined local authorities in England in 2017.

The constitutional reforms of the years since 1997 offer a spectacle perhaps unique in the democratic world, of a country gradually transforming its uncodified constitution in an ad hoc and unplanned way into a codified one, there being neither the political will nor yet sufficient popular consensus to produce such a constitution in one fell swoop. Nevertheless, these reforms are gradually creating a new constitution, the constitution of a multinational state.

The constitutional reforms have all served to limit the power of government. In 1972, government did not face pressures from directly elected devolved bodies in Scotland, Wales or Northern Ireland, each of which could claim a competing mandate in their respective territories. Before the Human Rights Act and the rise of judicial activism, governments had little to fear from the judges and little to fear from a House of Lords, the vast majority of whose members owed their position to hereditary succession and felt, therefore, that they lacked the legitimacy to offer more than a token challenge to government measures of which they disapproved. In 1976, shortly after Britain joined the European Union, Lord Hailsham, who had been Lord Chancellor in Edward Heath's Conservative government, characterized the British system of government in his Dimbleby lecture as an 'elective dictatorship'. That description is no longer appropriate. Constitutional reform has established the separation of powers as a de facto element of the British constitution, both at the centre of government and in the relationship between Westminster and the non-English parts of the United Kingdom and also in the relationship between government, the mayor of London and the metro-mayors in England. Liberty, it has been said, is power cut into pieces. From this point of view, the Britain of today is a land of much greater liberty than the Britain of 1972. So, although many Brexiteers feel with some confidence that Brexit will restore the sovereignty of Parliament, such a restoration would go against the trends of the last forty-five years. It is unlikely that Britain will revert to the constitutional position of 1972. The past is indeed another country.

But what Brexit does is to inject further uncertainty as to what the British constitution actually is, uncertainty that can only be resolved by a codified British constitution.

There are two reasons why Brexit strengthens the arguments for a codified constitution. The first is indeed the constitutional uncertainty which it brings in its train. The second is the fact that it will reveal the nakedness of our unprotected constitution.

There are three main uncertainties in the post-Brexit British constitution – uncertainties relating to the role and scope of the referendum, uncertainties relating to the scope of our rights and how they are to be protected, and uncertainties relating to the future of the devolution settlement.

The first set of uncertainties relates to the role and scope of the referendum. It may well have come to be accepted that the secession of any part of the United Kingdom or any transfer of the legislative powers of Parliament need to be validated by a referendum, as do major constitutional changes such as the introduction of a new electoral system for Westminster or the introduction of a major new political institution such as directly elected mayors. But there are many other issues concerning referendums which must be resolved. It is not, for example, clear *when* referendums are to be held nor how *frequently* referendums on a particular issue should be held. There has been no precise definition of which issues need to be put to the people nor when they should be put to the people. The great danger is that they come to be held, not for principled reasons, but at a time to suit the convenience of the government of the day.

Both of the referendums on Europe were prefigured in general election manifestos: the 1975 referendum in Labour's October 1974 manifesto and the 2016 referendum in the Conservative manifesto of 2015. But the original commitment to the 2016 referendum had been made earlier, in January 2013, when, in his Bloomberg speech, Prime Minister David Cameron signified that he would propose a referendum after he had secured 'fundamental reform' of the European Union. The commitment seems to have been made on the basis of a decision by the Prime Minister alone. The 2011 referendum on the alternative vote electoral system was decided upon as a result of post-election coalition negotiations between the Conservatives and the Liberal Democrats following the inconclusive general election result in 2010; it had no mandate from the voters. Indeed, most advocates of electoral reform would have preferred to have been given the chance of voting for a proportional electoral system rather than the alternative vote which is not a system of proportional representation. But they were not given that choice. It was instead determined by a post-election coalition agreement. The 2014 referendum on Scottish independence was decided upon by David Cameron after the 2011 election to the Scottish Parliament which yielded an overall majority of seats to the Scottish National Party. In that referendum, the franchise was significantly altered in an ad hoc manner to include those over sixteen as opposed to the over-eighteen franchise which was the rule in all other referendums and elections. Admittedly, in 2015, the Scottish Parliament was to enfranchise sixteen and seventeen-year-olds. Nevertheless, altering the franchise in this ad hoc manner for a single referendum could have caused serious problems if it had appeared that the result had been determined by the votes of the sixteen and seventeen-year-olds. The legitimacy of the outcome would have been questioned and some might not have respected it.

In addition, it has not always been clear why some referendums have been advisory, while others have been legally binding. There have been wide differences in what has been stipulated to follow the result in the various referendums that have been held. Some referendum legislation has imposed legal obligations upon ministers, others have not. The Scotland and Wales Acts of 1978 provided for devolution but stipulated that ministers should bring the Act into force if there were a majority for it in a referendum and if 40 per cent of the electorate had voted for it. If not, ministers were required to lay an order repealing the Act. The alternative vote referendum required the minister to bring the reform into force if approved in a referendum; if not, he was to repeal it. The 1998 Northern Ireland Act requires the minister to lay proposals for secession before Parliament if a majority voted in the province to join with the Irish Republic. But the 1975 and 2015 referendums on Europe stipulated no consequences at all for either possible outcome. These referendums, therefore, did not, of themselves, alter the law. The consequences, so it seems, were to depend entirely on political decisions by the government after the referendum.

Significantly, neither the Scottish referendum of 2014 nor the Brexit referendum of 2016 succeeded, in the minds of those on the losing side, as definitively and finally settling the issues that they were designed to resolve. Scottish nationalists argued that the Brexit vote of 2016 undermined the premise under which the 2014 referendum was conducted, to the effect that Britain would remain in the European

Union and that the best way to ensure Scotland's continued membership was to remain in a union with the rest of the United Kingdom. That is why some nationalists have argued for a second referendum in Scotland. Independence, they argue, would enable Scotland to re-join the EU. Irish nationalists have made a similar case for a referendum on Irish unity. Both referendum proposals have been rejected by the British government. But nationalists argue that such decisions on future referendums should not be at the discretion of ministers in the British government who, far from being neutral observers, are committed Unionists and therefore partisan. In a report on the constitution, entitled *A Constitutional Crossroads*, the Bingham Centre for the Rule of Law proposed a specific rule that referendums on secession should not be called more than once in a generation. It defined 'once in a generation' as meaning at least fifteen years. The adoption of a rule of this sort would constitutionalize the power to call referendums, removing it from ministerial discretion and might help, therefore, to resolve tensions between Westminster, Holyrood and Stormont.

There are also constitutional concerns relating to the 2016 Brexit referendum. Opponents of Brexit suggest that the outcome has left unclear the precise meaning of what Brexit entails. Would it allow Britain to remain in the European Economic Area together with Norway? Would it allow Britain to remain in a customs union with the European Union on the model of Turkey? It would, so Remainers argue, be unwise to buy a house before having evaluated the survey and contract and unwise, therefore, to end an existing relationship without precise clarity on the terms of what will replace it. Therefore, so the Remainers argued, there ought to be a referendum on the new relationship before Brexit is finalized. There is no clear understanding, then, as to when referendums should be held, nor on how frequently they should be held.

Some have argued that, on fundamental issues, such as perhaps Brexit or secession, a super-majority should be required or there should be a minimum turnout requirement, as in Poland, where a referendum in which fewer than 50 per cent have voted is declared void; or a threshold such as the requirement that, as well as a majority vote, 40 per cent of the *electorate* must also be in favour, the requirement in the Scottish and Welsh devolution referendums held in 1979. Are there issues which should require the consent of all four parts of the United Kingdom in referendums? Should referendums be advisory or binding? Under what circumstances can the principle of the sovereignty of the people legitimately override the wishes of Parliament? Almost all democracies use the referendum, but most of them have rules regulating its use. These rules are normally embodied in a codified constitution. With a flexible and elastic constitution, by contrast, there seems no alternative to an elastic referendum. Experience of the Scottish independence referendum and the Brexit referendum shows that this may not be an unmixed blessing.

A second area of constitutional uncertainty is that there is no agreed understanding on what our rights should be or how they should be protected. Despite the majoritarian, relativist and utilitarian doctrines which have found it so difficult to accommodate the conception of rights against the state it is, in fact, widely if not universally recognized in Britain that there should be such rights. Indeed, the existence of rights against the state was recognized by government as long ago as 1950 when Britain was one of the first countries to ratify the European Convention of Human Rights, the basis for the Human Rights Act of 1998. But two questions remain undecided: How extensive ought our rights to be? How ought they to be protected? As we have seen, the European Charter protects a far wider range of rights than the European Convention. For the protection of rights is a dynamic, not a static, phenomenon. Rights cannot remain forever fixed in the form in which they were set out in 1950 in the European Convention, which its founders surely intended as a living instrument, not as a document to be forever frozen in time. In 1950 indeed, few would have thought of a right to environmental protection or to the right of freedom from discrimination on grounds of sexual orientation in an era when homosexuality was illegal not only in Britain but in many other democracies. Is there not a case, therefore, for protecting a far wider range of rights than are protected in the European Convention and continuing to protect the rights guaranteed in the Charter?

How are our rights to be protected after Brexit? The effect of the European Union Withdrawal Act is that our rights will henceforth be protected primarily by Parliament. But Parliament cannot provide a legal remedy. Judges will lose the power to disapply legislation contravening human rights, a power which the European Charter of Fundamental Rights enabled them to exercise. The sense of British exceptionalism, a product of fortunate historical circumstances, has manifested itself, even in the Human Rights Act, in a belief that the rights which in other democracies are protected constitutionally by judges are in Britain best protected by legislators. Most other democracies, however, have decided that their legislators should not be entrusted with this vital function of protecting rights, a function better exercised by judges. We have to ask ourselves whether our MPs are so uniquely sensitive to the protection of human rights as compared with legislators in other democracies that they should be entrusted with this vital function. There is no evidence that this unique sensitivity exists. Indeed, the experience of Northern Ireland from the 1920s to the late 1960s and the experience of gay people until recently would seem to show that it does not. The Charter has exposed us, briefly, but with some effect, to a different model for protecting rights from that in the Human Rights Act, while survey evidence shows that judges enjoy more public trust than politicians. Should we not, therefore, continue with the model of the Charter after Brexit?

There is also a third source of constitutional uncertainty, an uncertainty on the precise constitutional relationship between Westminster and the devolved bodies. In Scotland, the establishment of a Parliament in 1998 was seen as recognition of the claim that Scotland was a distinct nation, with a right to self-determination, a claim that was seemingly reaffirmed in the independence referendum of 2016 implicitly accepting that Scotland's remaining in the United Kingdom depended on the consent of her people. Brexit, however, exposes the fact that the powers of the Scottish Parliament remain subordinate to Westminster; and that the Sewel convention, seems little more than a self-denying ordinance, which has no force in law and is not justiciable. The constitutional conflict over the Sewel convention has revealed, in addition, an uncertainty on the role of conventions in our system of government. Further, the panic-stricken extension of devolution in Scotland and the beginnings of devolution in England were implemented in an ad hoc and unplanned way, with insufficient consideration of the implications for the cohesion of the United Kingdom as a whole. The dangers of such an ad hoc process are twofold. The first danger is that of conceding too few powers to the devolved areas and thus failing to contain the grievances which gave rise to the demand for devolution. That, perhaps, has been the danger uppermost in the minds of governments since 1997. But the second danger, which has been insufficiently noticed, is that of conceding too much power to the devolved bodies and so weakening the cohesion of the state. The danger is lest a Britain, transformed into a multinational state and a multicultural and multidenominational society, might become so fragmented that the notion of a common identity, the whole idea of 'Britishness' comes to be lost. We have already noted the words of the European Union Select Committee of the House of Lords that the European Union 'has been, in effect, part of the glue holding the United Kingdom together since 1997'.[1] Perhaps a codified constitution can now help to supply that glue so that the United Kingdom does not now become unstuck. Devolution seemed to have transformed a constitution based on the absolutes beloved both by the traditionalist believers in parliamentary sovereignty and the separatists – a constitution based on either/or – to one based on both/ and – both the maintenance of the United Kingdom and respect for the autonomy of the constituent parts, respect for national identities and also for the notion of a shared union between the nations. Perhaps a constitution which recognizes that the doctrine of the sovereignty of Parliament is no longer its guiding principle could yield a third way between the traditionalists and separatists, one which offers constitutional recognition to the post-devolution post-Brexit United Kingdom. There is otherwise great danger that relationships between the four parts of the United Kingdom could become purely transactional, based on costs and benefits and that the sense of living in a shared multinational community comes gradually to be undermined. That danger was addressed in a different context by the then Chief Rabbi, Jonathan Sacks, in a lecture delivered at King's College London in May 2005, entitled 'How to Build a Culture of Respect'.[2]

Society, Sacks insisted, should be seen neither as a country house, nor as a hotel. Instead it ought to be regarded as a home. 'We have in Britain', he said, 'a series of sub-cultures, each with its own priorities, its own agenda but none of us can fully think clearly about what the

---

[1] HL 9, 2017–18, *Brexit: Devolution*, p. 12.
[2] Sacks's thoughts were to be further developed in his book, *The Home We Build Together: Recreating Society*, Continuum, 2007.

common good is'. Those sub-cultures include, no doubt, the four parts of the United Kingdom. In the past, Sacks went on, society was like a large country house with 'one single dominant culture'. This meant that if one wanted 'to belong, and not just feel a guest you have to get rid of your culture or play it very, very low profile indeed'. That perhaps was the position which many Scottish and Northern Irish nationalists felt they were in until recently. They felt that the unitary state provided no room within which they could express their identities. Part of the motive behind devolution was to allow those different identities to be expressed. But what had taken the place of the country house was not a home but a hotel: 'You pay for services rendered and in return you get a room, you get room services – beyond that, you are free to do whatever you like so long as you don't disturb the other guests.' But this model failed to generate loyalty. 'A hotel is somewhere you don't belong. It isn't a home. It's a convenience. And therefore when society becomes a hotel, as it has become in the past fifty years, you get no sense of national identity, of belonging, of common history, of common good, of moral concerns, of social solidarity – and that is where we are now.' What was needed, therefore, was to convert the hotel into a home that 'we build together', a home based not on 'who has the most persuasive voice or the largest number of votes' but something based on 'the collective good we make together'.[3] In a home, there is shared belonging and a duty to the whole. The implication is that devolution can only work successfully if there is an overall shared loyalty to the United Kingdom as a whole. That shared loyalty is difficult to achieve without a codified constitution laying out precise rules, rights and obligations.

If one was a member of a tennis club, had paid one's subscription and asked to be shown the rules, one would not be pleased to be told

---

[3] From a report of the lecture in *The Independent*, 31 May 2005.

that the rules had never been gathered together in one place, that they were to be found in past decisions of the club's committee over many generations and that they lay scattered among many different documents; nor would one be pleased to be told that some of the rules – some of the so-called conventions of the club – had not been written down at all, but that one would pick them up as one went along, with the implication that if one had to ask one did not really belong. Such a rationale would make it very difficult for anyone who wished to reform the rules. It might, perhaps, have been acceptable in the past when Britain was, in Sacks's terms, a country house, a more homogenous and deferential society. It will hardly do for the more assertive, multicultural country that Britain has now become, a Britain in which people are conscious of their rights and determined to assert them. In the 1950s, Britain rather resembled a very large and rather meandering country house without any guide as to where the main rooms were and how to find the facilities. A house of this sort might have been suitable for those prepared to live in it as guests and to accept the whims of the owner, who would find it easy to make up his own rules and even to bend them to suit his own particular needs. It would certainly be difficult for the guests to locate the various rooms for themselves. But a codified constitution could help in the process of making Britain a genuine home for all of its citizens.

This feeling that multinational and multicultural Britain was turning Britain from a country house into a hotel rather than a home seems to have been shared by Gordon Brown, Chancellor of the Exchequer in Tony Blair's government from 1997 to 2007 and then Prime Minister from 2007 to 2010. He appears to have favoured enacting a constitution which would help to confirm a common notion of what it meant to be British. Brown argued that just as the American constitution has helped to entrench a sense of American identity, of what it meant to be an American, so also a codified constitution might strengthen the sense of Britishness. A Green Paper issued shortly after he became Prime Minister in 2007[4] emphasized the 'need to ensure that Britain remains a cohesive society, confident in its shared identity' and the need 'to provide a clearer articulation of British values', values 'which have not just to be shared but also accepted'.[5] Britain, the Green Paper suggested, 'needs to articulate better a shared understanding of what it means to be British, and of what it means to live in the United Kingdom'.[6] There was, it added 'a growing recognition of the need to clarify not just what it means to be British, but what it means to be part of the United Kingdom. This might in time lead to a concordat between the executive and Parliament or a written constitution'.[7] The implication was, first, that a codified constitution would give the idea of Britishness greater legitimacy in the face of the nationalist challenge, but, also that a constitutional moment may have arrived. In a speech in February 2010, Gordon Brown expressed the hope that a codified constitution could be completed in time for the 800th anniversary of the Magna Carta in 2015.

But it was not to be; the defeat of Labour in the general election of 2010 meant that the constitutional moment, if there had been such a moment, was lost, since the Conservative-dominated coalition government which succeeded it, had far less interest in the issue. Nevertheless, the pressures of devolution have led to a revival of the argument for a constitution. Perhaps the first stage in that process ought to be a principled statement of which powers are suitable for devolution and which need to be retained at the centre so as to retain

---

[4] Green Paper CM 7170 *The Governance of Britain*, HMSO, 2007.
[5] Ibid, paras 125, 212 and 195.
[6] Ibid, para 7.
[7] Ibid, para 212.

not only the constitutional and political union but also the economic and social union, an economic and social union symbolized by the National Health Service under which treatment is intended to be available to all on the basis of need rather than geography. In May 2015, the report from the Bingham Centre, *A Constitutional Crossroads*, advocated, in its Foreword, 'a written constitution' that 'would most directly provide the advantage of clear ground-rules to serve as a framework for our territorial arrangements and to secure their permanence'.[8] But it felt that a constitution, inevitably a long-term project, should be preceded by a 'Charter of Union which would lay down the underlying principles of the UK's territorial constitution and of devolution within it. The Charter would help to provide guidelines, a road-map to the workings of government and the territorial distribution of power appropriate to a multinational state. It would be drawn up with the consent of the devolved legislatures and would establish a principled framework for the United Kingdom as a whole. It would be passed as a Westminster statute and would be a first step towards a codified constitution.

The view of the Bingham Centre was to be echoed in 2017 by the Welsh government which, in its policy document, *Brexit and Devolution: Securing Wales' Future*, proposed a Convention on the Future of the United Kingdom to consider constitutional questions following Brexit.[9] In its view, Brexit represented 'an existential challenge to the UK itself ... Can the Union survive EU exit in the medium and long terms? No one can be sure'. There was a need therefore for 'a major constitutional reconstruction'. The Convention would be charged with seeking 'effective constitutional arrangements

---

[8] British Institute of International and Comparative Law, 'A Constitutional Crossroads: Ways Forward for the United Kingdom', 2015, p. 8.
[9] Welsh Government, 2017. Available at: https://beta.gov.wales/brexit.

for a union of four nations'. It 'would be charged with putting in place appropriate, sustainable political institutions, recognising the quasi-federal nature of the United Kingdom, resolving questions around the way in which the interests of England, English regions (including the position of the London mayor and metro-mayors) are fully represented, and achieving clarity on the form and function of UK-wide political and governmental institutions, including the House of Lords'.[10]

The accumulation of unresolved constitutional problems in relation to use of the referendum, protection of rights and devolution could mean that Britain after Brexit will approach a crossroads in her constitutional development, perhaps even a constitutional moment.

II

In addition to constitutional uncertainty, Brexit will leave us with an unprotected constitution. While we were members of the European Union, we lived under what was, in effect, a constitution. The European Union is, as we have seen, a protected constitutional system, its institutions enjoying only the powers given to them by the Treaties, a system based upon a separation of powers between its institutions – notably the Council of Ministers, the Commission and the Parliament – as well as territorially between the EU and the member states and a system based on the judicial review of primary legislation, which, since December 2009, has included the European Charter of Fundamental Rights. The constitutional system of the EU, therefore, is, by contrast with the British system of government, protected against the abuse of governmental power.

---

[10] Ibid, pp. 19–20.

It is rare, if not unprecedented, for a democracy to exit from a major international human rights regime; no country has hitherto moved in evolutionary fashion as Britain is doing, from a protected to an unprotected system. The process of doing so raises profound constitutional questions. Britain will become once again a country which provides no legal remedy for breaches of human rights. The constitutional reforms enacted since 1997 mean that Britain will not return to the condition of 'elective dictatorship' identified by Lord Hailsham in 1976. Nevertheless, if 'taking back control' means a return to the sovereignty of Parliament, Brexit could easily become a paradise for an overweening executive.

It is sometimes asked whether there is any good reason why Britain should have a protected constitution. But it is misleading to put the issue in this way. The real issue is whether there is any good reason why Britain should *not* join the majority of democracies and enact a constitution. For it is not as if there are two classes of democracies, some with protected constitutions and some without. Almost every democracy has a protected constitution. Britain is one of just three which do not. The other two are New Zealand and Israel. But Israel has been working towards a protected constitution since the foundation of the state in 1948; in 1992, Israel's Basic Law: Human Dignity and Liberty provided that a law which contravened the rights enumerated in it would be unconstitutional and could be declared invalid by the courts. The President of Israel's Supreme Court, Aharon Barak, argued at the time that, in consequence:

> Israel's legislature itself is now bound by fundamental human rights. No longer can it be claimed that Israel has no (formal and rigid) "written constitution" regarding human rights. The new legislation has taken Israel out of its isolation and placed it in the larger community of nations in which human rights are anchored

in a "written and rigid" constitution, or in other words, in a document of normative supremacy or normative superiority.[11]

In his book, *Democracy in America*, the great French chronicler of democracy, Alexis de Tocqueville, declared that: 'In England, [he meant of course Britain], the Parliament has an acknowledged right to modify the constitution; as, therefore, the constitution may undergo perpetual change, it does not in reality exist; the Parliament is at once a legislative and constituent assembly.'[12] After *Factortame*, it seemed that Parliament was no longer a sovereign legislative assembly and no longer a constituent assembly, since it was bound by the European Treaties, which were, in effect, a constitution. But Brexit means that Tocqueville's statement once again becomes true and our rights will, once again, be at the mercy of Parliament.

Brexit, then, seems partially to reverse the progress of British constitutional development from an unprotected to a protected constitution. But it raises the question of how long we can remain satisfied with such a condition, a condition which Aharon Barak described as one of 'isolation' or whether we too should enter the 'larger community of nations in which human rights are achieved in a "written and rigid" constitution'. Brexit, by revealing the nakedness of our unprotected constitution, may, paradoxically provide a powerful impetus for the process of completing our constitutional development by enacting a codified constitution.

No other democracy except New Zealand now has a sovereign parliament, New Zealand, however, is hardly comparable to Britain, being a small country of just over 4.25 million people – a little over

---

[11] Aharon Barak, 'The Constitutional Revolution; Protected Human Rights', quoted on p. 30. Suzie Navot, *The Constitution of Israel*, Hart, 2014, p. 30.

[12] *Democracy in America*, Part 1, chapter 6.

half the population of Greater London – and a relatively homogeneous one. It is very much an exception amongst the world's democracies.

In my book, *The New British Constitution*, published in 2009, I argued that we had, without really being aware of it, begun the process of creating a codified constitution, but in a typically British unplanned and ad hoc way.[13]

We were, I suggested, following such reforms as devolution and the Human Rights Act, moving towards a codified constitution, but without any real consensus on what its final shape should be. In the course of a generous review of the book, Jeffrey Jowell, Emeritus Professor of Law at University College, London, argued that I had not followed through the logic of my argument by calling for a codified constitution.[14] He was right.

Countries normally adopt codified constitutions, however, not as a result of intellectual debate or ratiocination, but after a break in constitutional continuity, either when a colony achieves independence – as with the United States in 1776, Norway in 1814 or India in 1947 – or to mark a change of regime following defeat in war, as with Italy in 1947 or Germany in 1949. These breaks in continuity give rise to a constitutional moment and a new beginning. Scotland and Northern Ireland have had their constitutional moments – Scotland in the Scottish Constitutional Convention in 1989 and Northern Ireland in the process leading up to the Belfast Agreement. England, however, has never had such a constitutional moment, a national conversation concerning its place in post-devolution Britain – perhaps the Brexit referendum was the nearest the English have come to such a conversation – nor has Britain as a whole. One of the reasons why Britain lacks a codified constitution is precisely because we have

---

[13] Vernon Bogdanor, *The New British Constitution,* Hart, Oxford, 2009.
[14] *Public Law,* 2010, p. 627.

never had such a constitutional moment. England, the core of the United Kingdom, seems never to have begun as a nation, but to have evolved. England has not, since Roman times been a colony and Britain's fundamental regime has not been altered since the Glorious Revolution in the seventeenth century. Britain's last constitutional moment was in 1689. But, as we have seen, the Bill of Rights instead of providing a constitution, served to emphasize the principle of the sovereignty of Parliament. That principle has acted as a brake upon constitutional thinking and has served to inhibit it. For, if Parliament is sovereign and there can be no rule superior to that enacted by Parliament, a constitution or fundamental law can have no meaning. It is the principle of parliamentary sovereignty which prevented us securing, before passage of the European Charter of Fundamental Rights, an effective protection of rights. It is the principle of parliamentary sovereignty which has prevented us fully coming to terms with the constitutional implications of devolution. It is, indeed, arguable, as some Scottish jurists have suggested, that the principle of the sovereignty of Parliament has no part to play in an explicitly multinational state. A multinational state needs clear constitutional guidelines so that there is clarity about the place of each of the territories in the wider system of the United Kingdom. It is, however, certain that there is no point in having a constitution unless the principle of parliamentary sovereignty is explicitly abandoned. Britain has already, in my view, *implicitly* abandoned it. For one central argument of this book has been that Parliament did, in fact, abrogate its sovereignty in 1972 when it enacted the European Communities Act. It is now accepted, following the *Thoburn* case, that there is a class of 'constitutional' legislation with a different status from 'ordinary' legislation. A distinction of this type between different categories of legislation is something for which the doctrine of parliamentary sovereignty makes no provision. The European Charter of

Fundamental Rights made a further incursion into the doctrine by showing that rights can be entrenched against Parliament. Sovereignty, as we have seen, is like virginity. Once lost, it can never be recovered. So a codified constitution would not be so large a leap in the dark as it would have been before Britain joined the European Communities in 1972. But what is clear is that, if Britain is to have a constitution, Parliament must explicitly abdicate its sovereignty, something that Dicey, as we have seen, believed to be perfectly possible.

Brexit will be a new beginning and it will, in a sense, mark a change of regime, albeit a peaceful one, the ending of that short-lived regime, lasting from 1973 to 2019 during which Britain was a member of the European Communities and then of the European Union and was in consequence bound by its laws. It is just possible that we are now approaching a peaceful constitutional moment, one marked not by revolution or a struggle for independence, but by the concatenation of inter-connected constitutional problems, all pressing insistently for resolution. It is just possible that Brexit will prove to be that very break in continuity that will herald our own constitutional moment.

Index

Acheson, Dean, 10
Act of Settlement, 81
Acts of Union, Treaty of Union
    with Ireland, 31, 171–2
    with Scotland, 31, 164–5, 171–7
Adenauer, Konrad, 5
alternative vote electoral system, 107,
    127, 129, 262, 263
Amery, Leo, 116
Arden, Lady Justice, 189
Ashdown, Paddy, 245–6
Attlee, Clement, ix, 27, 89, 143

Bagehot, Walter, x
Baldwin, Stanley, 118, 120, 179
Barak, Aharon, 274–5
Barnett, Joel, Barnett Formula, 224–8
Belfast Agreement, 1998, 96, 106,
    156–7, 180, 190–8, 232–5, 238,
    242, 249–50, 258, 276
Belgium, 40, 41, 217
Benelux, 3, 9, 40
Benkharbouche v Secretary of State for
    Foreign Affairs, 2017, 149, 150
Benn, Tony, 12, 36–7, 91, 92, 93, 97,
    98–9, 101, 114, 123, 124,
    125, 170
Bentham, Jeremy, 140
Bernanos, Georges, 48–9
Bevan, Aneurin, 246

Bevin, Ernest, 24–5
Bill of Rights, 64–5, 136, 140–1,
    157–62, 192, 277
Bingham, Lord, Bingham Centre for
    the Rule of Law, 254, 264, 272
Birch, A.H., 87
Blair, Tony, Blair Government, 12,
    98, 106, 143, 148, 245–6, 252,
    258, 270
Booth, Albert, 125
Bretherton, Russell, 9–10
Briand, Aristide, 3
Bridge, Lord, 75–6, 77–8
British Empire, 5, 20–1, 22–3, 42
British-Irish Council, 194, 198
Brown, Gordon, 270–1
Brussels, Treaty of, 1948, 24
Bryce, James, 179
Buckland, Robert, 152
Burke, Edmund, 2, 92, 139

Cable, Vince, 127
Callaghan, James, Callaghan
    Government, 93, 94, 103, 108, 9,
    124–6, 133
Cameron, David, Cameron
    Government, 13, 16, 99, 100,
    108, 129, 131, 132, 152, 160, 184,
    202, 205, 251, 262
Canada, 161–2, 185, 217, 221

Castle, Barbara, 94, 114, 120–1, 123
Chamberlain, Neville, 23, 119
Chesterton, G.K., 198
Christian Democracy, Christian
    Democrats, 4, 5, 46, 47
Churchill, Winston, 3, 5, 6, 7, 23, 50,
    89, 119, 143, 160
Cities and Local Devolution Act, 2015,
    204–6
civil service, 132–3
Clarke, Kenneth, 12
class, social, 17–18
Clegg, Nick, 127
coalitions, coalition government,
    46–7, 108, 116–17, 124, 126–31,
    133–4, 136, 191–2, 262
codified constitution, xi, 29, 80, 81, 84,
    85, 86, 103, 111, 146, 161, 245,
    253, 260, 261, 263, 268, 269,
    270–2, 275–6, 278
collective responsibility, 113–34, 136
*Commission of the European
    Communities v United Kingdom
    of Great Britain and Northern
    Ireland,* 1979, 63–4
Common Agricultural Policy (CAP)
    11, 21, 222, 223
Common Fisheries Policy, 229
Commonwealth, 6, 21, 39, 55, 239–40
Conservatives, Conservative
    governments, 11, 12, 14, 15, 16,
    17, 18, 25, 26, 32, 33, 38, 59, 81,
    101, 105, 106, 108, 110, 117–18,
    120, 129–31, 157, 176, 201, 207,
    216, 226, 247, 252, 262, 271
conventions, constitutional, 88, 134,
    174, 182–3, 217–21, 232, 252,
    254, 267
Cook, Robin, 45
Cooper of Culross, Lord, 175–6
Corbyn, Jeremy, 15, 192

Costa/ENEL, 1964, 52–4, 57, 59,
    60, 70
Council of Europe, 24–5, 27, 51, 56,
    136, 158
Council of Ministers, 34–5, 43, 44, 45,
    142, 155, 273
Croatia, 40
Curtice, John, 18
Curzon, Lord, 20

Daily Express, 93
Dalyell, Tam, 202
Data Protection Act, 1998, 149–50
Data Retention and Investigatory
    Powers Act, 2014, 150
Davis, David, 150–1
De Gasperi, Alcide, 5
De Gaulle, Charles, 11, 21–2, 33,
    38, 40
De Smith, S.A., 54–5
Delors, Jacques, 44
De Maistre, Joseph, 111
Democratic Unionist Party, DUP, 195,
    225, 231, 234, 238
Denmark, 209–10
Denning, Lord 71–2
Devolution, 47, 82, 85, 98, 103, 104–6,
    109, 111, 134, 158, 169–255,
    257–8, 260, 261, 267–8, 271–3,
    276
Dicey, A.V., 30, 31, 32, 67, 68, 76, 79,
    84, 85, 86, 88, 112, 137, 140,
    141–2, 143, 145, 173–5, 220, 278
Dilhorne, Lord, 58
Diplock, Lord, 65, 69
direct effect, doctrine of, 51–2
Disraeli, Benjamin, 20, 110
Douglas-Home, Sir Alec, 55
Druon, Maurice, 4, 5, 6
Dunkirk, Treaty of, 1947, 23–4
Durkan, Mark, 236

Eden, Anthony, 22
Eliot, T.S., 49
England, English Parliament, English
    question, x–xi, 30, 32, 169–70,
    171–2, 177, 178, 179, 180, 185,
    186, 198–206, 223–7, 229, 246,
    267, 277
English votes for English laws, 203,
    260
Erskine May, 106–7
European Charter of Fundamental
    Rights, viii–ix, x, 136, 139, 140,
    146–58, 192, 193–4, 265–7,
    273, 278
European Coal and Steel Community,
    6, 9, 10, 25–6, 27–9, 33
European Commission, 26, 33, 36, 43,
    44, 45, 47, 92, 273
European Communities Act, 1972, 57,
    61–5, 69, 71, 72, 75, 77, 78, 79,
    80, 86, 97, 108, 173, 257–8, 277
European Communities and
    European Union, viii–ix, x, xi,
    1, 8, 9, 10, 11, 12, 16, 18, 21, 22,
    26, 32–5, 37, 38–9, 40, 42, 43,
    44, 45, 47, 48, 49, 50, 51, 52–4,
    56–7, 58–9, 60, 61, 62, 64, 67,
    69, 70, 72, 76, 82, 84, 85, 87,
    90, 91, 92, 93, 94, 95, 97, 98,
    100–1, 103, 107, 108, 110,
    111, 120, 121, 123, 135, 136,
    142, 146, 148, 152, 154, 156,
    157, 169–70, 189, 193, 206–7,
    208, 209–12, 213–14, 215–16,
    221, 223, 224, 231, 232–4, 236,
    238, 240, 241–4, 248, 257–9,
    260, 262, 264, 273, 278
European Convention of Human
    Rights, 24, 59, 136, 142–3, 144,
    145, 146–7, 151, 158, 160, 161,
    192, 259, 265–6

European Council, 236–7, 241
European Court of Human Rights,
    143, 145
European Court of Justice, 26, 43,
    51–4, 56, 58, 60, 61, 63–4, 72, 74,
    76, 154, 211, 214, 258
European Economic Area, EEA,
    209–12, 264
European Free Trade Area, EFTA,
    210–12
European Monetary System, EMS, 101
European Parliament, 34–6, 43, 44,
    45–8, 124–6, 134, 152,
    259, 273
European Peoples Party, EPP, *see*
    Christian Democracy
European Union Act, 2011, 46, 82–3,
    260
European Union (Legal Continuity)
    Scotland, bill, 220, 252
European Union Referendum Act,
    2015, 109–10
European Union Withdrawal Act,
    2018, 50, 152–4, 214–16,
    229, 266
eurozone, 98

Factortame case, 1991, 72–3, 75–7, 78,
    80–2, 83, 173, 275
Farage, Nigel, 13, 14, 109–10
fascism, 5
federal government, federalism, quasi-
    federalism, 35, 42, 79, 161–2,
    177, 182, 185–9, 216–17, 253,
    255
Fitzgerald, Garret, 197
Foot, Michael, 12, 101, 114, 125, 133fn
Foster, Arlene, 238
Fowler, Gerry, 102
France, French, 3, 5, 6–7, 8, 9, 12, 21,
    23, 26, 40, 41, 46

Gaitskell, Hugh, 12, 32–8, 48, 96
Gardiner, Lord, 58
Gearty, Conor, 138–9
general elections:
    1931, 117–18
    1970, 92, 93, 95
    1974, February, 92, 94
    1974, October, 105, 180, 262
    2001, 180
    2010, 46–7, 262
    2015, 13, 14, 18, 95, 132, 180, 262
    2017, 14–15, 16–18, 180, 195, 207,
        234
Germany, Germans, 3, 5, 8, 9, 23, 26,
    35, 40, 41, 47, 235–6, 276
Giddens, Anthony, 249
Gladstone, W.E., 114, 116, 181, 244
Goldsworthy, Jeffrey, 83, 84–5
Good Friday Agreement, *see* Belfast
    Agreement
Goodwin, Matthew, 200–1
Gove, Michael, 132
Government of Wales Acts, *see* Wales
    Acts
Grattan, Henry, 198
Grayling, Chris, 132
Greenland, 209–10, 243
Grieve, Dominic, 159
Greece, 41
Green Party, 14

Hailsham, Lord, 64, 65, 67, 68, 69, 118,
    260–1, 274
Hale, Lady, 164
Hart, H.L.A., 66–7, 80, 84
Heald, Sir Lionel, 59
Heath, Edward, Heath government,
    12, 28, 38, 55–6, 59, 61, 62, 91,
    94, 99, 121, 260
Heffer, Eric, 122
Heywood, Sir Jeremy, 132–3

Hitler, Adolf, 3–4, 6
Hockman, Stephen, 254–5
Hodgson, Lord Justice, 73
Hoffmann, Lord, 76
Hood Phillips, Professor, 65
Hope, Lord, 164
Howe, Sir Geoffrey, 59, 64, 65, 67, 68,
    69, 71–3
Huhne, Chris, 127
Human Rights Act, 1998, ix, 59, 82,
    85, 136, 137, 138, 139, 143, 144,
    145, 147, 151–2, 157–8, 159–62,
    165–6, 257–8, 259, 260, 265–7,
    276
Hume, David, 198
Hunt, Sir John, 133
Hunting Act, 2004, 163

implied repeal, 64–5, 70–2, 80
Ireland, Irish Republic, Irish
    Constitution, 31, 154, 155, 156,
    171–2, 179, 192, 193–5, 197,
    198, 230, 233–46, 249–50,
    263, 264
Israel, 160–1, 274
Italy, Italians, 3, 5, 8, 9, 40, 52–3, 276

Jackson and others v Her Majesty's
    Attorney-General, 2005, 163–4
James, Henry, 198–9
Jenkin, Bernard, 252
Jenkins, Roy, 12, 100, 102, 110–11, 124
Jennings, Sir Ivor, 120
Johnson, Boris, 12, 132
Jowell, Jeffrey, 276
judicial review, 136, 149–50, 165
Juncker, Jean-Claude, 44

Kant, Immanuel, 2
Khan, Sadiq, 206
Kilmuir, Lord, 55–6, 143

Labour Party, Labour governments, 12, 14, 15, 16, 17, 25, 32, 38, 57, 81, 91–5, 99, 101, 105, 111, 117–18, 121, 124, 129, 130, 143, 184, 207, 216, 242, 250–1, 252, 271

Lassalle, Ferdinand, 81

Laws, Lord Justice, 80–1

Lee, Sir Frank, 10

Leveson Committee, 131

Lewis, Sir Leigh, 157

Lib–Lab pact, 124–5

Liberals, Liberal Democrat Party, 14, 23, 101, 111, 116–19, 126, 127–31, 134, 181, 184, 216, 220–1, 245–6, 250–1, 252, 262

Lisbon Treaty 2008, 15, 42, 146, 230

Locke, John, 97–8

Low, Sidney, 31–2, 254

Luxembourg Compromise, 1966, 60

Maastricht Treaty, 1992, 13, 42, 101, 208

Macarthys v Smith, 1979, 70, 71, 78, 80, 83

MacCormick v Lord Advocate, 1953, 175

MacCormick, John, 175

MacCormick, Sir Neil, 176

MacDonald, Ramsay, 118

Macmillan, Harold, Macmillan government, 11, 12, 27, 32, 33, 38

Major, John, 101, 255

Maxwell Fyfe, Sir David, *see* Lord Kilmuir

May, Theresa, 14, 15, 16, 148, 155, 192

Melbourne, Lord, 115–16

Merchant Shipping Act, 1988, 72–3

Messina Conference, 1955, 9

'Metric Martyrs' case, *see Thoburn*

metro-mayors, 204–6, 260, 261, 273

Miliband, David, 148

Millan, Bruce, 125

Miller case, 2017, (*R (Miller) v Secretary of State for Existing the European Union*), 57, 75, 77, 218–19, 221

ministerial responsibility, 36–7, 43

Mitchell, J.D.B., 85, 177

Mitterrand, François, 47

Mollet, Guy, 7

Monnet, Jean, 6

Morley, John, 116

National Government, 116–17, 120

National Socialism, Nazism, 3–4, 5, 142

Neill, Lord Justice, 72–3

Netherlands, 40, 41, 51–2

New Zealand, 161, 274–6

North Atlantic Treaty Organisation, NATO, 1949, 24, 51

Northern Ireland, Northern Ireland Assembly, Northern Ireland Parliament, x, 47, 96, 97, 100, 106, 111, 156–7, 158, 169–70, 171, 178–9, 180, 183, 185, 188, 189, 190–8, 201, 212, 218, 223–7, 229, 230–44, 258, 259, 260, 266, 276

Northern Ireland Act, 1998, 191, 263

Northern Ireland Border Poll, 1973, 96

Northern Ireland Constitution Act, 1973, 96

Norway, 211–12, 264, 276

O'Neill, Sir Con, 39

Orme, Stan, 125

Osborne, George, 204, 208

Owen, David, 12

Palmerston, Lord, 114, 134
Parliament Act, 1911, 81, 160, 163,
    220–1
Patel, Priti, 132
Plaid Cymru, 180, 216
Poland, 40, 265
Pollock, Sir F, 88
Porter, Lord, 247
Portugal, 41
Powell, Enoch, 48, 104, 108
Prodi, Romano 47

*R v Secretary of State for Employment
    ex parte Equal Opportunities
    Commission*, 1995, 74
Rait, R.S., 173–4
Reed, Lord, 77
referendum, referendums, ix, 14, 15,
    16, 38, 82–3, 84, 87–112, 113,
    114, 121–4, 127, 131, 132, 135,
    169–70, 181, 182–3, 184, 187,
    190–1, 195, 202, 205, 206,
    207, 209, 230–2, 235, 251,
    252, 261–5
Reform Act, 1832, 31, 43, 92
Rey, Jean, 92
Reynaud, Paul, 7
Rifkind, Malcolm, 42, 103–4
Rippengal, David, 64–5
Robertson, George, 184
Rome, Treaty of, 1957, 9, 26, 33, 34,
    38–9, 55, 60–1, 69, 76–7
Rose, Richard, 178, 190, 200
Ross, Willie, 114
Royal Commission on the
    Constitution, 179,
    185, 187
Rule of Recognition, 82, 83–5, 166,
    253–4
Russell, Mike, 219
Russia, 3, 20, 41

Sacks, Jonathan, 268–70
Saint-Simon, Henri de, 2
Salisbury, Lord, 115
Samuel, Herbert, 119
Schuman, Robert, 5, 26, 27, 50
Scotland, Scottish Parliament, x, 15,
    18, 98, 100, 103, 104–6, 108–9,
    111, 155–6, 158, 164–5, 169–70,
    171–9, 180, 181–2, 184, 185,
    187, 188–9, 194, 201, 202,
    206–12, 213–21, 223–9, 235,
    246, 248, 250–2, 258, 259, 260,
    262–3, 265, 267, 276, 277
Scotland Acts, 181–2, 184, 202
Scottish Claim of Right, 250–2
Scottish Constitutional Convention,
    1989, 250–1, 276
Scottish National Party, SNP, 15, 18,
    170, 176, 180, 184, 207–9, 216,
    218, 251, 262–4, 269
separation of powers, 43, 260–1
Sewel Convention, 182–3, 217–19,
    221, 252, 267
Shore, Peter, 114, 123, 125
Short, Edward, 90, 97
Silkin, John, 114, 125
Sillars, Jim, 170
Simmenthal case, 1978, 70
Sinn Fein, 195, 230, 235, 237–8,
    249–50
Single European Act, 1986, 33, 42, 60
Slovakia, 40
Smith of Kelvin, Lord, 184
Smith, T.B., 174–5
Smith Commission, 184
Snowden, Philip, 117, 118–19
Soames, Sir Christopher, 94
Social Democratic Party, SDP, 12,
    15, 101
Socialism, Socialists, Social
    Democrats, 4, 15, 46, 47

sovereignty, national, 28–9, 40, 61
sovereignty of Parliament, xi,
    28–30, 32–3, 36, 48, 51–86,
    87, 88, 89, 135, 136, 140,
    151, 152, 153, 154, 163–7,
    171–6, 188, 221, 248–9, 252,
    253–4, 257–8, 261, 265, 275,
    277–8
sovereignty of People, 109–12, 135,
    141, 250–2, 258, 265
Spain, 41
St Andrews Agreement, 2006, 183,
    191, 192
Steyn, Lord, 145–6, 163–4
Stormont House Agreement, 2014,
    183
Stresemann, Gustav, 3
Sturgeon, Nicola, 209
Suez crisis, 1956, 7
Sumption, Lord, 137, 139–40, 149
Supremacy of European Law,
    Doctrine of, 52–4, 76

Thatcher, Margaret, 12, 33–4, 74–5, 78,
    102–3, 126, 208
Thoburn v Sunderland City Council,
    2003, 80–1, 173, 277
Tocqueville, Alexis de, 189, 254, 275
Tridimas, Takis, 109
Turkey, 242–3, 264

union state, 177–8
unitary state, 177–8, 248, 253
United Kingdom Independence
    Party, UKIP, 13, 14, 18, 95, 108,
    109–10, 185, 201

Van Gend en Loos, 1963, 51–2, 54, 57,
    59, 60, 70
Varley, Eric, 114
Vidal-Hall v Google, 2015, 149–50
Villiers, Theresa, 132

Wade, H.W.R., 76–7, 79, 81–2, 162–3
Wales, National Assembly for Wales,
    x, 98, 100, 103, 104–6, 108–9,
    111, 158, 169–70, 171, 178, 179,
    180, 181, 185, 187, 188, 216–17,
    223–9, 252–3, 258, 259, 260,
    265, 272–3
Wales Acts, Government of Wales
    Acts, 182–3
Watson, Tom, 150
West Lothian Question, 202
Wheare, K.C., 188, 220
Whittingdale, John, 132
Whyte, John, 197–8
Williams, Shirley, 12, 100
Wilson, Harold, Wilson governments,
    38, 57, 91, 93, 99–100, 102,
    108–9, 113, 120–2, 123–4